The Music of Angels

tHe MUSiC of AngELs

A Listener's Guide to Sacred Music
from Chant to Christian Rock

PATRICK KAVANAUGH

FOREWORD BY DAVE BRUBECK

 Loyola Press

Chicago

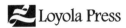 Loyola Press

3441 North Ashland Avenue
Chicago, Illinois 60657

Photos of Shirley Caesar (p. 232), Andrae Crouch (p. 234), Bill Gaither (p. 197), and Amy Grant (p. 252) courtesy of the Gospel Music Association. Photo of James Cleveland (p. 227) courtesy of the Gospel Music Workshop. Photos of Philip Paul Bliss (p. 159), Fanny Crosby (p. 162), Frances Ridley Havergal (p. 160), Martin Luther (p. 129), John Newton (p.140), Ira David Sankey (p. 161), Isaac Watts (p. 133), and Charles Wesley (p. 138) courtesy of Kenneth Osbeck. Photos of Steven Curtis Chapman (p. 249) and Twila Paris (p. 251) courtesy of the Sparrow Corporation. Photo of Sandi Patty (p. 250) courtesy of Word Music. Photos of J. S. Bach (p. 81), Ludwig van Beethoven (p. 102), Johannes Brahms (p. 114), Antonín Dvořák (p. 117), George Frideric Handel (p. 78), Franz Joseph Haydn (p. 92), Charles Ives (p. 179), Felix Mendelssohn (p. 112), Olivier Messiaen (p. 186), Wolfgang Amadeus Mozart (p. 96), Franz Schubert (p. 110), Igor Stravinsky (p. 181), Ralph Vaughan Williams (p. 177), and Antonio Vivaldi (p. 74) courtesy of the Zondervan Corporation. Photos of Duke Ellington (p. 276), Mahalia Jackson (p. 226), and Claudio Monteverdi (p. 70) courtesy of the Library of Congress. Photos of Michael Card (p. 275), Ralph Carmichael (p. 199), Jack Hayford (p. 200), Barbara Mandrell (p. 268), Dan Schutte (p. 201), and John Michael Talbot (p. 273) courtesy of the artists. Photos of Ambrose (p. 18), Augustine (p. 20), C. P. E. Bach (p. 90), William Byrd (p. 63), Guillaume Dufay (p. 47), Francis of Assisi (p. 39), Gregory the Great (p. 21), Guillaume de Machaut (p. 44), Hildegard von Bingen (p. 28), Josquin Desprez (p. 56), Francesco Landini (p. 46), Orlandus Lassus (p. 62), Giovanni Pierluigi da Palestrina (p. 59), Paul (p. 10), Plato (p. 7), and Pythagoras (p. 8) courtesy of the author.

Interior design by Jennifer Mindel

Library of Congress Cataloging-in-Publication Data
Kavanaugh, Patrick.
      The music of angels : a listener's guide to sacred music from chant to Christian rock / Patrick Kavanaugh.
     p. cm.
    Includes bibliographical references (p.   ) and index.
    ISBN 0-8294-1019-8 (pbk.)
    1. Church music. I. Title
    ML3000 .K44 1999
    781.71—dc21

                  98-45505
                     CIP
                     MN

Printed in the United States of America
99 00 01 02 03 04 / 10 9 8 7 6 5 4 3 2 1

This book is gratefully dedicated to Bill and Melanie Jeschke,
whose steadfast efforts have brought sacred music
into the realm of true ministry.

97702

CONTENTS

Foreword   viii
Preface   x
Acknowledgments   xii
Introduction: The River of Sacred Music   xiii

Part I: From Hebrew Psalms to the Renaissance

1. The Origins of Sacred Music (A.D. 1–400)   3
2. Chant (400–1000)   15
3. Medieval Polyphony (1000–1450)   33
4. The Renaissance (1400–1600)   51

Part 2: From Baroque to Hymnology

5. The Baroque Period (1600–1750)   69
6. The Classical Period (1750–1820)   89
7. The Romantic Period (1820–1900)   107
8. Chorales and Congregations (1500–1750)   127
9. The Growth of Hymnology (1750–1900)   147

Part 3: The Twentieth Century and the Advent of Recorded Music

10. Modern Classical Composers (1900–present)   171
11. Congregational Music and the Modern Church Choir
    (1900–present)   193
12. Gospel Music Performers and Composers (1900–present)   217
13. Contemporary Christian Music (1950–present)   239
14. Country, Folk, Jazz, and More (1950–present)   261

Afterword: Thoughts on the Future of Sacred Music   281
Further Reading   287
Index   315

FOREWORD

When I saw the title of Dr. Kavanaugh's book *The Music of Angels,* I was reminded of a Christmas many years ago when my oldest boy was a child of three. Because I was a working musician, in order for our family to be together we had to spend Christmas in a motel room in Salt Lake City. The Mormon Tabernacle Choir's performance of Handel's *Messiah* was on the radio.

The child was so moved by the music that tears rolled down his cheeks. When the announcer said that the program would be rebroadcast in the evening, he pleaded to be allowed to stay up past his bedtime because, he said, "I need to hear the angels sing." Thus music has the power to touch the soul of even the youngest listener.

Dr. Kavanaugh's book helps us to understand the significant role music has in expressing that which is deepest within our souls. Such is the wellspring from which the mighty river flows, fed by streams of melody and harmony, creating an endless flow of music throughout the ages.

Reading this book, I am reminded of my own experience studying Pange Lingua and eventually composing six variations on that ancient chant. Scholars speculate that the melody of Pange Lingua was first used in the sixth century by Fortunatus and was probably based on a Roman march that in turn was derived from a more ancient Hebrew chant. In the thirteenth century St. Thomas Aquinas wrote the famous Latin stanzas, which for generations scholars have considered perfect in theological content, poetic form, accent, and rhyme. To embellish or alter such perfection takes courage, but throughout the two-thousand-year history of this music there have been numerous settings of the melody, each one reflecting the era of the particular composer. (My own approach was to open each stanza with the Gregorian chant sung in Latin, followed by a contemporary musical variation based on that text.)

The Music of Angels will help not only the composers of church music but the listeners, too, to be aware of the scope and depth of the sacred music tradition. Throughout its history the church has had to accept change, first within its own walls and among its own musicians, later to adapt to the popular and contemporary music of each era in order to keep the church vital and relevant to society. When I hear criticism about the introduction of jazz or popular music into a worship service, I am reminded of the story that "O Sacred Head Now Wounded" was derived from a German drinking song that J. S. Bach knew would be familiar to his congregation. This book teaches us to understand that throughout Christian history there have been many meaningful approaches to glorifying and praising God.

DAVE BRUBECK

PREFACE

T *he Music of Angels* is about the two-thousand-year history of sacred music, an admittedly very large subject. Instead of filling a multi-volume encyclopedia, I have attempted to bring out the most important elements of sacred music in a short history that can be read and appreciated by the layperson. But in order to keep such a massive topic under control, I have imposed a number of restrictions on the material, two of which should be mentioned at the onset.

First, I will be examining only sacred *Christian* music. Certainly, other religions have their own music that they use in services of worship, but these fall outside the scope of this book. The only time they are explored is when they have a direct influence on sacred Christian music, such as the Jewish music of the pre-Christian era.

Second, I have limited the topic to the sacred music of Western civilization. The spread of Christianity was not, of course, limited to the West. There are magnificent sacred music traditions within the Greek and Russian Orthodox Churches as well as the Coptic, Ethiopian, and other African churches. But an East-versus-West comparison would be another book in itself. Therefore, we will stay within Western world history, which still covers the colossal period between early Christian chant and contemporary music of the late twentieth century.

In my research at the Library of Congress, I have found many volumes about even the most minute items mentioned in this book. Every composer, performer, and practically every composition has been studied and written about by scholars of the last one hundred years. In this single volume I have had to omit many lesser details about subjects that may be of great importance to some readers. Furthermore, I have avoided comment about the various controversies concerning different styles of Christian music today.

The most essential information in this volume is not the multitudinous details of so much music and so many musicians. Instead it is the critical connections—so significant, yet so seldom examined—that lie between the diverse genres represented here. If you want further information about any particular subject, you may refer to the "Further Reading" section in the back of the book.

My ultimate purpose, then, is to give the "big picture," to show the connections between one age and another, and the relationships between one genre and another—to put it all together in a medium accessible to musician and music lover alike. For this reason, the text is devoid of footnotes and musical technicalities, which might hinder the musical layperson. I have also used the English titles of most compositions, unless the original title has become so popular as to render translation unnecessary.

This topic, the totality of Christian music, is very important to me personally. As the director of the Christian Performing Artists' Fellowship, I have worked with hundreds of the world's finest Christian musicians. As both a professional conductor and an ordained minister, I have had the good fortune to experience sacred music in nearly every conceivable setting. I have conducted Christian opera at Moscow's Bolshoi Theatre and performed in Nashville recording studios. I have conducted mass choirs in classical masterpieces and led congregational singing in small storefront churches.

More important, I have had the misfortune of seeing music—or rather, the mishandling of music—create terrible schisms in the Christian church. It sometimes seems that there are more divisions occurring over musical tastes than biblical doctrine. Today, more than ever, there is a tremendous need for believers to have a deeper understanding of all forms of Christian music.

Therefore, I hope that this short guide will help all of us to examine where we have been in order to better see why we are here and where we are going. If it helps any reader to appreciate more fully the breadth of Christian music, it will have been worth my effort. If it then helps to bring people together in a spirit of Christian harmony, it will give me the greatest joy possible.

ACKNOWLEDGMENTS

A book of this scope is never created without the help of many talented people—more than I could possibly hope to thank—but I cannot forgo mentioning the following:

the directors of the Christian Performing Artists' Fellowship—Jim Kraft, Richard Lambert, Robert Sturm, and Nicholas Tavani—for their continued encouragement;

June Sawyers, Amy Schroeder, LaVonne Neff, Heidi Toboni, Vinita Hampton Wright, and the staff of Loyola Press, for superb editing and ongoing commitment to excellence;

the most resourceful of research assistants, Janice Norris, for resolving dozens of tricky problems and locating many obscure facts;

the incomparable staff of the Library of Congress for their help in locating research materials and photographs;

my four fantastic children—Chris, John, Peter, and David—for their understanding and love, even when Dad had to finish typing his book when he would rather have been playing ball with them;

and my best friend and dear wife, Barbara, for her unflagging support and invaluable companionship, not to mention tireless proofreading skills! May our Lord give us many more years together.

INTRODUCTION

The River of Sacred Music

Imagine a long, flowing river. It moves in a single direction for many miles before diverging into two distinct channels, each flowing in a parallel course for many more miles. One of these two streams begins to divide into additional streams. Ultimately, this delta flows out into the vastness of the sea.

This image represents the history of sacred Christian music. It is, of course, simply a visual aid and not the history itself. Like all generalizations, it contains exceptions and inconsistencies. But it will help us as we take a two-thousand-year tour in the time it takes to read a book.

For many centuries, sacred music existed almost entirely within the church walls. From its somewhat eclectic beginnings in the small meetings of the early church, it was eventually codified during the era of chant. Still later, with the rise of polyphony, sacred music continued under the control of the church musicians. Even the magnificent Renaissance masses and sacred motets remained the realm of musical church masters. For these long years, the image of the single stream is invoked.

With the Reformation and the Counter-Reformation, this musical river divides into two streams. These streams do not represent Catholics and Protestants. Rather, they indicate the different music created by professional musicians (both Catholic and Protestant) and the music created for the layperson in church congregations. In the first stream, you would find such works as Beethoven's *Missa Solemnis* for chorus and orchestra, while the second stream would contain the vast number of hymns, chorales, and anthems for congregations of every Christian church.

Finally, the advent of recorded music in the twentieth century further divides the second stream into many different musical styles. The classical traditions (the first stream) continue with modern sacred masterpieces like Stravinsky's *Symphony of Psalms*. But now the second, more popular stream divides into such new branches as sacred folk music, gospel music, and Christian rock as well as builds upon the already large repertoire of church choir and congregational music.

Thus, we have an image of two thousand years of sacred music. As we shall see in subsequent chapters, it isn't quite this simple. Whenever historians place "turning-point" dates and epochs onto the continuous flow of history, remember that events often overlap, and major changes occur gradually.

Nevertheless, this subdividing river is the course we follow through the centuries of sacred music. We begin in the headwaters—the obscure springs from which great rivers are born—and end our journey as the river finally flows into the future ocean of ultimate variety. It is a voyage well worth the taking.

PART
1

FROM HEBREW PSALMS TO THE RENAISSANCE

CHAPTER 1

THE ORIGINS OF SACRED MUSIC
(A.D. 1–400)

Sing and make music in your heart to the Lord.

Paul, Ephesians 5:19

How much do we know about the music of the early church? More than you might think.

Of course, we do not know exactly what the early church's music sounded like. We know little, for example, about particular melodies and rhythms, and still less about specific compositions. There was not much in the way of music notation available, and what little there was is impossible to decipher today with any accuracy.

You simply can't go to the local record store and purchase a CD of first-century Christian music. Unlike the music discussed in later chapters, for which specific music selections can be recommended, there are no CDs entitled *Saint Paul's Greatest Hits* or *David's Top*

3

40 Psalms. People have attempted to produce recordings of biblical music, but much of their efforts remain only guesswork. One point we can know for certain, though. Early church music sounded nothing like the background music Hollywood uses in its movies.

Yet we do know a good deal descriptively that can help us speculate on the music itself. Many of the primary descriptions are not about early Christian music per se, but rather about the two musical sources forming the seedbed from which Christian music began: the Jewish liturgy and the Greek musical traditions.

The Jews and the Greeks

Anyone who has read the New Testament has certainly noticed two major elements scattered throughout its pages: ancient Jewish history and the relatively newer influence of the Greek language and customs. Throughout the Gospels and letters, we find accounts and quotations from the Hebrew Scriptures told in the Greek language. The Acts of the Apostles, in particular, tells of the many conflicts that arose with the mingling of these two very different cultures.

Therefore, it should not be surprising to find that the major influences on early Christian music are the Jewish and Greek musical traditions. The first Christians were Hebrews who had grown up in the synagogues of Israel, singing the Psalms of David. Yet there were soon thousands of gentile believers who had never set foot in a synagogue and whose musical backgrounds were primarily Greek.

Some readers are probably wondering about the Roman musical influence. Didn't Rome conquer Greece long before the time of Christ? Yes, but the Romans were better soldiers than musicians. The Greeks had spent centuries building an impressive musical tradition. So when Greece fell to Rome, the conquerors found that their music couldn't hold a candle to that of the conquered. Therefore, the Greek musical systems were still "state of the art" in the world of the early church.

Let's examine what we know about these two musical traditions.

The Music of Jewish Worship

The Hebrew worshipers had been praising God with music since the time of Jubal, the "father of all who play the harp and flute" (Gen. 4:21). The many passages concerning the great choirs of the Jerusalem temple testify to the extensive use of music in Jewish worship. The words of the Psalms—notably Psalm 150—tell us that Jewish music was not only vocal but also employed a number of available instruments.

After the Babylonian exile of the sixth century B.C., the local synagogue replaced the temple as the usual place of worship for the Jewish believer. The worship lacked the sacrifices of the temple but still included prayer and psalm singing. Much of this singing was responsorial; that is, a cantor would sing a line of music, then the worshipers would respond in kind. For example, the first two verses of Psalm 136 could be sung in a responsorial fashion:

Cantor:	Give thanks to the LORD, for he is good.
People:	His love endures forever.
Cantor:	Give thanks to the God of gods.
People:	His love endures forever.

Many interesting variations of this technique existed, but its use represented a long-standing concept: the musical leadership versus the congregation at large. Obviously, the most difficult parts were given to the leader, who, hopefully, had more talent than the average congregant. The emphasis (or lack thereof) on this "clergy-versus-laity" concept would be a controversial factor in subsequent Christian worship, even to our present day.

Another practice that gave precedence to the leader was the singing of Scripture using accepted melodic formulas that could be varied to fit different lines of text. Still another Jewish practice that would later affect Christian worship was antiphonal singing. Two groups of singers would alternate verses or lines of text, thus enhancing the dramatic impact of the Scriptures on the worshipers.

Early synagogue worship differed sharply from that of the temple in one critical way: it was purely vocal. Some believe that the use of vocals mourned the destruction of Solomon's temple. Others think that it showed the dissimilarity between the worship of the "true" God and the practices of pagan temples, which used many instruments. Again, this argument against instrumental worship would be used in the early Christian church.

Greek Contributions

"Let me make the songs of a nation and I care not who makes the laws," **Plato** once said. The Greeks had recognized music's mystical powers many years before the Christian era. They had used it in artistic performances as well as in their own worship and had even invented the first systems of music theory. The major Greek philosophers speculated about music's powers, and the leading playwrights used music in the great plays that still move audiences today.

The methodical Greek mind focused on the acoustical and mathematical aspects of music. Struggling to understand the basic elements of sound, **Pythagoras** (fifth century B.C.) and his many followers divided strings into equal parts to create intervals and scale systems. A thousand years later, Christian melodies were categorized into Lydian, Dorian, and Aeolian modes, modes that were originally set down by early Greek musicians.

The Greeks produced a fascinating form of music notation, which looks nothing like the standard five lines we use today. There are no treble or bass clefs or, indeed, any indications of rhythm whatsoever. Instead, they wrote little words or symbols over each of the lyrics that indicated to the performer what pitch to sing for each word. Unfortunately, this imperfect system only works if you happen to know

PLATO

Born:
circa 427 B.C.
Athens, Greece

Died:
circa 347 B.C.
Athens, Greece

Occupation:
philosopher, scientist, teacher

Hobbies/Interests:
politics, psychology, art

Quotation:
"Musical training is a more potent instrument than any other, because rhythm and harmony find their way into the secret places of the soul."

PYTHAGORAS

Born:
fifth century B.C.
Samos, Greece

Died:
fifth century B.C.
Metapontum, Greece

Occupation:
mathematician,
scientist

Hobbies/Interests:
stargazing,
numerology, travel

Quotation:
*"Do nothing you do
not understand."*

exactly which pitch matches each symbol—and we do not!

Although the Greek and Hebrew cultures were worlds apart, some important similarities between their music did exist. For instance, in both cultures music was intricately linked with words. Both rhythm and melody were founded upon the poetry of a given text. Even the instruments of Greek music seemed to emphasize the words of the text it accompanied.

Speaking of Greek instruments, do not imagine that a Greek "orchestra" would sound anything like our modern orchestras. The ancient music of Greece was still monophonic. There is nothing to suggest harmony or polyphony as we know it. Instruments either doubled the vocal melody or embellished it in a dramatic style.

We also know that much of the music of the early Greeks was improvised. Therefore, no two performances were exactly alike. The composer and the performer were often the same person. For example, when a Greek bard sang a Homeric poem, he would superimpose his own style on the well-known story. This freedom of improvisation would affect the music of Christian worship until the Middle Ages. And, to some degree, it is still practiced in many churches, certainly in the performances of jazz, gospel, and rock music.

The Earliest Christian Music

In a manner of speaking, when Jesus "sung a hymn" at the end of the Last Supper (Matt. 26:30, Mark

*QUICK*TAKES
Recommended Recording

Music from Ancient Rome
Synaulia; A Research Group for Music, Dance, and Theater
(Amiata Records ARNR1396)

Although this recording is neither Greek, Hebrew, nor early Christian, it is one of the few recordings of ancient music that offers both competent scholarship and sensitive performances. Most selections are instrumental, encompassing a wide variety of unusual sounds—strange bamboo flutes, horns (literally the horns of animals), bells, buzzers, and drums. Undoubtedly, many of the notes are reconstructed by the players to simulate the forgotten melodies of Roman music, but the presentations are thoughtfully and skillfully crafted. The listener should be aware that this music of early Rome, closely related to that of Greece, is very different from what we are accustomed to hearing. Those willing to make the effort will discover a music that is truly fascinating.

14:26), he inaugurated the beginning of Christian music. Doubtless, the song he sang came from the Hallel group of Psalms (113–118) or some other Hebrew hymn. Since the earliest Christian worship services had much to do with reenacting the Last Supper, Jesus' hymn singing established an important precedent.

Much has been written about **Paul's** double reference to "psalms, hymns, and spiritual songs"

PAUL

Born:
circa A.D. 5
Tarsus, Asia Minor

Died:
circa A.D. 68
Rome (?)

Occupation:
tent maker, preacher, missionary

Hobbies/Interests:
traveling, poetry, letter writing

Quotation:
"Sing and make music in your heart to the Lord."

(Eph. 5:19, Col. 3:16). Rather than make dogmatic statements (which are mostly guesses that cannot be verified), it is probably best to say that Paul was simply describing all the possible music in a given worship service.

Paul's term *psalms* obviously refers to the singing of the various psalms from the Hebrew Scriptures. The Greek word *hymnis* simply means "a song written in praise or honor of God." It could have been composed by King David or by a local songwriter. Most of the millions of Christian songs today could fit into this very broad category.

Paul's spiritual songs have provoked much speculation, often bordering on musical and theological lunacy. There is nothing extramystical or magical about his terms, which are sometimes translated as "odes" or "canticles." Perhaps in contrasting the term *hymns* with the term *odes,* Paul used the second term to cover the improvised songs (possibly combined with ecstatic tongues) that were an integral part of the worship service. It may also refer to the phrase "sing with my spirit" that he used in his first letter to the Corinthians (1 Cor. 14:15).

In Paul's discussion of worship services, he recognized the somewhat improvisatory nature of music in the early church: "When you come together, every one has a hymn, or a word of instruction, a revelation, a tongue, or an interpretation. All of these must be done for the strengthening of the church" (1 Cor. 14:26). Paul's comment seems to indicate a strong musical involvement of the congregation, who freely chose the songs they would spontaneously sing.

It is probable that in Ephesians 5:14, Paul quotes the words to an early Christian hymn:

> Wake up, O sleeper,
> rise from the dead,
> and Christ will shine on you.

These words may have been the first two lines of a responsorial song, initiated by a music leader and answered by the Ephesian congregation. Or perhaps they were the chorus the congregation intoned between solo verses that told the story of Jesus' resurrection. If only someone had had a good tape recorder in those days!

Again, we see the difficulty of speculating on such early music pieces. Unfortunately, the New Testament manuscripts did not come with sheet music attached, and the first books never had CDs on their inside covers.

Music in the Persecuted Church

The Roman authorities outlawed the Christian faith; thus, the early worship services were held in secrecy and often had to move from place to place. Christians gathered together in homes, in forests, in caves, or underground. Consequently, the facilities for teaching new music were primitive or nonexistent. Perhaps the main rule for singing was "Keep it quiet."

In letters written about A.D. 112 to the Emperor Trajan, Pliny the Younger comments that the

Christians in Asia Minor "were in the habit of meeting on a certain fixed day before it was light, when they sang in separate verses a hymn to Christ, as to a god." The language he uses may refer to antiphonal singing or to a hymn sung by the congregation, a song leader, or both.

About the same time, Ignatius of Antioch, on his way to martyrdom in Rome, wrote seven letters to churches and friends. In one of the letters, he exhorted fellow believers: "Therefore by your concord and harmonious love Jesus Christ is being sung. Now all of you together become a choir so that being harmoniously in concord and receiving the key note from God in unison you may sing with one voice through Jesus Christ to the Father." Again, the emphasis is on unity, reflected in the monophonic melodies of praise.

As the great martyr Origen (185–253) so indicated, it is significant that early church congregations sang praises and recited prayers in their own languages. In fact, the church's first "songbook"— a collection of forty-two songs (text only, with no musical notation) from the early second century entitled *Odes of Solomon*—is not in Greek but in Syriac.

Many of the early hymns reflect the influence of the Psalms, as seen in this excerpt from the Greek Morning Hymn (from the second or third century):

> Each day I will bless you, and I will praise your name forever, and forever.

Yet the teaching through all the early hymns is clearly Christian, underscoring praise to the Trinity, as seen in the beautiful Greek Evening Hymn of the second century:

> Having come to the setting of the sun, seeing the evening light, we hymn the Father and the Son and the Holy Spirit of God.

An early Christian hymn with music notation as well as text finally surfaced when in 1922 a mangled piece of papyrus was found at the site of Oxyrhynchus, an ancient Egyptian city. This third-century fragment contained the last few lines of a hymn to the Trinity, with Greek notation above the text. But as mentioned earlier, this Greek notation is not much help to us, since we cannot know with any certainty which pitches are indicated by the notation.

What Next?

Fortunately, the Roman emperor Constantine legalized Christianity in 313 with the Edict of Milan. As the persecutions disappeared, the church began to codify its music for worship. Ironically, by suppressing the freedom of the early musicians, this codification did help to preserve some of the church's best hymns. Later, improved notation would record (at least on paper) the music as well as the words.

When the use of notation took place, we can say that the written history of sacred music truly began. Thus, both a song's text and its melody could be preserved for future generations. A singer could then look at a manuscript and perform it as it had been originally performed. Later it could even be recorded.

CHAPTER 2

CHANT
(400–1000)

Psalmody unites those who disagree, makes friends of those at odds, and brings together those who are out of charity with one another. Who could retain a grievance against the man with whom he had joined with singing before God?

Ambrose, bishop of Milan

Afbefore years of neglect, chant has recently made a well-deserved comeback. In the mid-1990s, chant suddenly sold millions of CDs and tapes. There is every reason to believe that this trend will continue and expand, and rightly so; it's about time that people discovered the beauties of chant.

The body of chant represents some of the greatest riches of Western art. Not only were chants used for Christian worship for over a thousand years, but they also inspired countless compositions in the centuries that followed their heyday. There are no parallels to chant in the history of music in terms of its longevity, importance, and influence.

Yet when people today first hear chant, they are often puzzled by it. Chant is simply a single melody sung in unison to a Latin text. Often there is considerable repeating of one "reciting tone." (Usually a chant will employ an "arch shape"; that is, start on a low tone, rise upward, and eventually fall back to the original low register.) There is no harmony, no accompaniment, no strong rhythm or accent. In other words, there is nothing to hide behind. It is the most straightforward, transparent music of all time. Its beauty is in its innocent simplicity.

Doubtless, it is this very simplicity that makes chant so attractive to us today. In our world of ever-growing complexity and speed, we develop a hunger for the uncomplicated, the unpretentious, the unadorned. After a long day spent at the office or in the factory, coming home to a soothing chant is in the same refreshing category as a relaxing hot bath, a walk through the woods, or an evening spent in front of a slow-burning fire.

The "Classical" Age of Chant

Yet such secular activities were not exactly what the church leaders had in mind when the liturgy of chant was first being established. After decades of Roman persecution, Constantine's Edict of Milan allowed the church to finally organize its music. As the Roman Empire began to decline, the power of the Roman bishop increased.

By the fourth century, Latin had become the official language of the Western church. The popes spent much of the fifth, sixth, and seventh centuries reviewing and ordering the music and liturgy. Thus, the first

Christian centuries of free and improvised worship gave way to an age of structure and organization.

If this organizing of music sounds too restrictive, let us examine an inherent trend in music history. Throughout the ages, composers typically adopt romantic, innovative, and fanciful tendencies until things get rather out of hand. Then an era of order and design counteracts earlier excesses. This "classical" age continues for a while, until composers eventually turn romantic once again, and the pattern repeats itself.

Sometimes called the pendulum theory of music history, this concept depicts long-term trends in musical ages as alternating between romanticism (greater freedom) and classicism (greater order). In a very general sense, it is a pattern that has always been with us and continues to be discernable even today:

Romantic Tendencies	**Classical Tendencies**
Pre-chant period	Gregorian chant
Medieval period	The Renaissance
Baroque period	Classical period
Romantic period	Neoclassical period

Many would even say that we are presently in a neoromantic period of classical music. Not every musicologist will agree with this pendulum theory, but it is offered here as a way of explaining the very natural process that took place when the varied music of the early church began to be organized in the world of chant.

AMBROSE

Born:
340
Gaul

Died:
397
Milan

Occupation:
bishop, writer,
composer

Hobbies/Interests:
hymn writing,
law

Quotation:
"The musician's fingers may often make mistakes on the small strings, but in the congregation, that Great Musician, the Holy Spirit, cannot err."

Different Types of Chant

All this organizing didn't take place overnight, of course. In fact, it took centuries before Rome's ecclesiastical authority finally won dominance over the whole musical world. Before then, there were a number of different styles of chant, depending upon what part of the globe you happened to be in.

For instance, there was Mozarabic chant from Spain, Gallican chant from France, Coptic chant from Egypt, Celtic chant from the British Isles, Byzantine chant from Byzantium (that is, Constantinople or Istanbul), and the well-known Ambrosian chant from Milan. Ambrosian chant was named after **Saint Ambrose, bishop of Milan** (340–97) and a champion of great music and worship.

The particular differences between these types of chant should not concern the average music lover who wants to increase his or her appreciation of sacred music. Indeed, the peculiarities are usually noticeable only to scholars. Each contains exquisite loveliness.

Chant is such a vast topic that it can be categorized in many different ways. For instance, each of the previously mentioned types of chant can be further divided into biblical and nonbiblical chant, depending on the text itself. Sometimes they are divided into categories called syllabic, with each syllable on a single note, and melismatic, with extended melodies on the same syllable. Often chant is divided into poetic texts and prose.

The Latest in Notation Technology

How did all these chants come down to us? Slowly but surely, music notation began to develop and improve. Remember those indecipherable words and symbols the Greeks placed over their vocal texts? Later, scribes would insert symbols above the texts that graphically represented how high or low the pitch should be sung. These looked a bit like notes floating in the air. Obviously, such imprecise notations gave only an approximation of the desired pitches; rather, they served to remind singers of a song's outlines, which they already knew fairly well.

Someone then got the idea of drawing a horizontal line to represent the main tone (often the beginning or ending tone) of the chant to be sung. Whenever a "note" was written on this line, the pitch would be the same. It was quite an innovation. Of course, all the other "notes" above the line were still only approximations. And rhythm was not notated; instead, it simply followed the poetry of the words. Even so, the simple addition of a horizontal line was an important turning point in the history of music.

Later, a second horizontal line was sometimes added for the highest pitch, and a little more precision was thus acquired. The notes (called neumes) were now becoming accurately related to one another. Over a number of centuries, even more lines were added, which eventually evolved into the five-line staff—with the various clefs—that we use today.

AUGUSTINE

Born:
354
Tagaste, Numidia
(North Africa)

Died:
430
Hippo (North Africa)

Occupation:
bishop, theologian

Hobbies/Interests:
writing, poetry,
philosophy

Quotation:
*"Understanding is the
reward of faith.
Therefore seek to
understand that you
may believe, but
believe that you may
understand."*

But we will leave such newfangled advancements to later chapters.

The Church Fathers and Sacred Music

The quotation by Ambrose that begins this chapter reflects the favor sacred music enjoyed under many of the church fathers. Ambrose was such an energetic champion of music that the chant from his native city is not known as Milanese but Ambrosian, in his honor. He believed worship encouraged lasting fellowship in the church: "The singing of praise is the very bond of unity, when the whole people join in the single act of song."

Ambrose had a strong influence on his friend **Augustine, bishop of Hippo** (354–430), another noted music lover. Legend has it that when Ambrose baptized Augustine, the two of them ecstatically improvised the celebrated hymn Te Deum laudamus ("We praise Thee, O God").

Augustine wrote a good deal about sacred music, including his six-book treatise, *On Music.* But his best-known words on the power of sacred music come from his *Confessions:*

> I wept at the beauty of your hymns and canticles, and was powerfully moved at the sweet sound of your Church's singing. These sounds flowed into my ears, and the truth streamed into my heart, so that my feeling and devotion overflowed, and the tears ran from my eyes, and I was happy in them.

Another notable advocate of chant was the great theologian Athanasius (296–373). He felt so strongly about singing that he insisted his followers "at midnight arise and sing praise to the Lord thy God." And the scholar Jerome (347–420) added, "Sing to God, not with the voice, but with the heart."

Perhaps the most avid fan of chant was Proclus, bishop of Constantinople (410–85). Long before Madison Avenue's hyperbole, Proclus claimed that psalmody

> calms the emotions, awakes courage, relieves grief, moderates the passions, drives away cares, consoles in affliction, leads sinners to repentance, provokes piety, peoples deserts, gives wise instructions to the State, founds converts, incites to a chaste life, teaches love of one's neighbor, praises charity, gives patience, affirms the Church, sanctifies the priest, banishes evil spirits, preaches the future, initiates us into the divine mysteries, and preaches the Trinity.

Gregory the Great

The real superstar of the chant era, though, was **Saint Gregory the Great** (540–604). Gregory was the driving force behind the standardization of chant and liturgy. In fact, his accomplishments were so momentous that many legends about him arose.

The principal myth claimed that Gregory singlehandedly composed all the hundreds of chants that were codified during his pontificate and after his death. There is even a famous illustration of Gregory and a scribe that depicts the Holy Spirit in

GREGORY THE GREAT

Born:
540
Rome

Died:
604
Rome

Occupation:
monk, abbot, pope

Hobbies/Interests:
music, writing, promoting missionary work

Quotation:
"If the work of God could be comprehended by reason, it would be no longer wonderful, and faith would have no merit if reason provided proof."

the form of a dove alighting on the pope's shoulder and whispering chant melodies into his ear.

Whether Gregory actually composed any specific chant is uncertain, but his contribution to the development of Christian worship is inestimable. For this reason, we have always informally labeled the entire body of chant literature Gregorian chant.

Later, these monophonic melodies would be given the name plainchant or plainsong (*cantus planus*) to differentiate them from the polyphonic music of the medieval period, which was referred to as measured song or figured song (*cantus mensuratus* or *cantus figuralis*).

Instrumentalists Need Not Apply

If you were a drummer or a piper during the centuries of chant, you had better have left your instrument at the church door. It may seem strange to us now, but all instruments were outlawed in church services. Even as late as 1160, when some churches were permitting occasional instruments, Aelred, abbot of Rievaulx, clamored against this: "Whence hath the Church so many organs and musical instruments? To what purpose, I pray you, is that terrible blowing of bellows, expressing rather the cracks of thunder, than the sweetness of a voice?"

How, you may ask, did church leaders justify this practice, which was in direct conflict with so many biblical references to instruments, such as Psalm 150? They would reply with numerous allegorical explanations: "The 'organ' is our body," or

*QUICK*TAKES
Recommended Recording

Gregorian Chant: Salve Regina
Benedictine Monks of the Abbey of Saint Maurice and Saint Maur
(Philips 420879–2)

The revival of Gregorian chant recordings makes it very difficult to select a favorite. The decision usually involves such choices as large choir versus small choir and cathedral ambiance versus studio acoustics. The Benedictine monks on this recording have chosen an admirable path between these extremes. Recording their moderately sized choir in a large church, they have carefully placed the microphones close enough to the voices to produce an intimate sound. Furthermore, these musicians sing with an emotion that is too often lacking in chant recordings. Wonderful examples of dramatic word painting are found in the Magnificat, Te Deum, and Ave Verum Corpus.

"Our tongue is the 'psaltery' of the Lord." Clement of Alexandria (circa 150–215) went so far as to interpret the "harp of ten strings" (Ps. 33:2) as simply a symbol for the Ten Commandments. These explanations may sound like double-talk to modern readers, but at that time, they served their purpose well.

There was another reason given for keeping the music exclusively vocal. Church leaders were understandably concerned with Christianity's many new

23

converts. A great deal of instrumental music was associated with pagan displays and rituals. To immediately distinguish the church from such paganism, the instruments had to go. As Saint John Chrysostom (circa 347–407) put it, "Everything must be banished which recalls the cult of pagan gods and the songs of actors."

You will remember from the previous chapter that Jewish synagogue leaders faced a similar problem with this kind of regulation. It was during the heyday of chant that the position of cantor was officially recognized in the Christian church. For that matter, scholars believe that many of the oldest chants developed from melodic formulas that originated in the music of the synagogue. Certainly the florid "Alleluia" chants had their roots in the euphoria of Hebrew worship.

The Offices

Gregorian chant was a practical and functional music to be used in worship services. The two primary services are the offices and the mass. So much has been written about them that we need only to explore the most important aspects that relate directly to music.

Most of us today know little about life in a functioning monastery, let alone the monastic life of the Middle Ages. Yet those very monks were the sole preservers of everything we know about early sacred music. These dedicated Christians lived a highly structured existence. Eight times every day

they worshiped the Lord together in song. Specific
chants were written for each of these canonical
hours, or offices:

Matins (very early morning)
Lauds (sunrise)
Prime (approximately 6 A.M.)
Terce (approximately 9 A.M.)
Sext (approximately noon)
Nones (approximately 3 P.M.)
Vespers (sunset)
Compline (evening or immediately
        following Vespers)

All of these offices represent dozens of beautiful
chants, but the one that has had the greatest musical
importance is Vespers. This office contains such
matchless hymns as the Magnificat (from Luke
1:46–55) and has been inspiring composers long
after the age of chant. One immediately thinks
of the magnificent Vespers of such masters as
Monteverdi (1567–1643), Mozart (1756–91), and
Rachmaninoff (1873–1943).

Numerous chants would be sung at the offices,
including psalms, hymns, and antiphons—there
are more antiphons than any other type of chant—
as well as chanting through various passages of
Scripture. Medieval monks probably sang more in
a given day than any professional singer of the
twentieth century.

The Mass

Depending upon your background, you either know very little about the mass or most everything about it. If you're Catholic, you've probably been to thousands of masses and can, more than likely, skip ahead to the next section. But if you're not, then you will be given enough information here to appreciate the mass's musical and historical significance.

This liturgical commemoration of the Last Supper is not only the primary worship service of the Catholic Church but also the inspiration for the finest masterpieces of hundreds of composers. And it should be noted that not all of history's greatest mass composers were Catholic—some were Protestant, Jewish, agnostic, or even atheist.

Certain parts of the mass change at different times during the liturgical year. These parts are called the proper of the mass because they are proper—appropriate—to specific days and seasons. The sections that remain in every mass, regardless of time of year, are collectively called the ordinary of the mass. It is the ordinary that contains the parts that are usually set as separate movements to music. The names of the movements are derived from the Greek or Latin words that begin the particular movement. Here is a list of parts of the mass that are frequently set to music:

Kyrie (from Kyrie eleison: "Lord, have mercy")

Gloria (from Gloria in excelsis Deo: "Glory to God in the highest")

- Qui tollis (from Qui tollis peccata mundi: "Who takes away the sin of the world")
- Quoniam (from Quoniam tu solus Sanctus: "For You alone are holy")
- Cum Sancto Spiritu ("Together with the Holy Spirit")

Credo ("I believe")
- Et incarnatus ("And was made flesh")
- Et resurrexit ("And he rose again")
- Amen ("Amen")

Sanctus ("Holy")

Benedictus (from Benedictus qui venit in nomine Domini: "Blessed is he who comes in the name of the Lord")

Agnus Dei ("Lamb of God")
- Dona nobis pacem ("Grant us peace")

A special mass called a requiem mass (or mass for the dead) has a specific place in music history. Its dramatic texts have inspired composers to create sensational works of almost operatic drama, especially in the eighteenth and nineteenth centuries. But in the requiem mass, there is no Credo or Gloria. Rather, it adds the following movements:

Requiem aeternam ("Eternal rest")
Lux aeternam ("Eternal light")
Dies irae ("Day of wrath")

Often, parts of the proper of the mass are also put to chant music, such as the Gradual, the

HILDEGARDE VON BINGEN

Born:
1098
Benersheim,
Rheinhessen

Died:
1179
Rupertberg

Occupation:
abbess, preacher

Hobbies/Interests:
poetry, music,
medicine

Quotation:
*"Let all the heavens
hear it and praise
God's Lamb in great
harmony."*

Alleluia, the Tract, the Offertory, the Preface, the Pater Noster, and the Communion.

Anonymous Composers Only Need Apply

Can you name five chant composers? No one else can either. We simply don't know who wrote the vast majority of chants. Many may have been spontaneously "composed" in improvised worship. Yet even when there was a specific composer, custom dictated that he (and, yes, it virtually was a male domain) remain anonymous.

A fascinating exception is **Hildegarde von Bingen** (1098–1179). This remarkable woman was pledged by her parents to the church, and from the tender age of eight, she lived a monastic life. She rose to the position of Mother Superior and even founded a convent where she served as abbess. A woman of poetic visions, Hildegarde wrote both the music and the words to many beautiful chants, most of which have only become well known in the late twentieth century. Borrowing elements from folk music, her chants contain innovations that feature melodies spanning two and a half octaves.

Later developments in the world of chant made this music even more interesting. Sometimes clever monks created additions to the antiphonal chants in the proper of the mass. These new melodies were called tropes. Once monks found that they could get away with it, the practice of "troping" became the rage in monasteries all over Europe, especially in the tenth and eleventh centuries.

Another innovation was the sequence. These were long melodies—apparently very well known in their day—that appeared virtually unchanged in a wide variety of diverse settings. Sequencing is much like inserting a long line from a popular tune into different songs. Sometimes sequences were extended melisma passages—that is, very long and fast melodies in one voice à la Alleluia—but often they contained long texts.

Legend has it that sequencing began with a monk named **Notker Balbulus** (840–912), known as the Stammerer. Supposedly he had a hard time learning the long melismas sung in his monastery of Saint Gall. So he quietly wrote extra words under them as an aid in memorization. In doing so, he—accidentally—invented the sequence.

Musical Missionaries

If all this seems a bit overwhelming, let us look at these forms in a different light. Chant, the offices, and the mass were more than simply an organization of sacred music. More important, they became the backbone of a powerful missionary movement.

Between the time of Constantine and the end of the first millennium, Christianity spread over the whole of Europe and beyond. Thousands and thousands of new converts—almost all illiterate—needed to be grounded in the Christian faith. One of the best vehicles for the teaching of Christian doctrine was this growing body of sacred music.

Music was for the masses of new Christians what books were to the few scholars of the time. The church fathers quickly grasped the evangelistic possibilities of sacred music and encouraged its universal use. As Ambrose boldly admitted, "Some claim that I have ensnared the people by the melodies of my hymns. I do not deny it!"

When Charlemagne became head of the Holy Roman Empire in 800, he sought to bring Gregorian chant into his entire realm. At times he had to reprove his leaders "to return to the fountain-head of Saint Gregory, since you have clearly debased the ecclesiastical chant." By the end of the tenth century, though, missionaries had taken the simple beauties and the Christian teachings of chant to every corner of Europe.

So when you are relaxing after a long day with a good recording of chant, do not simply imagine a group of nameless monks in their cells. Picture a group of peasants hearing the Christmas story in song for the first time. Imagine a group of singers energetically intoning the celebration of Easter for assemblies of new Christians who were thrilled to hear that "Christ is risen!" Virtually every Bible story would find its way into chant and liturgical dramas. In short, it was this sacred music that kindled the faith of the Western world.

Other Listening Recommendations

Only a few decades ago, most recordings of chant were by nonprofessional choirs that were often so dreadful that Pope Gregory would have placed them under papal arrest. Fortunately, recent years have given us a plethora of fabulous chant recordings, and they continue to get better. One hardly knows where to begin.

Let's keep it simple at this point. In later chapters, you will encounter many specific pieces (that is, you will be directed to Bach's Magnificat, Brahms's Requiem, Stravinsky's *Symphony of Psalms,* and so on). With chant, all the composers are anonymous anyway. So for now, you should simply hear some recordings of chant, period.

It does not matter if it is Gregorian chant or Byzantium chant or whether it is *Music for Septuagesima Sunday* or a recording of Christmas chant. It may be by a group of professional musicologists or by the Choir of the Abbey of [name your favorite monastery]. Find a good CD at the store or library and sample chant for yourself.

What is important is that you delve into the world of chant, that you experience the musical faith that moved Ambrose, Augustine, Gregory, and countless other Christians. Close your eyes and let yourself slip back a thousand years or so. And when you've savored chant's innocent glory for a while, then let's move into the next phase of sacred music: polyphony.

CHAPTER 3

MEDIEVAL POLYPHONY
(1000–1450)

We do not mean to prohibit the use of harmony occasionally on festive days. . . . We approve of such harmony as follows the melody at the intervals, for example, of the octave, fifth, and fourth, and such harmony that may be supported by the simple chant of the church.

Pope John XXII, Edict of 1325

We now enter an enigmatic part of music history. Nearly every music lover knows about the works of composers from Bach to Bernstein, that is, from the baroque to the twentieth century. And most people have heard some Gregorian chant. Yet between the eras of chant and baroque, there are two outstanding periods of music that are generally known as medieval (1000–1400) and Renaissance (1400–1600). (Again, these dates are very approximate and subjective.)

The medieval period was a fascinating time for the growth of music. The eleventh century saw dozens of major improvements to society, from the rise of modern cities and economic stimulation to the growth of universities and culture. Musically, the lightbulb seemed to turn on for the first time: music at the beginning of the medieval period sounds very strange to modern listeners, but music composed at the end of this period sounds like "normal" music.

The Supreme Innovation

The most important of many musical changes following chant is the addition of polyphony. This term simply means "many sounds," as opposed to monophony, or "one sound." For centuries sacred music was limited to the monophony of chant, with one note sung at a time without harmony or accompaniment. Soon, however, medieval composers would write for two different parts to be sung simultaneously . . . or three parts or four parts or more! That's polyphony.

You have to stop and ponder for a moment to realize the magnitude of this incredible innovation. Virtually every piece of music you have ever heard has been affected by it. Without polyphony, all you have is one melodic line. That's all. No harmony, no counterpoint, no chords, no pianos, no guitars, no orchestras. In fact, without polyphony, all you have is chant.

Short experiments in polyphony turned into extended compositions around the turn of the millennium. Actually, polyphony was doubtless used as far back as the seventh century, but we have only fleeting hints of it. The first simple indications of its practice are found in a ninth-century treatise called *Musica enchiriadis* ("Handbook of Music").

Organum

The first time you hear organum, an early polyphony, you shouldn't expect much. In its simplest form, a chant melody was sung while someone else sang exactly the same melody at a higher interval.

This may seem very elementary to you, but these musicians had to start somewhere. By the eleventh century, though, things became more interesting. Now there were several types of organum: parallel, contrary, and oblique.

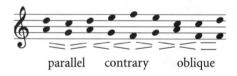

parallel   contrary   oblique

Numerous organum examples are found in a twelfth-century manuscript from Milan, which must be regarded as *the* how-to book in music history. When you see titles like *How to Read Music* or *How to Play Guitar,* remember it all began nine hundred years ago with this sublimely titled treatise, *Ad organum faciendum,* ("How to Make Organum").

Another type of organum, usually called florid organum, caught on like wildfire in the twelfth century. In these pieces, one singer continued the practice of singing a slow chant, while another singer sang a much more elaborate part. Like the jazz riffs of a later age, this upper part gave a talented singer something special to sing, while the less talented singers (or the congregation) plodded along on the slower chant part.

The slow chant melody became known as the cantus firmus ("fixed song"). In later compositions, the person who sang this chant was called the tenor, a term still in existence. The word *tenor* comes from the Latin *tenere,* meaning "to hold," and refers to holding very long chant tones. Sometimes in florid organum, the singer of the elaborate upper part may sing through forty or fifty fast notes while the tenor holds a single chant tone!

The Need for New Rhythmic Notation

The idea of florid organum posed a new problem: notation for rhythm. As we saw in the earlier examples, the initial organum had two singers (or vocal parts) singing the exact same rhythm. In those days, the old nonrhythmic chant notation still sufficed. But when long notes are mixed with short ones, clarity is suddenly needed. You can almost imagine the monks who sang the cantus firmus asking, "How long do you want us to hold this tone so that when you're finished with all those fast notes, we come out together?"

The medieval musicians came up with a solution called the rhythmic modes. These were short rhythmic patterns that were repeated to give the composition structure and rhythmic certainty.

I ♩♪   II ♪♩   III ♩. ♪♩

IV ♪♩ ♩.   V ♩. ♩.   VI ♪♪♪

As always, the example is given in modern notation for the sake of clarity. In medieval manuscripts, the actual notes were often compounded into ligatures. These obscure little squiggles were part of the evolution of notation, which still had a long way to go.

The basic hypothesis was that a melody in, shall we say, Mode II would have to continue that single rhythm until the piece was over! Fortunately, a degree of flexibility was allowed, and the rhythmic mode would change often in one piece. This somewhat unwieldy system worked better than before, but it would eventually need an overhaul.

A Musical Tribute to the Trinity

Any musician reading these descriptions will have noticed that all of the six rhythmic modes are in divisions of three, always producing music that sounds to us like 3/4 or maybe 6/8. The reason for this lies in the musician's respect for the Trinity and the number three. A theorist named Johannes de Muris wrote in 1319:

> That all perfection lies in the ternary number is clear from a hundred comparisons. In God, who is perfection itself, there is singleness in substance, but threeness in persons; He is three in one and one in three. . . . Three is the first odd number and the first prime number. It is not two lines but three that can enclose a surface. The triangle is the first regular polygon.

A threefold rhythmic pattern was called a *perfectio.* It was not until the fourteenth century that the "imperfect" modes were employed, producing the duple patterns of 2/4 that became so fundamental to later music composition.

Léonin and Pérotin of Notre Dame

Léonin and **Pérotin** are the first composers of polyphony whose names have come down to us. The Notre Dame where they worked was in Paris, but their church building was the predecessor to the famous cathedral we know today, whose cornerstone was dedicated by Pope Alexander in 1163.

We know that Léonin was a choirmaster at Notre Dame in the first half of the twelfth century. He wrote a huge volume of two-part compositions for the entire church year, called the *Magnus liber organum* (*The Great Book of Organum*). Unfortunately, the book in its original form has been lost to history. The bits and pieces that have survived demonstrate masterpieces of florid organum, with ornamental melodies of a solo part over the long tones of the congregation.

Pérotin picked up where Léonin left off, becoming Notre Dame's choirmaster around 1183. He and his contemporaries offered another improvement on organum: three and four parts instead of the usual two. This resulted in several complicated vocal lines, which must have sounded pretty wild to the hundreds of chant-singing monks all around Europe. Furthermore, having three or four parts often produced "chords," which sometimes sounded amazingly like the major and minor triads so important to later composers.

Now that we are finally out of the age of anonymous composers, we find a name you will already know: **Francis of Assisi** (circa 1181–1226). His beautiful *Canticle of the Sun* exists in a manuscript that has caused many a musicologist to tear out his hair. This battered manuscript clearly shows the famous text, and underneath the words is a large space that had apparently held the actual music notation. Unfortunately, this space has been blank for centuries.

FRANCIS OF ASSISI

Born:
circa 1181
Assisi, Italy

Died:
1226
Assisi, Italy

Occupation:
soldier, preacher, missionary

Hobbies/Interests:
music, nature, poetry

Quotation:
"Let those who belong to the devil hang their heads—we ought to be glad and rejoice in the Lord."

New Musical Forms

The conductus was a new form of music in the first half of the twelfth century. A piece in two, three, or four parts, it used Latin poems as texts. Instead of the long tones of chant, the words of a conductus were usually set syllabically. And instead of giving the tenor part an ancient chant, the composer usually supplied an original melody.

Then came the motet, which captured composers' imaginations in the second half of the century. One of the interesting aspects of these three- and four-part compositions had to do with their texts. The words in the various parts were usually from different texts and often in different languages. One singer might sing a French love ballad, while another might simultaneously sing a sacred chant text in Latin. This made for some odd titles, since the first line of a motet was generally taken for its title. But what happens if the first lines of all parts are different and simultaneous? Then you have compositions with such multi-titles as *Pucelete-Je Langui-Domino*.

If this practice seems scandalous to you, remember that in the Middle Ages there was not the great chasm between the secular and the sacred that we have today. Nevertheless, there were those who scorned these new ideas. John of Salisbury, for example, condemned the modern singers, who he believed sought "with the lewdness of a lascivious voice and in a singularly foppish manner, to feminize all their spellbound little followers with the girlish way they render the notes and end the phrases."

Yet the novelties continued. One of the most unusual was the hocket. This term is derived from the Latin word for hiccup, and for good reason. Using this technique, notes would be left out of one melody and supplied in another part so that the melody itself would be divided between the different voices. This back-and-forth technique became very popular, but it, too, gave the conservative crowd one

more thing to denounce. One of the most exagger-
ated denunciations of the use of hocket was given
by that lovable abbot, Aelred of Rievaulx:

> Sometimes thou mayst see a man with an
> open mouth, not to sing, be as if to breath out
> his last gasp, by shutting in his breath, and by
> a certain ridiculous interception of his voice to
> threaten silence, and now again to imitate the
> agonies of a dying man, or the ecstasies of
> such as suffer.

Franco of Cologne's Great Idea

Remember those rhythmic modes? Well, they worked
for a while but still left much to be desired. Enter
Franco of Cologne, a fine musician and theorist.
Around 1280, he summed up his ideas about notation in his *Ars cantus mensurabilis* (*The Art of
Mensurable Music*). Mensuration simply refers to the
temporal relationships between different note values. Musical history is profoundly indebted to Franco
for his ideas, since the theory behind them
is still in use today.

If you took piano lessons as a child, you learned
that one whole note equals two half notes or four
quarter notes or eight eighth notes and so on. The
concept behind this equal subdivision of time came
from Franco and his contemporaries. Their notation
gave us four types of note values:

⌐	the double long	■	the breve
⌐	the long	◆	the semi-breve

Depending on the specific composition, these note values still retained flexibility. For instance, a long might equal three breves (called perfect— again, note the tribute to the Trinity and the number three) or only two breves (called imperfect). This system gave composers much more room in which to experiment.

Franco's *Ars cantus mensurabilis* was more than just a theory book. It offered a generation of composers encouragement and instruction on their craft. For example, when writing about the composition of a conductus, Franco begins with a flourish that could not have been written in the Dark Ages: "He who wants to write a conductus should first compose as beautiful a melody as he can." Good advice for hundreds of years to come.

The "New Art"

As the fourteenth century rolled in, many things in the medieval world seemed destined to change. Archaic systems were soon to give way to the enlightenment of the Renaissance. Musically, this era is known as the *ars nova* ("new art"), in contrast with the *ars antiqua* ("old art") of the late thirteenth century.

It may seem strange and amusing today to call a centuries-old period the *ars nova*. The name was actually taken from the 1315 treatise of a French musician (and bishop of Meaux) named Philippe de Vitri. When he called the music of the previous century old fashioned, he apparently didn't think about the fact that his *ars nova* wouldn't always be the latest fad.

But this new music contained several unmistakably fresh ideas. One was a greater acceptance of "imperfect" rhythmic modes, that is, music in duple meter. Instead of the triple rhythms of the thirteenth century, the *ars nova* presents divisions of the beat into two parts. At the time, it was still experimental, but one day it would become the norm.

Isorhythm ("same rhythm") was another new idea. The concept was to use similar rhythms in a given melody at various places in a composition, particularly a motet, to give the music more organization. This germ of an idea would later evolve into the nineteenth-century, idea-fixed concept and the leitmotif of Richard Wagner. Some have even noted parallels between isorhythms and the tone rows of twentieth-century serial composers such as Arnold Schoenberg. A good idea may travel a long way indeed.

Still another innovation of the medieval period was the frequent use of *musica ficta* ("false music"). This does not refer to incorrect music or immoral music. In fact, *musica ficta* has opened the door for centuries of compositions.

To put it in nontechnical terms, a typical piece of music has not only notes on five lines but also a number of accidentals, which are called sharps (♯) and flats (♭).

If you have the opportunity, look at a piano. Notice the white keys and the black keys. You might

GUILLAUME DE MACHAUT

Born:
circa 1300
Machaut, France

Died:
April 13, 1377
Reims, France

Occupation:
notary, priest, composer, secretary to the king of Bohemia

Hobbies/Interests:
poetry

Quotation:
"May God give you perfect joy of all that your heart loves, and a good life and a long one."

say that the black keys are the sharps and flats. Therefore, without these accidentals, all we have are white keys. They are fine keys, of course, but those black keys help make some interesting music.

Now let's get back to the Middle Ages. Before the *ars nova*, almost all music was "white-key" music, meaning it had virtually no flats or sharps. All those centuries of chant can be played on your piano even if all the black keys are broken. (Chant occasionally uses a B♭, but seldom any other accidentals.) Yet in the fourteenth century, composers began using many sharps and flats, and the trend has never abated.

The First "Big-Name" Composers

Since so much of the *ars nova* music revolved around Paris, it is not surprising that the period's main composer was a Frenchman. **Guillaume de Machaut** (circa 1300–77) was certainly the most important composer of the fourteenth century, and he has a unique claim to fame. Machaut is surely the only musician in all of history who can be indisputably called the most important of his century. All later centuries had a number of claimants to that title.

Machaut was not only a musician but also a poet, a priest, and the secretary to King John of Bohemia. He followed his king in military campaigns throughout Europe and later served in the courts of France. Yet in all his extramusical duties, he found time to write a huge amount of music,

*QUICK*TAKES
Recommended Recording

Guillaume de Machaut
La Messe de Notre Dame
Oxford Camerata
Jeremy Summerly, director
(Maxos 8.553833)

The first "must-hear" of the medieval period is Machaut's celebrated *La Messe de Notre Dame*. The singers of the Oxford Camerata, under the authoritative direction of Jeremy Summerly, capture the rich open sounds of the medieval cadences while bringing out the occasional sharp dissonance without apology. The mass was recorded in Reims Cathedral, so the ambience is full and vibrant while the small size of the ensemble keeps the counterpoint clean. The result is enchanting, and the precise, pure tone given by the lower parts is especially noteworthy. Although many listeners may find this early piece unusual and unpredictable, give it a chance. Listen with open ears and open minds, for *La Messe de Notre Dame* is the culmination of the *ars nova*, a fourteenth-century masterpiece that belongs in the collection of every serious music lover.

including motets, songs, ballades, and the first famous mass in the annals of music.

Machaut's *La Messe de Notre Dame* is a true masterpiece. Not only is it beautiful to hear, but it is the first major work with structural integrity in its different movements. A short motive of chant is

FRANCESCO LANDINI

Born:
circa 1325
Fiesole, Italy

Died:
February 9, 1397
Firenze, Italy

Occupation:
composer, organist

Hobbies/Interests:
poetry, music theory

Quotation:
"Your song, which moves the heart, I send again to you in its new dress, that it may go and wander o'er all the earth, singing its strain."

found throughout the mass, and its Credo is particularly striking for the emotional setting of its words of testimony. This mass in four voices would be the standard for measuring all similar work for many years.

France may have been the center of fourteenth-century sacred music, but other countries had composers as well. Italian madrigals are usually associated with secular topics, but many of them also employed sacred texts. In England the composer **John Dunstable** (circa 1385–1453) was writing motets, songs, and hymns that inspired the faith of many of his contemporaries. Indeed, there is an English collection of music from this period that lists among its composers a "Roy Henry," commonly known as King Henry IV, who ruled England from 1399 to 1413.

Certain medieval composers who worked in secular song had a profound effect on composers who stayed within the church walls. A good example is the blind musician **Francesco Landini** (circa 1325–97). Although we know of no sacred compositions by this Italian master, he is credited with creating several musical innovations, including triadic chords and the melodic formula that bears his name—the Landini cadence—in which the sixth degree of the scale is inserted between the leading tone and the final octave.

Music of Burgundy

The dukes of Burgundy were fantastic patrons of music during the first seven decades of the fifteenth century. Their lands covered much of what is modern Belgium, Holland, and northern France. They sought out outstanding musicians for their courts, and their patronage helped create many masterpieces, both sacred and secular.

The leading composer of this musical movement is **Guillaume Dufay**, who was born about 1400 and lived until 1474. Like Machaut, Dufay was a well-educated man who traveled throughout Europe and eventually became a priest. Our principal interest in him is simple: he composed some very beautiful sacred music, notably his masses and motets.

Dufay's chief contribution to the ongoing progress of music is harmony. Earlier composers had written interesting melodies that sounded fine by themselves but often clashed when the entire piece was put together. Dufay was very concerned with a piece's overall effect and carefully wrote parts that together formed a harmonic entirety. The splendid result is amazingly similar to the chords of modern harmony.

Heading toward the Renaissance

The boundaries between musical ages are very fluid. It is not as though all composers woke up one morning and said, "Hey, I'm tired of writing medieval music. Let's start a renaissance!"

GUILLAUME DUFAY

Born:
circa 1400
Bersele, Belgium

Died:
November 27, 1474
Cambrai, Belgium

Occupation:
clerk, priest, composer, choirmaster

Hobbies/Interests:
traveling, scholarship

Quotation:
"With our Lord's help, may He grant you a good life and long, and heaven at last."

Change came very gradually in those times before modern forms of communication existed. A composer, say from Italy, might write something very innovative. Yet it would be months or years before a fellow composer in England might hear it and be inspired to use this innovation in his own music.

We associate the great rise of musical instruments with the Renaissance (and even more so with the baroque), yet there were more and more instances of their use in the fourteenth century. This is especially true of the organ, which was being added to many churches in Europe. Indeed, a number of the old organs in cathedrals had even added pedals.

Granted, the Renaissance era preceded the popularity of instrumental solo works, and instruments were still relegated to double vocal parts. Nevertheless, the use of an organ in sacred music was significant. A few centuries earlier these instrumentalists would probably have been thrown out of the church!

Another trend rises notably as we leave the medieval period: the growth of secular music. This does not necessarily mean that the composers of this era were irreligious; on the contrary, they were usually very devout. But for centuries all music had revolved around the church. Now composers began to use music to express topics and themes on all aspects of life, especially romantic love.

Other Listening Recommendations

Guillaume Dufay
Missa se la face ay pale

All Dufay masses are worth hearing, but this one is especially beautiful. The cantus firmus on which the movements are based is not an old chant, but a lovely song by Dufay, "If My Face Is Pale." You may not recognize the specific melody, but you will certainly note the beautiful harmony that permeates Dufay's work.

Also look for any recordings of the medieval period, with music by Léonin, Pérotin, Franco, Dunstable, or anyone else "medieval" you can find. As you hear the first great attempts at polyphony, isorhythm, and *musica ficta,* try to imagine the difficulties the composers had to contend with while breaking this new ground. It may sound new to you—perhaps even strange at first—but it possesses the beauty of transition, moving us from one musical period to another.

CHAPTER 4

THE RENAISSANCE
(1400–1600)

Modern Church music is so constructed that the congregation cannot hear one distinct word.

Desiderius Erasmus

Today we tend to think of the Renaissance as an idyllic time when everyone happily sat around painting, sculpting, writing great books, and thinking great thoughts. But as indicated by the above quotation, it was also a time of controversy and contention over the tremendous new arts coming forth. Most certainly, it was an exciting age in which to be alive. The same Erasmus who complained about the sacred music of his day admitted that "the world is coming to its senses as if awakening out of a deep sleep."

The word *renaissance* means "rebirth," and this awakening is most clearly seen in the visual arts. The master artists of this time saw their work as a rekindling of the glories of ancient Greece and Rome.

Leonardo da Vinci, Raphael, Botticelli, Michelangelo, and many others used ancient Greece as an inspiration to create many of the finest works of all time.

Yet their contemporaries' knowledge of the music of ancient Greece was inadequate, and this music was not very easy to emulate. Renaissance musicians sought instead to look forward and to glory in the innovations of their time. In fact, the Flemish musician Johannes Tinctoris made this startling comment in 1477: "There does not exist a single piece of music, not composed in the last forty years, that is regarded by the learned as worth hearing." Fortunately, his opinion did not persevere.

The Secular in the Sacred

Many modern books mention the conflict between the secular and the sacred in the Renaissance. For the musicians themselves it wasn't so much a conflict as an amalgamation, a constant mingling of the two. More composers began to write both sacred and secular songs, as has been the case in classical music to our own day.

Renaissance composers saw no conflict whatsoever between the secular and sacred realms, even when they brought the two forces into the same composition. One of the most popular practices was to compose a sacred mass using a popular tune of the day, which the composer invariably entitled *L'Homme Arme* (*The Armed Man*, that is, a man armed for battle). Dozens of Renaissance composers wrote at least one *l'homme arme* mass, from Dufay to Ockeghem to Josquin.

This practice would later be discouraged following the Reformation and Counter-Reformation. So many reforms were being called for that a composer had to be careful not to offend. Thus, a Renaissance composer might write a mass built around a secular tune or model but simply name the work *Missa sine nomine,* meaning "Mass without a name"!

Another "sacred-versus-secular" aspect of the Renaissance concerns instruments. For centuries the church had kept instruments outside the church walls, so most instrumental pieces became associated with secular composition. By the end of the Renaissance, however, choirs would not only use an organ but would also often employ brass, strings, or even orchestral accompaniment.

Much has also been written about the "Renaissance sound." The composers of this period loved a smooth, homogeneous tone color, preferably from a four-part vocal ensemble—the different parts being of equal importance. Naturally, there are many exceptions, but this four-part-chorus trend would eventually become the "SATB" (soprano, alto, tenor, bass) we have today. Of course, in the Renaissance, only men and boys were allowed to sing these parts. We still had a long way to go.

The Printing Press

It is impossible to exaggerate the tremendous impact that the invention of the printing press had on the music world. When Johannes Gutenberg (1390–1468) built his movable-type masterpiece in 1450, he was thinking about printing words only. But within twenty-five years the printing press was being used to produce books of plainchant.

A few years later someone tried printing music using woodblocks, but this was very difficult and time consuming. Finally, in 1501, a Venetian printer named **Ottaviano dei Petrucci** (1466–1539) published a collection of polyphonic music printed from a musical movable type.

Now copies of a new composition from one city could be copied en masse and taken throughout the Continent. Composers could be assured of accurate parts instead of the many errors that had crept into hand copies. The new printing technique was still tedious and expensive, far removed from our photocopying machines and computer graphics. But it was a great step in the right direction.

The printing press came at the perfect time for the musical world. The Renaissance refined the trend toward functional harmony. Renaissance composers really began to imagine each part simultaneously, seeing their pieces as a whole. Instead of writing out individual parts, they wrote out full scores from which parts could then be extracted. And the new printing presses could print the entire score in bountiful numbers.

Ockeghem and Obrecht

Remember how there were virtually no composers to note from the chapter on chant? Not any more! Starting with the Renaissance, many composers entered the scene, so we have to be rather selective in our focus. The first composer we will examine is a Netherlander who followed in the Burgundian footsteps of Dufay, **Johannes Ockeghem** (circa 1410–96).

For more than half his life, Ockeghem worked in the chapel of the king of France. He influenced many younger musicians and was so beloved that many composed laments in commemoration of his death. One of them described him as "learned, handsome in appearance, and not stout."

Like so many Renaissance masters, Ockeghem wrote motets and chansons, but his forte was the mass. His twelve masses are distinctive for their incredibly long, protracted melodies, which have exhausted singers for centuries. He also loved to extend the bass range very low, creating a darker, richer sound than that of his contemporaries.

Another great composer of the early Renaissance was **Jacob Obrecht** (circa 1452–1505). He wrote twice as many masses as Ockeghem as well as many beautiful sacred motets. Continuing the emphasis on harmonic expansion, Obrecht's work is sprinkled with what are now called dominant-tonic cadences. He also loved to insert secular tunes into his sacred works. His *Mass carminum* contains more than twenty examples of these "unholy tunes."

**JOSQUIN
DESPREZ**

Born:
circa 1440
Condé, France

Died:
August 27, 1521
Condé-sur-l'Escaut,
France

Occupation:
composer, singer,
choirmaster

Hobbies/Interests:
humor, traveling

Quotation:
*"Oh Lord, you have
dealt graciously with
your servant."*

Josquin Desprez

Much of the Renaissance belongs to one musician, **Josquin Desprez** (circa 1440–1521). He was such a cosmopolitan composer that it is difficult to pin him down to one area or style. In his lifetime he traveled all over Europe, and his music seems to have impressed everyone who heard it. It still does.

Martin Luther gave Josquin a profound tribute: "He is the master of the notes, which must do as he wills; other composers must do as the notes will." His talent was extraordinary, and he was well compensated for it. In a letter of 1495, a duke who needed a new court composer was advised to hire Flemish composer Heinrich Isaac instead of Josquin because "Josquin asks 200 ducats while Isaac is pleased with 120." The duke knew that quality was worth it and hired Josquin.

What was it that everyone loved about Josquin's music? He was one of the first great masters of emotion in music. Like Beethoven a few centuries later, Josquin openly sought to move his audience. This desire is especially evident in his hundred or so motets, many of which are based on Bible stories. But the emotional element is also found in his twenty masses, in which he skillfully uses word painting and imitation to inspire his contemporaries anew with the ancient Latin text.

It is difficult to find live performances of Josquin's work, but much of it is now recorded. When you hear the beauty of his perfectly balanced voices, you may

*QUICK*TAKES
Recommended Recording

Giovanni Pierluigi da Palestrina
Missa Papae Marcelli

Choir of Westminster Cathedral
David Hill, director

(Hyperion CDA66266)

Palestrina's mass represents the high-water mark of Renaissance music. It has been said that this single work saved polyphony from being outlawed by the Council of Trent. Anyone who has heard this recording can understand why the council was won over to Palestrina's side: it was and remains an inspired work of timeless beauty. Without the excesses of chromatism, this "white-key" music is nevertheless highly passionate. David Hill's singers are not afraid to wring out the emotional content of the work, and their pure-tone Renaissance vocal style is enhanced by their evident love of the music. The magnificent ambience of the Westminster Cathedral is the perfect setting for this pinnacle of cathedral music.

think you are hearing heavenly music. At the least, you will agree with Luther's assessment.

The Reformation
Speaking of Luther, you will recall that in the middle of the Renaissance came the Protestant Reformation. This colossal movement had an unprecedented effect not only on the history of Christianity but

also on the history of sacred music. From this time forward, nothing would ever be quite the same.

This does not mean that now we will be studying Protestant sacred music versus Catholic sacred music. It's not that simple. For one thing, both Catholic and Protestant composers throughout the centuries would often compose sacred music from traditions outside their own. Hence, the Lutheran Bach wrote the Mass in B Minor and the Catholic Haydn wrote such nonliturgical (and non-Latin) sacred music as *The Creation*.

Rather, the Protestants' new emphasis on the role of the laity introduced an entirely new stream of music for their emerging congregations (Lutheran, Baptist, and so on). Of course, the Catholic congregations had been singing every Sunday for years, but their parts were usually subservient to the more exalted melodies of the choir and the trained musical leadership. Now the new Protestant congregations wanted everyone to sing, which meant composing a huge and popular genre of unpretentious music suitable for those who were not only unable to read music but also illiterate.

Therefore, the two streams of sacred music that emerged might well be viewed as the "popular" versus the "classical," or perhaps the music of the congregation versus that of the sophisticated music lover and professional musician. The former includes the entire genre that began with Lutheran chorales and the rise of hymnology. The latter continued in the classical tradition and would later be found as frequently in the concert hall as in the church.

Of course, the Protestant musicians had a monumental task before them: to quickly create an entire body of music for their new congregations to sing. They would be busy with this for some time, and it would be years before great Protestant "classical" composers such as Heinrich Schütz or Johann Sebastian Bach would make their mark on the musical world. In the meantime, Catholic composers continued to produce masterpieces within the classical tradition.

Palestrina and the Counter-Reformation

Soon after Luther and his colleagues began breaking away from the church in Rome, the Catholic authorities launched the Counter-Reformation. Few modern readers of any faith can fully comprehend all the ramifications of these ecclesiastical matters, but every music lover is certainly thankful for the greatest musical representative of the era: **Giovanni Pierluigi da Palestrina** (circa 1525–94).

Palestrina was one of the greatest composers of all time, on a par with Bach, Mozart, and Beethoven. His music has been loved and studied so intently that the phrase "Palestrina style" is synonymous with the pinnacle of High Renaissance music. Even today, over four centuries after his death, every college music student has to learn the basics of Palestrina-style counterpoint.

Why is this? Simply because his music is extraordinarily beautiful. Unlike many of his colleagues, Palestrina strove for the purity of each individual

GIOVANNI PIERLUIGI DA PALESTRINA

Born:
circa 1525
Palestrina, Italy

Died:
February 2, 1594
Rome, Italy

Occupation:
composer, teacher, choirmaster

Hobbies/Interests:
business

Quotation:
"If men take such pains to compose beautiful music for profane songs, one should devote as much thought to sacred song, nay, even more than to mere worldly matters."

59

line, with little chromaticism. Even though he often used four or six parts in his masses, he arranged the words of the singers to coincide so that the text could be easily understood. He composed a huge volume of sacred music: more than 100 masses, 56 spiritual madrigals, and 450 liturgical motets.

With so much to choose from, we need a good starting place: Palestrina's magnificent *Missa Papae Marcelli* (*Mass of Pope Marcellus*). The story goes that during the Council of Trent (1545–63), a faction of the clergy was so bent on reformation that they advocated the complete abolishment of polyphony in favor of nothing but chant. Palestrina composed this mass to show that chant was not the only way to worship God through music, and the council warmed to his side. Whatever the historical significance of origin, this beautiful mass is one of the crowns of the Palestrina epoch (see description in this chapter's "Quick Takes").

The Rise of National Styles

In studying sacred music written before the Renaissance, one doesn't often think in terms of English music versus French music versus German music. Virtually all pre-Reformation composers were controlled by the authorities in Rome. And before the invention of the printing press, new manuscripts didn't circulate very quickly around the Continent.

But the Renaissance produced a rebirth of national identity that surfaced in the visual arts, in literature, and in music. Italy remained, of course, the leader of sacred music in the Catholic Church. But now we find stylistic differences in the music from the Netherlands, France, Spain, England, Germany, and the lands of eastern Europe. We even find music composed in the vernacular instead of Latin, such as in the French chanson and the German lied.

Many new forms of music were created, some of which found their way into sacred music. Since instrumental compositions now consisted of such forms as the canzone, ricercar, theme and variation pieces, and dozens of dances, sacred works might include the *frottola* (a simple chorus form with multiple verses), the *lauda* (popular devotional songs), and the *Madrigali spirituali* (a sacred-text version of the celebrated madrigal). All of these represent the efforts of composers to express their devotion with greater latitude than found in the standard mass or motet.

Another important innovation of the era will surprise modern readers. The composers called it *musica reservata* ("reserved music"), but we might call it simply fitting the music to the meaning of the words. This may seem like an obvious thing to do nowadays, but it was quite a milestone in vocal composition and has been a rule of thumb ever since.

Many composers of sacred music emerged during this time, and you ought to know a few names.

ORLANDUS LASSUS

Born:
1532
Mons, Belgium

Died:
June 14, 1594
Munich, Germany

Occupation:
choirboy, composer,
court musician

Hobbies/Interests:
publishing, business

Quotation:
*"God by His grace
guide us and lead us
to safety."*

Orlandus Lassus

Orlandus Lassus (1532– 94), sometimes called
Orlando di Lasso, roamed around much of Europe
in his youth but eventually settled in and spent most
of his adult life at the Ducal Chapel in Munich. He
was the first truly great composer to emerge from
the Germanic lands. In contrast with the clarity of
Palestrina's music, Lassus's work is almost Beethoven-
like in its emotional unpredictability. He composed
volumes of sacred work, the finest examples of
which are his motets, especially the 1604 collection
he entitled *Magnum Opus Musicum* (*Great Work
of Music*). Yet his most famous works were of an
earlier period, such as the moving *Penitential Psalms*
of 1560.

William Byrd

Owing to Henry VIII's separation from Rome,
it should not surprise us that **William Byrd**
(1543–1623) would be the last great Catholic composer from England for quite a while. Because the
religious mood of his country was against him, he
only wrote three Latin masses, but they are excellent. He also composed music for the Anglican
Church and worked for years in the Royal Chapel as
the only Catholic. Byrd seemed to get along with
everyone in an age when having both Catholic and
Protestant friends could be dangerous. One of the
great loves of his long life was the setting of biblical
passages to music. He would often employ the imi-
tative counterpoint of his Continental colleagues,

adding a highly original smattering of sharp dissonances. A fascinating example is Byrd's motet *Laudate pueri dominum,* in which he allows the lovely contrapuntal melodies to clash at unexpected points and so keeps the listener's interest.

Giovanni Gabrieli

Most every brass player today loves the music of **Giovanni Gabrieli** (circa 1556–1612) of Venice. Gabrieli began a "big-is-beautiful" tradition that many composers still adhere to. Gabrieli didn't just write for a chorus, but for double choruses, triple choruses, even as many as five choruses singing with one another antiphonally. He often combined large instrumental ensembles, not just to accompany the choruses but to answer them in turn. Gabrieli was also one of the first composers to indicate forte (loud) and piano (soft) in his scores—quite an innovation in those days. The love of contrast is evident in many of his works and is especially notable in the motet *In Ecclesiis,* which is frequently performed today.

Heading toward the Baroque

So what has happened to bring us out of the Renaissance and into the baroque? One answer is to look at the differences between the early Renaissance and the late Renaissance. The very trends that transformed this epoch are those that move us into the next.

WILLIAM BYRD

Born:
1543
London, England

Died:
July 4, 1623
Stondon, Essex

Occupation:
composer, organist, choirmaster

Hobbies/Interests:
art, poetry

Quotation:
"Since singing is so good a thing, I wish all men would learn to sing!"

One of the most important, at least to musicians, is often overlooked by the layperson: the evolution of modality to tonality.

This is not the book to explain all the theoretical implications of modality versus tonality. Suffice it to say that during the Renaissance and earlier, a composer would work within a framework of modes, such as the Dorian mode or the Ionian mode. After the Renaissance and up to the twentieth century, composers wrote in major or minor keys, such as C major or E minor.

Hence, older music has such titles as *Mass in the Aeolian Mode* or *Motet in the Lydian Mode*. From the baroque era onward, you don't find these titles. Instead, you'll see Suite in B Minor or Mass in D Major.

Of course, this is much more than simply a matter of titles. Under the modal system, virtually every note played or sung was just as important as the next. No system of hierarchy was necessary. In fact, the piece seemed to end wherever it wanted, and we are often rather surprised and perplexed at the place where it actually does end.

But as the baroque style approached, the music gained more direction and order. Certain pitches— we call them tonic and dominant—became more important than others. Since the most important pitch usually began and ended the composition, the listener got a feel of purposeful progression: one began in one place, proceeded away from it, and finally returned home.

Texture and rhythm were also "modernized"
by the end of the Renaissance. In the texture of early
works, no one part was more important than the
other. Usually one part (today we often refer to it as
the melody) took prominence over the other parts,
which melded into the harmony.

Rhythmically, the haphazard multirhythms of
the medieval and Renaissance ages began to group
themselves in one of two basic categories. Musicians
often notice that the bar lines placed in modern
editions of Renaissance compositions don't seem as
obtrusive toward the end of the period as they did
earlier. By the baroque era, rhythms were either
found in groups of three (the beginnings of 3/4
time, 3/8 time, and so on) or groups of two (the
beginnings of 2/4 time, 4/4 time, and so on).

Toward the end of the Renaissance period,
composers began to offer tantalizing bits of detail.
Specifically, they tended to say which instrument or
voice part they wanted to play or sing a certain line
of music. Again, providing such concrete instruc-
tions may seem like an obvious thing to do from
today's viewpoint, but in most early music compositions these indications of specific instrumentation
were left unwritten. A piece of music could be
played by practically any available instrument. Not
any more. Composers were now more specific: this
line for the violin, this line for the flute, and so on.

Even the use of the human voice changed.
The straight choral sound that is so characteristic
of the Renaissance succumbed to a new way of solo

Other Listening Recommendations

William Byrd
Sonets and Songs of Sadness and Piety

Giovanni Gabrieli
In Ecclesiis

Josquin Desprez
Missa Pange Lingua

Orlandus Lassus
Penitential Psalms

Jacob Obrecht
Missa Caput

Johannes Ockeghem
Missa Prolationum

singing, full of dramatic expression, which led to another new musical form: opera. We soon will see this dramatic new musical form entering the picture as well, from Bach's Mass in B Minor to Handel's *Messiah*.

FROM BAROQUE TO HYMNOLOGY

CHAPTER 5

THE BAROQUE PERIOD
(1600–1750)

Music's only purpose should be for the glory of God and the recreation of the human spirit.

Johann Sebastian Bach

In this wonderful period of music we begin to hear familiar names like Bach and Handel as well as famous pieces like the "Hallelujah Chorus" and the *Brandenburg Concertos.*

Suddenly we feel that we have entered the modern era, as if we have turned a corner in the history of music. It was a fantastic time for sacred music, especially the latter half of the period, and nearly all great composers of the baroque created sacred masterpieces that are frequently performed today.

Claudio Monteverdi
Bach and Handel may have been the most famous musicians of the baroque era, but they weren't the only great ones. If fact, they do not appear until the last

CLAUDIO MONTEVERDI

Born:
May 15, 1567
Cremona, Italy

Died:
November 29, 1643
Venice, Italy

Occupation:
composer, conductor, choirmaster

Hobbies/Interests:
poetry, drama

Quotation:
"The modern composer builds his work on the basis of truth."

third of this 150-year period of music. The first two composers of note, Claudio Monteverdi and Heinrich Schütz, form a link to the Renaissance, from both the Catholic and the Protestant points of view.

Claudio Monteverdi (1567–1643) may not get as much play as Bach and Handel, but he was one of the most innovative composers in history. Today he is principally remembered for writing the first masterpiece of opera, *Orfeo* (1607). One of its many novelties was an orchestra of some forty players. (Remember, Monteverdi lived long before the days of Berlioz or Wagner.)

But he also wrote sacred music, including three beautiful masses and his most acclaimed work, the *Vespers*. The *Vespers* consist of a collection of contrasting movements that culminate in a splendid Magnificat, whose text was taken from the well-known passage in the first chapter of Luke's Gospel. Sometimes we hear an organ solo, sometimes a double choir whose orchestral accompaniment includes sensational trombone passages. The work contains as much raw drama as any opera.

Heinrich Schütz

Do you remember in the last chapter when we discussed the Reformation? You may recall that Luther and his followers had a huge task before them. They all wanted music, but they wanted nothing to do with the music of Roman Catholicism—that is, *all* of the sacred music of Christendom up to that time!

So they had a lot to do to create their own version of sacred music.

Developing a new genre of popular church music was no easy task, of course, and it took a while for the Protestants to produce their first great "classical" composer. His name was **Heinrich Schütz** (1585–1672), and he began a great Germanic tradition of composition that soon included Bach, later Beethoven, and the many German composers of the nineteenth and twentieth centuries.

Schütz wrote huge amounts of sacred music, including four settings of Christ's Passion, the "Resurrection" and "Christmas" oratorios, twenty-six *Psalms of David,* and a very moving *Seven Last Words of Jesus.* This last piece was composed during the ravages of the Thirty Years' War and used chorale tunes in a way that presupposes the work of Bach. The suffering of the Passion is underscored by an instrumental movement called the "Trauer-Symphonie" ("Grief Symphony"). Schütz may still be considered early baroque, but he seems a world away from the purity of a Palestrina mass.

Henry Purcell

We now come to the last great English composer until the advent of the twentieth century: **Henry Purcell** (1658–95). The same country that gave us so much magnificent literature seems to have missed music class for a few centuries. Music composition class, that is—there have always been many fine English performers.

71

Many theories have discussed this dearth of composers, but none completely explain it. Perhaps England's geographical location separated it a bit too much from the compositional activities on the Continent. Perhaps the fact that England was so often at war with its European neighbors prevented artistic pursuits.

Fortunately, Purcell could not foresee the turbulent future of his country, and so he simply concentrated on writing excellent music. He served for many years as the organist of Westminster Abbey and became the leading composer of the Anglican Church. His best-known work, the opera *Dido and Aeneas,* is still performed often, as are his two Latin motets, *Beati omnes qui timent Dominum* and *Jehovah quam multi sunt hostes.*

Purcell's *Dido and Aeneas* was composed for a girls' boarding school in Chelsea and has long been recognized as a turning point in opera history. It tells a story based on Virgil's *Aeneid* with drama and pathos. Particularly moving is the famous death scene "Dido's Lament," in which the dying heroine intones, "Remember me, but ah! forget my fate!"

Purcell was also a master of shorter pieces—anthems, odes, and beautiful songs—some of which are the finest in the English language. His choral writing is especially joyous, particularly his *Ode for Saint Cecilia's Day* and the ever-popular "Rejoice in the Lord." Purcell was in many ways the English counterpart of Heinrich Schütz in that they both made emotional expression the focal point of their sacred music.

Vocal Parts and Their Accompaniment

Let's take a short break between composers and look at an important musical difference between the Renaissance and the baroque. In the former, composers typically worked within a chorus of equal voices (think of a mass by Josquin or Palestrina). Those beautiful voices, with their polyphonic melodies so intertwined as to form one resounding tone color, epitomized the Renaissance sound.

This model gives way to a different concept in the baroque era. The outermost vocal parts (soprano and bass) become most important, with the inner parts serving a complementary role. This model further evolved until the typical baroque sound consisted of a treble melody, a solid bass line, and a harpsichord or lute strumming through chordlike accompaniment.

Baroque composers began a novel way of notating this new combination. They would often write out only the soprano melody and the bass line, the latter containing little numbers next to each note. These numbers constituted a basso continuo, or figured bass part, which a skillful accompanist would interpret to add the inner parts.

Of course, the actual notes might differ with each performance, but this did not seem to bother baroque composers, who were always skillful performers themselves. This semi-improvisational art has largely died out today, and modern editors of

ANTONIO VIVALDI

Born:
March 4, 1678
Venice, Italy

Died:
July 27, 1741
Vienna, Austria

Occupation:
teacher, composer, violinist, priest

Hobbies/Interests:
traveling, business

Quotation:
"*I have not been saying Mass for the last twenty-five years, nor shall I ever say it again, not because of any prohibition or command, but at my own election, and this because of an illness I have been suffering from birth, which keeps me oppressed.*"

baroque music usually write out the genuine notes in accompaniment parts instead of leaving us to figure out all those little numbers.

Antonio Vivaldi

In the meantime, let's move back to Italy. Although the northern Protestants were making headway in their music, Italy still exercised a profound influence on baroque sacred music, producing a number of excellent composers such as Corelli, Tartini, Torelli, and, especially, Vivaldi.

The music of **Antonio Vivaldi** (1678–1741) brings us into a new century. The son of a prominent violinist, Vivaldi entered the priesthood in his twenties but spent most of his life involved in music. His flaming red hair earned him the nickname *il prete rosso* ("the red priest"), a moniker he retained even after he became famous throughout Europe.

For thirty-five years Vivaldi worked as the director of music at Venice's Conservatory of the Pietà, a huge, well-endowed orphanage for girls that offered music education. The result was a musical extravaganza, and the orphanage's many performances were enthusiastically praised by their audiences. One of Vivaldi's contemporaries remembered that the students were "reared at public expense and trained solely to excel in music. And so they sing like angels, and play the violin, the flute, the organ, the violoncello, and the bassoon."

As you might imagine, these talented teenagers kept their music director quite busy. Vivaldi composed with lightning speed, priding himself on being able to write a new piece faster than the copyist could reproduce the individual parts! He is best remembered for his instrumental concertos (more than four hundred have survived), which were usually performed by his best students at the frequent church festival services.

Somehow Vivaldi also found time to compose forty-nine operas, dozens of sonatas and sinfone, and a host of sacred music—motets, oratorios, and cantatas. His best-known sacred work is the *Gloria,* for soloists, chorus, and orchestra. From the opening shouts of "Gloria!" this work conveys the joy of singing to the glory of God. The duet Laudamus te contains such ebullient music that in several passages the interplay between the two vocal parts seems to suggest the sounds of laughter.

Oratorios, Cantatas, and Passions

Every new era has its own musical forms. Of course, many forms—such as the symphony—are used for centuries and therefore transcend the musical ages. The three genres listed above have been used by composers of other ages but not to the extent that baroque composers employed them. The oratorios of Handel and the cantatas and passions of Bach are so celebrated that these forms will always be associated with baroque sacred music.

A typical definition of the word *oratorio* reads as follows: "An extended composition for vocal soloists, chorus, and orchestra, sung without costumes, scenery, or action. Usually of religious character." We could add that an oratorio is somewhat like an opera but without the costumes, props, and acting. In other words, the singers simply stand there and sing the various movements, rather like a cast of players reading aloud the script of a play but not acting it out.

The roots of the oratorio date back centuries to the medieval mystery plays, in which biblical subjects were acted out in a combination of music and drama. But the form really became popular in the eighteenth century, and its greatest exponent was Handel. In fact, the most popular choral music in history is one of his oratorios, *Messiah*. The oratorio and the mass are the two pinnacles of choral music from 1700 onward, as they employ the greatest forces: chorus, orchestra, and a number of vocal soloists.

The cantata is similar to the oratorio but shorter and smaller in scope. Some cantatas involve secular themes, such as the well-known *Coffee Cantata* of J. S. Bach. But the majority of cantatas' themes involve biblical subjects and, in the case of Bach, span the vast gamut of Christian theology. Like its big brother the oratorio, the cantata uses a number of contrasting movements, employing chorus, orchestra, and soloists but in smaller quantities.

Another member of this family is the passion, which concerns the death of Jesus Christ. The texts were originally verbatim accounts from any of the four Gospels (Matt. 26–27, Mark 14–15, Luke

22–23, and John 18–19), though later examples also add poetic text by contemporary writers. The earliest musical passions date back to ninth-century chants, but the greatest examples of this genre come from the pen of J. S. Bach.

Comparing the Lives of Handel and Bach

Whenever two great men appear almost simultaneously in history, it is always interesting to compare them. The comparison between Handel and Bach is quite common in music books, as it is fascinating to note their similarities and differences. But as you will see, at least one area in their lives is often misinterpreted in contemporary accounts.

Let's begin with their resemblances. Both were born in 1685 within one month of each other (Handel on February 23, Bach on March 21), and both were steeped in a rich Germanic tradition of local music (Handel in Halle, Bach in Eisenach). Their primary instruments were the organ and the harpsichord, though both were excellent violinists as well. And both became masters of composition in many of the same genres—choral music, orchestral music, and chamber music.

Now the differences, and they are considerable. Bach came from a family of musicians dating back generations, whereas Handel's father hated music and thwarted his son's study. Bach never moved far from the place of his birth and was only known locally; Handel traveled widely—living for years in Italy and later in England—and became world famous.

**GEORGE
FRIDERIC
HANDEL**

Born:
February 23, 1685
Halle, Saxony

Died:
April 14, 1759
London, England

Occupation:
composer, organist

Hobbies/Interests:
business, art

Quotation:
"*Whether I was in
the body or out of
my body when I
wrote it [Messiah],
I know not.*"

Furthermore, Bach worked principally for churches, while Handel received commissions from kings, courts, a variety of patrons, and other secular sources.

At this point most musicologists falsely conclude that Bach was a religious composer and that Handel was a secular composer. At least one author has even proposed that Handel was an atheist. Such conjecture is not backed up by fact. Both men were devout Christians, as documented by their own words and by those who knew them. Both composed sacred as well as nonsacred works. Just because Handel did not feel called to work at a church did not mean that he didn't take his faith seriously. The composer of *Messiah* was certainly not an unbeliever.

George Frideric Handel

Since he was born a few weeks earlier than his Saxon counterpart, let's examine Handel first.

Handel's father did all he could to discourage his son's musical abilities, yet the boy became the organist at Halle's Cathedral, his first job while still in his teens. Handel lived a few years in Hamburg, mostly composing for the opera house, but it was here where he created his first sacred work, the *Saint John* Passion. Even at such a young age, the composer's love of melodrama is evident, especially in the "crowd scene" choruses.

Late in 1706 he moved again, this time to Italy. In this musical land Handel learned a great deal and spent most of his composition time producing Italian operas. Three years later he accepted a post

*QUICK*TAKES
Recommended Recording

Johann Sebastian Bach
Saint Matthew Passion

**Chicago Symphony Orchestra and Chorus
Sir Georg Solti, conductor**

(London 421177–2)

It can be said that the culmination of the baroque era was in the person of J. S. Bach and that the culmination of Bach's work was his *Saint Matthew* Passion. Certainly this work most powerfully expressed the faith of the composer and his age. Of the many worthy recordings of the Passion, the above was specifically selected for its impeccable chorus. The German of the chorus members is crisp and weighty, and when they shout "Barabbas" during the demanding crowd scenes, the effect is overwhelming. Solti's dramatic control of the symphony is superb, and the soloists' performances are also noteworthy, especially the lovely soprano of Kiri te Kanawa and the strong tenor of Hans Peter Blochwitz, who sings the challenging role of the evangelist.

in Hanover and during this time made a visit to London that changed his life. Discovering that Italian opera—his specialty—was the rage in London, he was determined to live there himself.

Thus, from 1712 until his death, Handel lived in England. Unfortunately, it so happened that London audiences tired of Italian opera just about the time Handel arrived. Nevertheless, the determined composer wrote opera after opera until he almost starved to death. It finally dawned on him that this would never work, and he turned his attention to a new genre, the oratorio. It was in this field that he would compose his greatest works.

Most of Handel's oratorios are based on biblical stories and include *Esther, Samson, Belshazzar, Saul,* and *Israel in Egypt.* Even though they involve no staging, costumes, or acting, these oratorios are so dramatic that if you close your eyes during a performance, you will think you are actually at an opera. The London audiences adored these pieces and attended hundreds of performances. Although Handel's oratorios are still performed today, one stands out above the others: *Messiah.*

Much has been written about the amazing twenty-four days in which Handel composed the 260-page manuscript of the world's most popular choral masterpiece. Suffice it to say that *Messiah* was truly a divinely inspired work, a work that has brought more people into the Christian faith than any other piece of music in history. Handel biographer Robert Manson Myers wrote that *Messiah* "has probably done more to convince thousands of mankind that there is a God about us than all the theological works ever written."

The text of this celebrated oratorio consists of a series of fifty-six excerpts from the King James Bible. It is divided into three sections: the first part describes the coming of Christ to earth, the second Christ's sacrifice and victory, and the third the hope and faith of Christianity. *Messiah* features a dramatic mix of choruses, recitatives, and arias. It includes such famous arias as "Every Valley" and "I Know My Redeemer Liveth" as well as the rousing choruses "For unto Us a Child Is Born," "Hallelujah," "Worthy Is the Lamb," and many others.

Despite the tragic renditions by many under-rehearsed choirs and the grotesquely overblown reorchestrations we hear so often (once it was performed using almost one thousand players!), *Messiah* still reigns supreme within the choral repertoire. Perhaps this is as it should be. A comment the composer made following the first London performance of *Messiah* shows us his urge to bless others. When Lord Kinnoul congratulated Handel on the excellent "entertainment," Handel immediately replied, "My Lord, I should be sorry if I only entertain them; I wish to make them better."

Johann Sebastian Bach

Handel's *Messiah* is a tough act to follow. Nevertheless, our friend J. S. Bach is up to the task. (Incidentally, we usually call him "J. S." instead of simply "Bach" because there are a number of other Bachs who were also noted composers. Most of these were his own sons, such as Carl Philipp Emanuel Bach and Johann Christian Bach. But in this book, if the name "Bach" appears alone, be assured that it is a reference to **Johann Sebastian Bach.**)

JOHANN SEBASTIAN BACH

Born:
March 21, 1685
Eisenach, Thuringia

Died:
July 28, 1750
Leipzig, Germany

Occupation:
choirmaster, composer, conductor, organist

Hobbies/Interests:
numerology, pipe smoking

Quotation:
"I was obliged to work hard. Whoever is equally industrious will succeed just as well."

In many ways Bach himself represents the pinnacle of sacred music. This genius lived most of his life working for obscure churches, and little of his music was published during his lifetime. He had one great desire, which he announced even as a young man: to create "well-regulated church music to the glory of God."

Bach worked in a number of towns in Germany, but his career can be thought of as being divided into three principal positions. His first major position was that of organist and concertmaster in the chapel of the duke of Weimar, where Bach wrote his greatest organ music. He later worked for several years as music director in the court of Cöthen, where most of his superb instrumental works were created. Finally, he moved his family to Leipzig when he became the cantor of the Saint Thomas Church. It was here that he composed his finest choral works, including most of his cantatas.

Bach composed an immense number of masterpieces that represent most every genre, but his work shows a special emphasis on sacred music. He wrote more than two hundred church cantatas (the vast majority of which were written during a three-year period!), at least three massive passions, the great Mass in B Minor as well as many smaller masses, the Magnificat, three huge oratorios, motets, hymns, and dozens of organ chorale preludes. It took forty-six years for the editors of the Bach-Gesellschaft publishing company to collect and publish all of the surviving Bach scores, and the completed edition filled sixty huge volumes.

Where does one begin? It's like walking into the Library of Congress and trying to decide which book to read first. Since entire volumes have been dedicated to Bach's sacred music, this short guide will simply whet your appetite by examining a few of his "greatest hits": one of his finest cantatas, *Sleepers, Awake!*; the Magnificat; the Mass in B Minor; and the *Saint Matthew* Passion.

Cantata no. 140 (*Wachet Auf!*), known in English-speaking countries as *Sleepers, Awake!* is an example of Bach the evangelist. It was composed for the twenty-seventh Sunday after Trinity Sunday, which by the Lutheran calendar meant that the sermon text was Christ's parable of the wise and foolish virgins (Matt. 25:1–13). Bach interwove an old chorale (*Wachet Auf!*) into the new cantata. The opening chorus movement announces the joyful coming of the bridegroom to meet his beloved. In subsequent movements the composer eloquently develops this theme with his Lutheran theology of "longing" for death, a meeting with the Lord. The final chorale—like hundreds of other Bach chorales—brings the chorus together in an ebullient celebration of joy.

Bach's Magnificat, taken from the first chapter of Luke's Gospel, is surely the greatest setting in history of Mary's prayer. Its exhilarating opening segment—which also closes the work—sets the joyous tone for the entire work. Larger than a cantata but smaller than an oratorio or a passion, Magnificat contains many unforgettable moments and splendid word paintings. Particularly memorable is the way in which Bach treats the text "he has filled the hungry with good things, but the rich he has sent away empty." To depict the word *empty* (Latin, *inanes*), Bach orders the flutes to an abrupt stop, leaving only the note of the cello and the keyboard to fill the emptiness of the final bar. Indeed, the entire work is imbued with many imaginative touches.

That the Lutheran Bach wrote the Catholic Mass in B Minor (which is far too huge a work to be used for liturgical purposes) demonstrates the vastness of the composer's spirit. The opening Kyrie Eleison ("Lord, Have Mercy") explodes with religious drama that is sustained through the final resolution of the Dona Nobis Pacem ("Grant Us Peace"). One of its most famous moments is found in the two movements of the Credo: "Cruxifitus" and "Et Resurrexit." After the passion of the Crucifixion, the Lord's body is quietly lowered into the tomb as the quiet pitches descend lower and lower. Then comes the Resurrection, and the chorus and orchestra seem to explode with joy—a breathtaking effect that composers have imitated for many years.

And who can forget the sublime *Saint Matthew* Passion? This is the perfect portrait of the suffering Savior, the epitome of symbolic sacred music. Even the titles of the movements—"Break in Grief," "For Love My Savior Now Is Dying," "Come, Healing Cross"— express the fervor of Bach's convictions. A classic point is the so-called halo effect given by the hushed upper

strings that always play when Jesus sings. These strings
are abruptly removed at the words "My God, my God,
why have you forsaken me?", their absence accentuat-
ing Christ's humanity. It is no wonder that Felix
Mendelssohn declared it "the greatest Christian music
in the world."

There is much more that could be said about this
great composer of sacred music, but we will end here
on an enigmatic note. Although so venerated today,
Bach was all but forgotten after his death in 1750.
Though Bach was one of the last great masters of the
baroque period of composition, musical tastes—
which were often related to such extramusical events
as court intrigues, political struggles, and the whims
of kings—changed quickly, and audiences wanted to
forget the old and embrace the latest musical style.

Performances of Bach's music ceased altogether.
Precious manuscripts—priceless today—were lost,
thrown away, or sold for a pittance (such as the bundle
of cantatas that once sold for the equivalent of forty
dollars). The great *Brandenburg Concertos* were valued
at ten cents apiece by the margrave of Brandenburg's
librarian. Some of Bach's manuscripts were even used
as wrapping material by local merchants and butchers!
Many manuscripts vanished forever.

But Bach would not be forgotten forever.
Beethoven greatly admired Bach's keyboard works.
Concerning the richness of Bach's huge output,
Beethoven once exclaimed, "Not 'Brook' [the Ger-
man word for "brook" is *bach*] but 'Ocean' should

be his name!" Almost exactly a century after its premiere, Bach's *Saint Matthew* Passion, would be rediscovered by a young composer named Felix Mendelssohn in 1829, initiating the great Bach revival of the nineteenth century, a revival that continues to the present day.

Other Listening Recommendations

Johann Sebastian Bach
Magnificat
Cantata no. 140 (Wachet Auf!)
Mass in B Minor

George Frideric Handel
Messiah
Esther

Claudio Monteverdi
Vespers

Henry Purcell
Ode for Saint Cecilia's Day

Heinrich Schütz
Seven Last Words of Jesus

Antonio Vivaldi
Gloria

CHAPTER 6

THE CLASSICAL PERIOD
(1750–1820)

Since God has given me a cheerful heart, He will forgive me for serving him cheerfully.

Franz Joseph Haydn

T ransitional periods in music are always confusing, and the classical era is no exception.
For a while, composers toyed with a whimsi-
cal yet often melodramatic style of composition.
Usually called the rococo period of music (borrowing a term from architecture), the early part of the
classical period involved many lesser composers, including several of J. S. Bach's musical sons: C. P. E.
Bach, W. F. Bach, and J. C. Bach.

But the enormous genius of Franz Joseph
Haydn (1732–1809) and Wolfgang Amadeus Mozart
(1756–91) would soon appear, ushering in the so-
called classical age of classical music. Such terminology will doubtless sound confusing to readers who
thought the word *classical* simply refers to this entire

CARL PHILIPP EMANUEL BACH

Born:
March 8, 1714
Weimar, Germany

Died:
December 14, 1788
Hamburg, Germany

Occupation:
composer, conductor, choirmaster

Hobbies/Interests:
drama, poetry

Quotation:
"Dissonances are generally played more loudly and consonances more softly, because the former stimulate and exacerbate the emotions, while the latter calm them."

category of music. It does. But many books still refer to the classical age of Haydn and Mozart, if only to confuse young music students.

The Classical Mass

Much of the music of the classical era comes from Austria and its very musical capital, Vienna. Austria remained Catholic despite the close proximity of its Protestant neighbor Germany. Therefore, it is not surprising that much of the sacred music of this time was composed for use in the Catholic Church.

Three types of masses were employed by both the faithful and their faithful composers. On ordinary Sundays, when the mass was somewhat shortened, many compositions under the descriptive title *Missa Brevis* were used. On feast days the high mass was used. Most composers preferred this genre, with its longer movements (and usually larger orchestras).

Then there is the requiem mass. If you are not from a Catholic background or know little of church history, the idea of a mass for the dead may rub you the wrong way. But this specific form has inspired dozens of different composers—from very different theological viewpoints—to create many of sacred music's greatest works.

In this chapter we will discuss the wonderful sacred music composed by the two classical masters—Haydn and Mozart—as well as that of the genius Ludwig van Beethoven (1770–1827). Of course, it was Beethoven who brought us into the next era, the romantic period. Many books might

*QUICK*TAKES
Recommended Recording

Ludwig van Beethoven
Missa Solemnis

Vienna Philharmonic, Leipzig Rundfunkchor
James Levine, conductor

(Deutsche Grammophone 435770–2)

Vienna was Beethoven's home for many years, so it should come as no surprise that the Vienna Philharmonic would produce one of the most profound recordings of Beethoven's *Missa Solemnis*. Yet this sacred masterpiece seems too colossal for one country, and as if to underscore its universality, the Vienna Philharmonic is joined by an American conductor, a German chorus, and soloists from several other nations. Uncommonly striking performances are given by alto Jessye Norman and tenor Placido Domingo. James Levine's intrepretation combines elegant lyricism, particularly in the soloists' passages, with electrifying tempos and climactic drama, culminating in the Credo and at the end of the Gloria.

have placed him in the chapter that deals specifically with this epoch. But it is really a toss-up; Beethoven's earlier music sounds classical, and his later sounds romantic. He has been placed here for a very practical reason: there are already too many composers to deal with in the chapter on romantic music!

FRANZ JOSEPH HAYDN

Born:
March 31, 1732
Rohrau, Lower
Austria

Died:
May 31, 1809
Vienna, Austria

Occupation:
choirboy, pianist,
composer, conductor

Hobbies/Interests:
poetry, pranks, art

Quotation:
*"Oh God, how much
is still to be done
in this splendid art,
even by such a man
as I have been!"*

Franz Joseph Haydn

Haydn deserves a special place in sacred music. Throughout his long life he remained sincerely pious and wrote his sacred music from a devotional point of view. Although he is still known as the father of the symphony and the string quartet, it is in his sacred music that he reveals his innermost being to us.

Franz Joseph Haydn was born and raised in the Catholic faith, and he composed some of the most beautiful masses of his day. As a youth he belonged to the famous Vienna Boys' Choir—until his voice broke and he was promptly tossed onto the streets to fend for himself. His simple faith sustained him through such troubles, and he eventually was hired by the wealthy Prince Pál Esterházy. Haydn worked for this Catholic music lover for three decades, during which time he became the most famous musician of his day.

It may seem odd today, but Haydn was sometimes criticized by his fellow Catholics for the liveliness and enthusiasm of his music. Once he even had to justify himself before Empress Maria Theresa of Austria, explaining that the cheerful melodies in his works were truly from his heart. He declared simply, "Since God has given me a cheerful heart, He will forgive me for serving him cheerfully."

Even familiar and somber words from the mass provoked an exuberant response in Haydn. When he was composing a melody for the words "Agnus Dei, qui tollis peccata mundi" ("Lamb of God, who takes away the sins of the world"), he said that he was seized by an "uncontrollable gladness" and that his heart "leapt for joy" whenever he contemplated God's love for him.

Exhilaration is present in hundreds of Haydn's compositions, but we will limit ourselves to his sacred works. We will look at his great oratorio, *The Creation,* which crowned his long life, as well as two of his most profound masses, the *Imperial* Mass (commonly known as the *Lord Nelson* Mass) and the *Paukenmesse.*

Haydn's *Paukenmesse,* so named because of its prominent use of the tympani, is also known as the *Missa in tempore belli (Mass in Time of War).* This dramatic composition reflects the spirit of revolution that troubled Haydn's world, even though Haydn himself was somewhat isolated from it while living in the palatial Esterházy estate. Its celebrated Agnus Dei is so heartrending that it seems to foreshadow the emotional music of the next century. Its timeless cry for mercy from the injustice of war was powerfully demonstrated almost two centuries later, when Leonard Bernstein conducted a performance of it as a musical form of protest during the Vietnam War.

Haydn's goal in his sacred music was to "depict Divinity through love and goodness." In the tradition of Bach, he liked to begin his scores with the words "In Nomini Jesu" and end them with "Laus Deo" or "Soli Deo Gloria." He prayed earnestly, even while composing. "If it [the music] soon comes without much difficulty, it expands," Haydn once explained. "But if it does not make progress I try to find out if I have erred in some way or other, thereby forfeiting grace; and I pray for mercy until I feel that I am forgiven."

In a similar vein, Haydn later revealed his musical theology:

> I prayed to God—not like a miserable sinner in despair—but calmly, slowly. In this I felt that an infinite God would surely have mercy on his finite creature, pardoning dust for being dust. These thoughts cheered me up. I experienced a sure joy so confident that as I wished to express the words of the prayer, I could not express my joy, but gave vent to my happy spirits and wrote above the Miserere, "Allegro."

The famous *Lord Nelson* Mass was composed in 1798. Trumpet calls at the end of the Benedictus are said to commemorate Nelson's victorious Battle of the Nile. It is interesting to note that Nelson visited Haydn at the Esterházy castle in 1800. But today it is not the histrionics but rather the remarkable music that causes us to admire this mass. It is Haydn's only mass in a minor key (D minor), and each movement, particularly the Kyrie and Qui tollis, portrays the noble and majestic side of this usually cheerful composer.

Perhaps Haydn's greatest sacred work, though, is the grand oratorio *The Creation*, which he completed at the age of sixty-six. Haydn said that it was composed to inspire "the adoration and worship of the Creator" and to put the listener "in a frame of mind where he is most susceptible to the kindness and omnipotence of the Creator." Haydn would later recall,

> Never was I so devout as when I composed *The Creation*. I knelt down each day to pray to God to give me strength for my work . . . When I was working on *The Creation* I felt so impregnated with the Divine certainty, that before sitting down to the piano, I would quietly and confidently pray to God to grant me the talent that was needed to praise him worthily.

His prayers were thoroughly answered, for *The Creation* is a sublime masterpiece. Like Handel's great opus, *Messiah*, Haydn's work is in three parts, which deal with (1) the first four days of the Creation, (2) days five and six, and (3) the coming of Adam and Eve. *The Creation* opens with an amazing orchestral introduction; its depiction of chaos sounds as wild as anything produced in the twentieth century.

One of its most stirring moments is when the chorus intones, "Let there be light!" The orchestra virtually explodes, and the divine creator of light is musically revealed. This, of course, was deliberate, as evidenced by a comment the composer made on March 27, 1808, in Vienna at the last performance he ever attended of *The Creation*. When the piece concluded and the listeners began their thunderous applause, Haydn lifted his hands toward heaven and

WOLFGANG AMADEUS MOZART

Born:
January 27, 1756
Salzburg, Austria

Died:
December 5, 1791
Vienna, Austria

Occupation:
composer, teacher, pianist

Hobbies/Interests:
billiards, cards, games

Quotation:
"Let come what will, nothing can go ill so long as it is the will of God; and that it may so go is my daily prayer."

declared, "Not from me—from there, above, comes everything."

Wolfgang Amadeus Mozart

It is unfortunate that certain modern writers and filmmakers have overlooked (or even disparaged) Mozart's sincere Christian beliefs. Thankfully, dozens of letters in Mozart's own hand have been preserved that show the true heart of this composer:

> God is ever before my eyes. I realize His omnipotence and I fear His anger; but I also recognize His love, His compassion, and His tenderness towards His creatures. He will never forsake His own. If it is according to His will, so let it be according to mine. Thus all will be well and I must needs be happy and contented.

Wolfgang Amadeus Mozart was an incredible child prodigy, who even as a very young boy astounded the pope with his talent and was awarded the Vatican's Cross of the Order of the Golden Spur. Like his friend Haydn, Mozart was a devout Catholic, but he was less successful at being received by his church. The notorious archbishop of Salzburg humiliated Mozart and did all he could to damage his career. He even had Mozart physically tossed out of his cathedral.

Although Mozart was famous throughout Europe at a young age, his good fortune did not continue into adulthood. The novelty of a child prodigy was more fascinating to the public than that of a talented young man. Lack of finances became increasingly problematic, and when he died at the age of thirty-five, Mozart was penniless. Yet in this brief time, he composed a huge amount of the world's greatest music, including sacred music.

Like Haydn before him, Mozart's music and faith were intricately linked. He confided in his letters that several of his compositions, including the great Mass in C Major and the oratorio *Davidde Penitente,* were the consequence of sacred vows he had privately made before the Lord. The composer saw his talent as a gift from God and developed a profound confidence in his heavenly Father. He wrote:

> Let us put our trust in God and console ourselves with the thought that all is well, if it is in accordance with the will of the Almighty, as He knows best what is profitable and beneficial to our temporal happiness and our eternal salvation.

This confidence is evident in Mozart's masses, and especially in the Credo movements. In order to sample the riches of his sacred music, we will discuss both a small and a large mass (the *Missa Brevis* K. 192 and the later *Coronation* Mass K. 317) as well as the illustrious Requiem Mass in D Minor, K. 626, the last work of this prolific man.

When writing a *missa brevis* in eighteenth-century Austria, a composer did not have huge orchestral forces at his disposal. It is typical that Mozart's *Missa Brevis* K. 192 has no violas in the score, probably for the simple reason that none were procurable for a small Sunday mass. Yet Mozart used the small work to focus on intimacy, and he filled this mass with creative contrast. Consider the somber minor key of the Agnus Dei, followed by the joy of the Dona nobis pacem.

If Haydn was occasionally faulted for too much cheerfulness in his sacred music, Mozart has been criticized for not having enough—for sounding too secular. It certainly is true that the same lovely melodies might have been used in a Mozart mass or a Mozart opera. Yet such disapproval would have puzzled him, since he considered all of life to be submitted to God. He once wrote his father:

> It will greatly assist such happiness as I may have to hear that my dear father and my dear sister have submitted wholly to the will of God, with resignation and fortitude—and have put their whole confidence in Him, in the firm assurance that He orders all things for the best.

Mozart's faith is best seen in his larger masses, such as the matchless *Coronation* Mass K. 317. This work uses a full string section and organ in addition to oboes, bassoons, trumpets, horns, trombones, and tympani. After a spacious Kyrie, the Gloria explodes with music that is unmistakably Mozart. The rapid violin passages and unusual modulations are carefully designed to enhance the exhilaration of the text. Later, in the "Et incarnatus" section of the Credo, the descending violin lines become an enchanting illustration of the Incarnation of Christ.

Yet even these dramatic devices are ordinary compared to the magnitude of Mozart's last work, the sublime Requiem. Mozart's health had never been robust, and it declined rapidly as he composed this masterpiece. During its creation the composer told his wife that he was writing the requiem for himself. He died before its completion, but his stamp is firmly upon every movement. When someone asked Beethoven about questionable parts in the Requiem's conclusion, the master commented, "If it wasn't all written by Mozart, then it must have been written by another Mozart!"

The theme of death in Mozart's work was not the macabre one that haunted many other composers. Mozart's faith was strong as he faced his own mortality. A few years before he died, he wrote:

> I never lie down in my bed without reflecting that perhaps I—young as I am—may not live to see another day; yet none of all who know me can say that I am socially melancholy or morose. For this blessing I daily thank my Creator and wish it from my heart for all my fellow men.

The Requiem is brimming with spectacular moments: the intensity of the "Dies irae," the dramatic contrasts of the "Confutatis," the exquisite counterpoint in the "Recordare," and the painful throbbing of the "Lacrymosa" create a tragedy of Shakespearian proportions. One can well imagine the sorrow of Mozart's last night, when friends gathered around his bedside for an informal rehearsal of this last work. Mozart reportedly burst into tears during the "Lacrymosa," concluding, in a sense, the composer's last rehearsal.

This sacred masterpiece—and indeed all of Mozart's work—has had a penetrating effect on subsequent composers of the nineteenth century. Decades after Mozart's death, the French composer Charles Gounod proclaimed, "Mozart is to Palestrina and Bach what the New Testament is to the Old in the spirit of the Bible, one and indivisible."

From Eighteenth-Century Classicism toward Nineteenth-Century Romanticism

In the chapter on chant we examined a way of looking at music history: the pendulum theory. According to this view, each succeeding epoch of music is a reaction against its predecessor, granting a noted contrast in musical styles. To some degree these styles tend toward either a classical or a romantic tradition, going back and forth between the two like a pendulum.

Whether or not one agrees with placing all of musical history within such restrictions, this theory most certainly applies to the beginning of the nineteenth century. In hindsight it seems that the romantic period openly tried to throw out everything that was enjoyed in the classical period. Much of the transition between these two ages is found in the life of Beethoven, who almost singlehandedly brought music into the era of romanticism.

The classical period was the age of clarity and objectivity in composition. The romantic style exalted subjectivity, imagination, even mystery. The beauty of classical music is in its simplicity; romanticism's beauty is in its complexity, particularly in its harmonies. A typical title of the classical style was Sonata in B-flat Major (absolute music). A typical romantic title might be *A Faust Fantasia* (program music).

The romantic composer Robert Schumann once characterized the music of his day as "not a matter of figures and forms, but of the composer's being a poet or not." As we enter the freedom of the nineteenth century (especially the latter half), you will sense a new spirit of rebirth, of individuality, of independence. For this reason the music is often thought of as being more akin to secular than to sacred musical forms. Yet some of history's greatest sacred masterpieces were composed during this period.

Before we turn to the romantic era, we need to examine the marvelous and curious master who, more than anyone, ushered us into it: Beethoven.

Ludwig van Beethoven

Like Mozart before him, **Ludwig van Beethoven** is another composer who has received a lot of bad press in the twentieth century, at least from a spiritual point of view. To see some modern movies, one would think that Beethoven was a maniacal, promiscuous, depraved, self-centered cretin. This is certainly not the case. Indeed, although he was

LUDWIG VAN BEETHOVEN

Born:
December 16, 1770
Bonn, Germany

Died:
March 26, 1827
Vienna, Austria

Occupation:
composer, pianist, teacher

Hobbies/Interests:
walking, pranks, poetry

Quotation:
"Beethoven can write, thank God; but do nothing else on earth."

clumsy, unorthodox, and thoroughly misunderstood, he also had a deeply profound faith in God.

As Beethoven's hearing deteriorated, he wrote his famous *Heiligenstadt Testament,* in which he poured out his deepest yearnings:

> Almighty God, you look down into my innermost soul, you see into my heart and you know that it is filled with love for humanity and a desire to do good.

Even while suffering this terrible malady, Beethoven's faith was steadfast:

> Therefore, calmly will I submit myself to all inconsistency and will place all my confidence in your eternal goodness, O God! My soul shall rejoice in Thee, immutable Being. Be my rock, my light, forever my trust!

Beethoven will always be remembered for his great symphonies, piano pieces, and string quartets, but his faith also found its way into some of his most significant vocal works. It is true that he never obtained the vocal lyricism of a Mozart or a Schubert and that his inclination tended more toward the instrumental medium. And yet he composed the majestic *Missa Solemnis,* which is considered by many to be the absolute pinnacle of sacred music.

Unlike Mozart, who composed very rapidly and never had to write out sketches for his works, Beethoven worked sluggishly. Sometimes he would carry around themes in his notebooks for years before they would find their way into a composition. Before he created such a masterpiece as *Missa Solemnis,* Beethoven seemed to be "warming up" his choral expertise with two other works that also merit our attention: *Christ on the Mount of Olives* and the Mass in C Major.

At the turn of the century Beethoven was at work on his only oratorio, *Christ on the Mount of Olives.* If you're expecting an oratorio like Handel's *Messiah,* you'll be quite surprised. Beethoven's work is much more like a grand opera without the costumes and sets. The melodramatic choral writing, the emotional orchestral interludes, and especially the theatrical solo parts certainly evoke the opera house rather than the concert hall. But the drama of the suffering Savior is serious and moving and indicates that the young Beethoven had the promise of a brilliant future.

If this oratorio seems a bit overdone, you must remember that Beethoven never did anything halfway. He was a man of strong opinions and even stronger convictions. Arguing against the growing irreligion and atheism of his day, he insisted that "it was not a fortuitous meeting of chordal atoms that made the world; if order and beauty are reflected in the constitution of the universe, then there is a God."

In 1807 Beethoven embarked on another sacred work, the beautiful Mass in C Major. Quite different from the earlier oratorio, the mass begins quietly and, despite its bombastic moments, leaves you with a feeling of peace and simple faith. No wonder the composer wrote that this piece "is dearer to my heart and in spite of the coldness of our age to such works."

As Beethoven matured, he retreated more and more into his devout relationship with God. In his diary, fervent prayers appear: "In whatsoever manner it be, let me turn to Thee and become fruitful in good works."

He once wrote an acquaintance:

> I have no friend; I must live by myself. I know, however, that God is nearer to me than others. I go without fear to Him, I have constantly recognized and understood Him.

To the Grand Duke Rudolf, Beethoven wrote, "Nothing higher exists than to approach God more than other people and from that to extend His glory among humanity." It was in this noble spirit that Beethoven composed *Missa Solemnis* and its sister work, the Ninth Symphony. In the high mass, every movement is penetrating in its own distinct way. The grandeur of the Kyrie gives way to an explosive Gloria, which ends with a choral shout that seems to go on forever. The Credo is certainly one of the greatest musical statements of the Christian faith ever written. The grief of the Cruxifitus and the power of the Et resurrexit bring the listener to a new depth of faith.

Other movements—the stirring Sanctus and the tender Benedictus—continue to move us. But it is the final prayer, Dona nobis pacem, that epitomizes

Missa Solemnis. Beethoven inscribed these words in its score: "A prayer for inner and outer peace." It is with this prayer that the tragically misunderstood composer concludes his sacred music, and we conclude this chapter on the classical period.

As you may have gathered from Beethoven's later music, the nineteenth century brings us into an innovative and revolutionary period of romanticism. But before you strap yourselves into your seats for this wild ride, we will again visit the second stream of sacred music, which brings us to the zenith of hymnology and delivers us at the door of the twentieth century.

Other Listening Recommendations

Ludwig van Beethoven
Christ on the Mount of Olives
Mass in C Major

Franz Joseph Haydn
Imperial Mass (the Lord Nelson Mass)
Paukenmesse (Missa in tempore belli)
The Creation

Wolfgang Amadeus Mozart
Missa Brevis, K. 192
Coronation Mass, K. 317
Requiem in D Minor, K. 626

CHAPTER 7

THE ROMANTIC PERIOD
(1820–1900)

Do not wonder that I am so religious. An artist who is not could not produce anything like this. Have we not examples enough in Beethoven, Bach, Raphael and many others?

Antonín Dvořák

You may have noticed that as the centuries roll forward, the two streams of sacred music—popular congregational singing and the classical tradition—move farther apart from each other.

To understand this widening split, we must go back to the earliest philosophy behind congregational singing: to embrace every person in the church. Therefore, it had to exist on a much simpler level of musical sophistication. Thus, the concept behind congregational hymn writing contrasts substantially with the classical concept of continual innovation, summarized by Beethoven's famous declaration "Art demands that we not stand still!"

The end result? Hymn writers remained careful to not "lose the crowd," while classical composers became increasingly "ahead of their time." These are, of course, generalizations, but they explain why the two streams had become so unrelated by the nineteenth century. Indeed, their continued separation into the twentieth century actually helped to create a new stream that flowed between the two. But that must await a later chapter.

The Nineteenth Century's Crisis of Faith

Much has been said and written about the "crisis of faith" among the romantic composers, poets, and writers. It is not as though complete atheism had taken hold, but this epoch was full of doubts, uncertainties, and questions. The Protestant churches had permanently established themselves, so neither the Catholic nor the Protestant hierarchy could claim absolute authority over people of faith.

Perhaps it was such division that encouraged the disillusionment among the nineteenth century's artists. Or perhaps the growing industrialism and depersonalization of society contributed to the trend. Whatever the cause, the simple faith of the medieval mind was hard to find in the romantic period, at least in artistic spheres, and this uncertainty had a strong influence on the direction of sacred music.

For example, we see in this period a number of strange contradictions, an unexplainable separation between many composers' religious beliefs (which, of course, affected their work) and their private lives:

- **Hector Berlioz** was an outspoken unbeliever, yet he composed a very convincing sacred work, *The Infancy of Christ,* which would have hardly been possible a century or two earlier.

- **Franz Liszt** considered himself a "serious sacred composer" and created magnificent biblical works from a sincere Christian faith, yet he openly carried on one notorious love affair after another.

- And **Richard Wagner**? With all his insane beliefs and lifestyle aberrations, he composed the incredible *The Love Feast of the Twelve Apostles* and attempted, but didn't quite complete, an opera on the life of Jesus Christ.

It was a curious century, especially in the world of classical music.

Yet there were still composers whose beliefs and music corresponded to genuine Christian principles. Some were Catholic, others Protestant. This stream of sacred music rolled onward, and some of history's finest masterpieces are found in this bizarre, outrageous, but not religionless century.

Schubert's Masses

Franz Schubert (1797–1828) lived a very short life, mostly in obscurity and poverty, yet he created hundreds of wonderful compositions for almost every musical genre. His instrumental works—symphonies, chamber music, and piano pieces—are all part of the standard repertoire today. Still, most of us consider Schubert's vocal music to be his

FRANZ SCHUBERT

Born:
January 31, 1797
Vienna, Austria

Died:
November 19, 1828
Vienna, Austria

Occupation:
teacher, composer

Hobbies/Interests:
poetry

Quotation:
"It sometimes seems to me as if I did not belong to this world at all."

greatest accomplishment, since he had such a tremendous gift for lyric melody.

Schubert's many songs, most of which are secular love songs, are so popular that it is almost impossible to hear a vocal recital without encountering at least one of them. But Schubert also gave us several beautiful masses and a number of smaller works that clearly express his Catholic faith. These include his *Hymn to Faith, Hope, and Charity,* his cantata *Miriam's Song of Victory,* and his *Hymn to the Holy Spirit.* He also left behind an unfinished Easter cantata based on the biblical account of Jesus raising Lazarus from the dead.

But his masses represent his finest sacred music. Four of them were composed during the years 1814–16: Mass in F Major, Mass in G Major, Mass in B-flat Major, and Mass in C Major. All of these are lovely, but the most performed piece is the Mass in G Major, whose warmth is displayed in its opening Kyrie and whose vocal serenity is evident in every movement.

Schubert's faith was sincere but unpretentious. In a letter to his father, he once told of the effect a hymn he had composed had on listeners: it "grips every soul and turns it to devotion." Then he recounted how his audience "wondered greatly at my piety." He explained that he "never forced devotion in myself and never compose hymns or prayers of that kind unless it overcomes me unawares; but then it is usually the right and true devotion."

After a break of a few years, Schubert wrote of the powerful Mass in A-flat Major in 1822. It is an innovative work and leaves behind a sweetness that, it must be admitted, almost overwhelms the listener of his earlier masses. This mass may begin and end in A-flat major, but it changes keys so frequently (and so cleverly) that it reminds one of the remote chromaticism of the twentieth century.

Schubert's most exalted sacred masterpiece, written in the last year of his life, was the Mass in E-flat Major. The cry of the chorus at the beginning of the Gloria perhaps found its origin in the distress of the composer's own life. The Credo is passionately intense, and the triple forte chords during the Crucifixion convincingly portray the thunder at Calvary. Schubert may have died tragically—he left this earth penniless and in relative obscurity at a very young age—but his great mass ends in a triumphant testimony of victory over death.

Mendelssohn's Oratorios

The next major composer of sacred music was the Protestant **Felix Mendelssohn** (1809–47). Except for the unfortunate fact that they both had very short lives, there is little in common between Schubert and Mendelssohn. The latter was wealthy, almost continually happy, and enjoyed a wonderful married life.

Born into a prosperous Jewish family, Mendelssohn became a Christian at an early age and was a faithful Lutheran all his life. He inaugurated the important Bach revival of the nineteenth century when

FELIX MENDELSSOHN

Born:
February 3, 1809
Hamburg, Germany

Died:
November 4, 1847
Leipzig, Germany

Occupation:
composer, pianist, conductor

Hobbies/Interests:
billiards

Quotation:
"I know perfectly well that no musician can make his thoughts or his talents different to what Heaven has made them; but I also know that if Heaven had given him good ones, he must also be able to develop them properly."

he produced the first performance of Bach's *Saint Matthew* Passion since Bach's death. He even imitated Bach's habit of marking his scores with prayers and exclamations, such as "Let it succeed, God!" or "Help along."

Mendelssohn's sacred compositions include many splendid psalms and the well-known *Hymn of Praise,* but his finest works in this genre were oratorios. The first was the stalwart *Saint Paul,* which received its inaugural performance in 1836. As a converted Jew himself, Mendelssohn was deeply moved by Paul's story from the Book of Acts. He studied everything he could find on the subject and worked with extra fervor on the project, insisting that he "must not make any mistakes."

The composer was soon pondering another topic, the life of Saint Peter. Unfortunately, this project was never realized, as Mendelssohn was so preoccupied with his multifaceted musical career. Despite his Lutheran background, he also toyed with the idea of composing a mass, although the inspiration behind this idea was rather negative. Mendelssohn was so disappointed with the masses he heard during a trip to Rome that he wrote, "Were I a Catholic, I would set to work at a mass this very evening; and, whatever it might turn out, it would at all events be the only mass written with a constant remembrance of its sacred purpose."

Ten years after *Saint Paul* was first performed, Mendelssohn premiered another oratorio that would become his magnum opus: *Elijah.* From its opening page we feel its forceful drama: Elijah the prophet proclaims his stormy entrance before the overture can even begin! So many magnificent choruses: "He Watching over Israel," "Thanks Be to God," "His Mercies on Thousands Fall," "Blessed Are the Men Who Fear Him." So many magical moments: the duet with Elijah and the Widow, the scene with the Prophets of Baal, the poignancy of the boy soprano solo—all of these and more are in *Elijah*!

In many ways, Mendolssohn's *Elijah* did for the oratorio what Beethoven's Ninth did for the symphony. It was so spectacular, such a tough act to follow, that it seemed to intimidate composers into seeking other musical avenues of expression. It would be a long time before others would attempt the oratorio form with much success. In the meantime, many masses would continue to be composed, especially the variety known as the requiem mass.

The Brahms Requiem

In the chapter on the classical period, we looked at the concept of a requiem, specifically referring to Mozart's Requiem. This form actually goes back centuries earlier and was used in Catholic funeral services. It uses the same Latin text as the mass, with a few exceptions: The requiem omits the Gloria and the Credo and adds three new movements: Requiem aeternam ("Eternal rest"), Lux aeternam ("Eternal light"), and Dies irae ("Day of wrath").

**JOHANNES
BRAHMS**

Born:
May 7, 1833
Hamburg, Germany

Died:
April 3, 1897
Vienna, Austria

Occupation:
pianist, teacher, composer, conductor

Hobbies/Interests:
walking, traveling, tin soldiers, business

Quotation:
"When I feel the urge to compose, I begin by appealing directly to my Maker, and I first ask Him the three most important questions pertaining to our life here in this world—whence, wherefore, whither."

Now that we have all this straight, let's look at a famous requiem that breaks all the rules. It's not in Latin but German. It doesn't use the standard text or even the standard movements, and so it really isn't a requiem at all. Yet it is perhaps the most beloved and frequently performed piece of music by that name. It was written by **Johannes Brahms** (1833–97).

Brahms's *Ein Deutsches* Requiem was composed in memory of his mother. But Brahms was not from a Catholic background and had no affinity with the Latin requiem, which he considered a bit heavy on hell, judgment, and other rather bleak themes. Instead, he went to his German Bible (translated by Martin Luther) and chose some of his favorite passages that accentuate the peaceful and joyful facets of death.

The work begins and ends in serenity, framed by thoughts of blessing: "Blessed Are They Who Mourn, for They Will Be Comforted" and "Blessed Are They Who Die in the Lord from Now On." The second movement, "For All Flesh Is as Grass," contains some of Brahms's most dramatic climaxes. The famous "How Lovely Is Thy Dwelling Place" combines elegance and a superb lyrical line. And the sixth movement, with its depiction of the final trumpet and its fugal hymn of praise and glory, is Brahms at his most majestic. This requiem may not be very typical, but its inspiring consideration of such a serious theme makes it the best of its genre.

QUICKTAKES
Recommended Recording

Johannes Brahms
Ein Deutsches Requiem

**Philharmonic Orchestra and Chorus
Otto Klemperer, conductor**

(EMI Classics CDC 56218)

Otto Klemperer has a well-deserved reputation for the interpretation of Brahms's symphonies, and this extends to *The German Requiem* as well. To make the recording, he teamed up with two of the finest singers of the twentieth century, soprano Elizabeth Schwarzkopf and baritone Dietrich Fischer-Dieskau. The latter's vocal strength carefully contrasts with the exquisite beauty of the soprano's aria, "Therefore now you have sorrow, but I will see you again and your hearts will rejoice." Klemperer coaxes a huge sound from both the orchestra and the chorus. In the climaxes of the second movement, "For All Flesh Is as Grass," the listeners are virtually lifted out of their seats.

Other Requiems

Within a decade of the premiere of Brahms's unique Requiem, another example of this genre was created by the Italian opera composer **Giuseppe Verdi** (1813–1901). Verdi, a musician from the most Catholic country in Europe, naturally used the standard Latin text that Brahms had declined. Of course, a sacred work by the master of Italian opera sounds more like rigoletto than a pious cantata. Someone once described the Verdi Requiem as "a bunch of opera singers let loose in a cathedral!"

But this composition also offered deep glimpses into Verdi's faith. The serenity of the Lux aeterna, the power of the offbeat bass drum in the Dies irae, the resplendent quartet writing of Domine Jesu Christe, and the prayerful duet in the Agnus Dei all paint a vivid picture of the quiet piety of the composer and his country. Verdi has equal fervency in his other sacred works, including the energetic Te Deum and his heartrending Stabat Mater.

For the next famous requiem, we move to 1885 France. Again, we find a Catholic requiem, but one of a completely different style. **Gabriel Fauré** (1845–1924) created a work that is austere, heavenly, almost weightless in its French simplicity. Fauré once stated, "It has been said that my *Requiem* does not express the fear of death and someone has called it a lullaby of death. But it is thus that I see death: as a happy deliverance, an aspiration towards happiness above."

The orchestra used in this work is rather spare, without violins (except for a beautiful solo in the Sanctus) and with little playing from the wind sections. The choral writing evokes the sound of distant angelic choirs, and several of the melodies are rooted in Gregorian chant. The result is ethereal and innocent, portraying a childlike faith that is epitomized in the celebrated movement "Pie Jesu," sung by a boy soprano.

Now we turn east to Bohemia, where the great composer **Antonín Dvořák** (1841–1904) created his Requiem in 1890—again, a very different work from a very different musician. Dvořák was a simple man of the soil with a simple but profoundly strong Catholic faith. He took the Latin text very seriously, and, like Bach, Haydn, and Mendelssohn before him, would often begin his scores with the marking "With God" and end with the benediction "God be thanked."

Yet his way of expressing his faith in this work must have raised a few eyebrows at its premiere. Do you recall how Haydn sometimes set somber theological text to lighthearted, cheerful music? Similarly, the Bohemian Dvořák loved the Slavonic folk tunes of his native countryside and used them throughout the Requiem, even with such solemn texts as "Requiem aeternam." He also created a good deal of other sacred music, so we will hear more from this distinctive composer later in the chapter.

Incidentally, some readers may wonder why we haven't examined Hector Berlioz's 1837 Requiem. This book is, of course, only a short survey of sacred music, so everything can't be mentioned! But if you want to hear a work for 4 flutes, 2 oboes, 2 English horns, 4 clarinets, 4 bassoons, 12 trumpets, 4 cornets, 12 horns, 16 trombones, 6 tubas, 2 bass drums, 4 gongs, 16 tympani, 5 pairs of cymbals, 50 violins, 20 violas, 20 celli, and 18 basses—not to mention 300 to 900 singers—then try it. But be prepared. Instead

ANTONIN DVOŘÁK

Born:
September 8, 1841
Nelahozeves,
Bohemia

Died:
May 1, 1904
Prague,
Czechoslovakia

Occupation:
composer, teacher,
conductor

Hobbies/Interests:
trains, pigs, traveling

Quotation:
*"I am just an ordinary
Czech musician."*

117

of a mass for the dead, musicians have nicknamed this requiem a mass to wake the dead.

Gounod, Liszt, and Bruckner

Not every romantic composer wrote a requiem. Now we will look at a few who created some excellent sacred music in forms other than the requiem. The contrasts found within the nineteenth century are astounding.

French composer **Charles Gounod** (1818–93) is best known for his famous opera *Faust* as well as the popular song "Ave Maria," in which he composed a lovely melody using Bach's Prelude no. 1 in C Major as its accompaniment. But he also wrote some ambitious sacred works.

Gounod's sacred music includes masses, sacred songs, hymns, a requiem, and his two greatest oratorios, *Redemption* and *Mors et Vita.* The former is about the Passion and death of Christ, and the latter deals with Christ's life on earth between Resurrection and Ascension. And for that matter, Gounod's two secular operas, *Faust* and *Polyeucte,* also have much to do with spiritual subjects and might themselves be said to be within the genre of sacred music.

And what about the enigma of **Franz Liszt** (1811–86)? This intensely romantic concert pianist and notorious womanizer insisted that he had "taken a serious stand as a religious, Catholic composer," and he certainly created some powerful sacred music. He claimed that he composed his *XIIIth Psalm* while "weeping blood." Concerning his *Solemn*

Mass, he insisted that he had "prayed this mass rather than composed [it]."

Liszt's greatest sacred work was the gargantuan oratorio *Christus,* which is seldom performed today because of its length. As Brahms had done for his Requiem, Liszt compiled the text for *Christus* himself, taking dozens of excerpts from the Latin Bible. Again, we may be tempted to expand our definition of sacred music to include such beautiful piano pieces as Liszt's *Harmonies poetiques et religieuses,* the two *Legendes,* and the *Annees de pelerinage.* Certainly, their composer considered them to be within the realm of sacred music!

Finally, another example, this one from Austria. **Anton Bruckner** (1824–96) was a quiet man with a strong Catholic faith. A great organist, he refused to mount the bench until he had knelt and prayed. His nine symphonies are all in the standard repertoire today, and his sacred music—especially his two masses—becomes more popular every decade.

His Mass in F Major is the larger of the two masses and is warm and sturdy in character. The Mass in E Minor is extremely chromatic, but its small size keeps the difficult vocal parts from becoming abstruse. The festive Psalm 150 and his excellent Te Deum are also testaments to Bruckner's devout faith. Concerning this latter piece, the composer once asserted, "When God calls me to him and asks me, 'Where is the talent which I have given you?' then I shall hold out the rolled up manuscript of my *Te Deum* and I know he will be a compassionate judge."

Dvořák, Franck, and Elgar

The nineteenth century saw the rise of many nationalistic musical styles. No longer did the Germanic instrumental tradition or the Italian vocal tradition reign unchallenged in musical Europe. Composers felt pride in their multicultural roots, and we find new works from such lands as Finland, Norway, and Czechoslovakia. These nationalistic trends become apparent as we explore the works of the last three great romantic composers of sacred music.

We have already examined Antonín Dvořák's Requiem, but this composer made such a unique contribution to the world of sacred music that we need to discuss him further. Dvořák came from the most humble of households in Bohemia but went on to achieve international fame, especially in America, where his *New World* Symphony found acceptance and acclaim. But he never forgot his folk ancestry nor his religion. After completing his massive Mass in D Major, Dvořák declared, "Faith, hope and love to God Almighty and thanks for the great gift of being enabled to bring this work in the praise of the Highest and in the honor of art to a happy conclusion."

One of Dvořák's most touching works is Stabat Mater. The music was set to the poem by Jacopone di Todi, and in it the grief of Jesus' mother echoes Dvořák's own grief at the loss of three of his children within a very short time. A different type of his sacred music is found in his exquisite *Biblical Songs*, which have been called "ten variations on the theme of God." These were not liturgical pieces but rather interpretations of ten of the composer's favorite psalms.

His most dramatic sacred work is the oratorio *Saint Ludmila,* which celebrates the conversion of the Czechs to Christianity. Its libretto is quite theatrical: during a pagan festival for a goddess, the hermit Ivan shatters her statue and calls upon all present to worship the one true God, whose son died upon the cross. Ivan wins the young princess and her future husband, Borivoj, to Christ. The work culminates with their joyous baptism into the new religion. With its folk melodies and Slavic flavor, the work is a monument to both the faith and the music of Antonín Dvořák.

Now we move on to an organ loft in France, where another Catholic composer, **César Franck** (1822–90), is at work. This amicable man wrote a great deal of music using Scripture as his text, from solo songs to biblical scenes with orchestra such as *Ruth* and *Rebecca.* But his greatest contributions to this genre were his two oratorios and his cantata *Redemption.*

This "cantata" was actually a three-part oratorio whose libretto embraced virtually all of biblical history. From the origins of sinful man to the final culmination of Christ's reappearance, this massive work is almost overwhelming in its scope. Like so many works from the nineteenth century—an age for which the motto might be "Big is beautiful"—

Franck's *Redemption* is seldom produced for today's audiences, who are desirous of short sound bites.

But his other great works are still in the modern-day classical repertoire. *The Tower of Babel* not only conveys the biblical story but also reminds audiences of their need for God. Franck's other oratorio, *The Beatitudes,* is perhaps his most effective sacred work. Devoting a full decade (1869–79) to this score, the composer presents the words of Christ in an ecstasy of French lyricism. He actually planned to set the entire Sermon on the Mount to music, but, alas, did not meet his goal. At least, though, he was able to complete this jewel.

Finally, for the first time since Handel died there in 1759, we move to England. **Sir Edward Elgar** (1857–1934) is perhaps the last great composer of the romantic era to create sacred music. Elgar had it in mind to set virtually the entire New Testament to music, quite an ambitious and lofty goal. Failing this, he did musically represent some of its finest portions.

Elgar composed an oratorio entitled *Lux Christi* (*The Light of Christ*), which contains a sublime selection of the sayings of Jesus. Another sacred work is *Scenes from the Saga of King Olaf,* which is about the Norwegian monarch's conversion from paganism to Christianity. But Elgar's greatest contribution to this genre, *The Dream of Gerontius,* premiered in 1900, taking us to the end of the romantic era.

The text for this popular composition is not from the Bible but from an 1865 poem by John Henry

Cardinal Newman. It relates the vision of a Christian named Gerontius as he travels from this life to the next, encountering both angelic choirs and the demons of hell. One of the reasons for the work's powerful impact is the stark realism Elgar chose over easy sentimentality. He once wrote, "Look here: I imagined Gerontius to be a man like us, not a priest or a saint, but a *sinner,* a repentant one of course but still no end of a *worldly man* in his life, and now brought to book."

Although *The Dream of Gerontius* remains Elgar's most popular sacred work, his three New Testament oratorios, over which he labored so long, also demand our attention. The first part of this enormous trilogy, *The Apostles,* appeared in 1903. Three years later, Elgar finished the second part, *The Kingdom.* *The Apostles* concerns the period of Jesus' ministry and ends with his Ascension; *The Kingdom* continues the story, telling of the early church. Sadly, the composer died before finishing the final part of the trilogy, entitled *The Judgment.* But the profound masterpieces Elgar left behind bring us well into the innovations of the twentieth century.

Bringing Classical Music into the Twentieth Century

You have surely noticed that the music of the late nineteenth century is more complex than that of a century earlier. This trend continues into the twentieth century. The two streams of sacred music grow farther apart through the ages, becoming so dissimilar in the twentieth century that many new streams begin to emerge.

The classical stream will continue to become more innovative and therefore less accessible to the average listener, moving from the postromantics like Mahler and Strauss, through the beautiful blur of French impressionism (Debussy, Ravel, and others), into the neoclassical adventures of Stravinsky, past the cerebral world of serialism (Schoenberg and his followers), and through the experimental language of the late twentieth century.

The sacred music of this period also weaved through these new worlds. Many of the greatest twentieth-century composers created sacred music, from Stravinsky's *Symphony of Psalms* to Penderecki's *Passion according to Saint Luke.* It may not sound much like Mozart's masses anymore, but it is certainly a legitimate form of sacred music, sincerely composed to express a contemporary faith.

As we enter the twentieth century, especially the realm of classical music, be aware of sacred music's place in the history of the last two millennia. Not all the music will appeal to you, but be careful not to reject it out of hand. Much of the music through the ages was rejected by its contemporaries and was not fully appreciated for many years. Doubtless this will be the case for many twentieth-century masterpieces.

Other Listening Recommendations

Anton Bruckner
Mass in E Minor

Antonín Dvořák
Requiem

Sir Edward Elgar
The Dream of Gerontius

Gabriel Fauré
Requiem

Franz Liszt
Christus

Felix Mendelssohn
Elijah

Franz Schubert
Mass in E-flat Major

Giuseppe Verdi
Requiem

CHAPTER 8

CHORALES AND CONGREGATIONS
(1500–1750)

Why should the devil have all the good music?

Martin Luther

When the Protestant Reformation began in the sixteenth century, it brought not only theological changes but musical ones as well. As we saw in chapter 4, one of the results of the Reformation was the growth of a new stream of sacred music. This new stream consisted of an explosion of popular, unpretentious music for the untrained layperson to sing in a congregational setting.

As we look back from our modern vantage point, we see that this new stream of sacred music is not really "Protestant versus Catholic." It is simply the emergence of an original genre of common music written to enable the average person in a church congregation to praise God in song. Instead of such musical forms as the cantata, the oratorio, or the motet, we will now hear about the chorale, the anthem, and the hymn. Instead of "classical" composers such as Palestrina or Handel, we will look at great hymn writers such as Isaac Watts and Charles Wesley.

At this juncture some readers might point out that popular hymns were written long before the sixteenth century. It is true that lovely hymns, such as Saint Francis's "All Creatures of Our God and King" and Bernard of Clairvaux's "O Sacred Head Now Wounded," were composed and sung centuries before the Reformation. Indeed, we know of hymns dating to the beginning of the Christian era.

But few of these early hymns were written to be sung by the general populace. For that matter, most of the hymns we still know consist of the text without the music itself. And these hymns were usually sung in Latin, which would not have been understood by the vast majority of Christian worshipers.

Furthermore, congregational singing as we think of it had been banned as early as 367 by the Council of Laodicia and again in 1415 by the Council of Jerusalem. Since the Catholic congregations of the Renaissance continued to worship while listening to the chant and organum of earlier centuries, virtually all of the great pre-Reformation composers spent their time creating the newer, more "classical" forms of music we have examined in the last few chapters.

The Influence of Martin Luther

Martin Luther and his followers formed an entirely
new tradition of Christian worship. Since one of their
basic tenets involved the "priesthood of all believers,"
they wanted every man, woman, and child in their
new congregations to be directly involved in each
worship service. Too often in the past, even the most
devout congregants had understood little of what
was being said or sung in the Latin masses.

Luther's solution involved the replacement of
Latin singing with vernacular hymns, which were
often unabashedly set to the tune of local folk songs.
In the same way in which he insisted that every word
of Scripture readings and sermons should be understood by all, he also maintained that the music of his
churches should be able to incorporate every individual, whether educated or illiterate.

Since such drastic innovations would mean
beginning a complete overhaul of sacred music as
they then knew it, one wonders whether these reformers might have balked at the enormity of their task.
That such a task was undertaken and fulfilled was in
large part because of the incredible influence Luther
himself exerted. A musician in his own right, he realized and openly acknowledged the indispensable role
of music in the life of the Christian church.

Martin Luther believed that "next to the Word
of God, music deserves the highest praise." He once
wrote:

> I have always loved music. Whoever has skill in
> this art is of a good temperament and fitted

MARTIN LUTHER

Born:
November 10, 1483
Eisleben, Germany

Died:
February 18, 1546
Eisleben, Germany

Occupation:
monk, theologian,
preacher

Hobbies/Interests:
composing

Quotation:
"*Music is one of the
greatest gifts that
God has given us: it
is divine and therefore
Satan is its enemy.
For with its aid many
dire temptations are
overcome; the devil
does not stay where
music is.*"

for all things. We must teach music in schools.
A schoolmaster ought to have skill in music or
I would reject him. Neither should we ordain
young men as preachers unless they have been
well exercised in music.

Such enthusiasm for the art of music, intrinsic-
ally coupled with the theological genius and courage
Luther possessed, had a long-lasting effect. It virtually
assured the preeminent place music would have
in the diverse Protestant church movements. Its
emphasis on involving the entire body of worshipers
would eventually have a profound effect on *all* forms
of sacred music, even in the Catholic Church.

Congregational Music in the Early Reformation

The chorale was the foundation of Luther's new
church music. Unlike chant melodies that often
joined many notes to a single syllable of text, Luther's
chorales applied only one note to each syllable.
Again, we see the emphasis on simplicity and on the
congregation's clear understanding of the words.
Later, these strong, straightforward tunes would be
harmonized and elaborated.

This tradition continued with the work of
such German hymn writers as **Nicolaus Decius**
(1458–1546), **Philipp Nicolai** (1536–1608), **Hans
Leo Hassler** (1562–1612), and **Lucas Osiander**
(1534–1604). Osiander published a hymnal in 1586
that supplied both the chorale melodies and an
elementary harmony as accompaniment. But this

modernization does not obscure the editor's determination to follow the Lutheran model, as is seen in
the book's title: *Fifty Sacred Songs and Psalms arranged
so that an entire Christian congregation can sing along.*

Reformers in other parts of Europe also experi-
mented with the new sacred music. **Huldrych
Zwingli** (1484–1531) of Zurich initially forbade
music in his church but later reconsidered and allowed the use of songs and psalms back in the liturgy.
Likewise the great **John Calvin** (1509–64) of Geneva
removed music from his services—in a reaction
against what he considered excesses of Catholicism—
but was so moved by the psalm singing he heard in a
Strasbourg church that he tempered his opinion.
Calvin set a number of psalms to preexisting tunes,
and his congregations became well known for the
singing of the Genevan Psalter.

More Controversies

In England, Henry VIII's reason for breaking
from the established church may have had more
to do with politics than religion, but the resulting
Anglican Church soon established its own musical
traditions. Although Henry was a musician himself,
he was more interested in marrying Anne Boleyn
than reforming church music. In fact, for some
years after his break with Rome, Anglican churches
continued using the Roman mass.

In 1549 the English *Book of Common Prayer*
was published, and the Anglican Church began
to develop its own customs. Then came the reign

of Mary I (1553–58). She was nicknamed Bloody
Mary for her persecution of Protestants, and under
her rule, all church worship reverted once again
to Catholicism. Finally, Elizabeth I aspired to bring
the traditions of both Catholics and Protestants together. The subsequent Anglican worship was the
closest to Rome that could be found within the
Protestant tradition. Anglican musicians spurned the
chorales of Lutherans, often worshiped in Latin, at
times employed large trained choirs, and later even
created an Anglican chant that contained plainsong
harmonized into four parts.

But during the brief return to Catholicism under
Mary's reign, many English Protestants fled to the
European mainland, where they were strongly influenced by the anti-Rome preachings of John Knox
and John Calvin. The sacred music that was allowed
in their churches was unadorned psalm singing.
Hence, when these Protestants returned to their native
English and Scottish soil, they brought with them
a dislike for the moderation and "Romanizing" tendencies of Elizabeth I.

By the end of the sixteenth century, various
conflicts produced radical groups of Christians
known as Puritans and Separatists. (Later these
groups would produce the traditions we now call
Baptist, Congregational, and Presbyterian.) These
dissenters rejected the vestments, altars, and cathedrals of the Anglican Church, and they initially
allowed no music whatsoever. But believers always
long to sing their praise to God, and soon even the

most radical Separatist gatherings included psalm singing and, later, hymn singing.

A similar controversy raged in Germany during the first half of the seventeenth century. Just as the Separatists rebelled against the more conservative Anglican Church tendencies, a movement known as Pietism rejected what its adherents perceived as a lack of fervor in the Lutheran Church. These Pietists condemned all "highbrow" music—including such masters as J. S. Bach!—as a "sinful abomination." Again, their emphasis was on the simplest of hymnody. Almost none of these simple hymns have survived.

The First Master of Hymn Writing

Amidst so much controversy, many dedicated Christian musicians must have been torn by what seemed to be a terrible dilemma: either to pursue their desire to make great music or to attend a church that maintained the highest scriptural standards. (In various ways this dilemma still haunts many contemporary church musicians. Indeed, most of today's musical controversies have centuries-old roots.)

Finally, there arrived on the scene a man to put things together. He came from a surprising source. From the most radical of Separatist movements—in which most music, especially if it had any redeeming quality, was outlawed—emerged a creator of beautiful, meaningful hymns. His name was **Isaac Watts** (1674–1748).

ISAAC WATTS

Born:
July 17, 1674
Southampton,
England

Died:
November 25, 1748
London, England

Occupation:
pastor, writer

Hobbies/Interests:
astronomy, geography, psychology

Quotation:
"Do not hover always on the surface of things, nor take up suddenly with mere appearances; but penetrate into the depth of matters, as far as your time and circumstances allow, especially in those things which relate to your profession."

133

An old story relates how young Isaac fidgeted in his seat during the interminably long church service of the Dissenters. He especially loathed his church's music, which usually consisted of a one-note psalm. When he complained, his father challenged him to "give us something better, young man."

Fortunately, he did. Even as a boy, the brilliant Watts began composing psalm melodies and complete hymns. During his life, he created more than six hundred hymns, and, for this and other reasons, he is considered the father of English hymnody. He would become a fine preacher too, but his greatest genius was in hymn writing, creating such master-pieces as "When I Survey the Wondrous Cross," "Alas and Did My Savior Bleed," "Joy to the World," "Jesus Shall Reign," "Am I a Soldier of the Cross," and "There Is a Land of Pure Delight."

Is a Hymn Writer a Composer, a Poet, or Both?

Until this chapter, such a question would not need to have been asked. In the other stream of sacred music, the principal creator of music was a composer. If he wrote vocal music, he seldom considered himself competent to write the words to be sung. The text might come from the Bible, a preexisting Christian poem, or even material put together by a friend. The composer was the person who wrote the melodies, the harmonies, the *music*.

Some of the early hymn writers, including Luther himself, often did create both the words and the music. Sometimes a composer and a hymn writer would work together to produce music and lyrics, a combination very fashionable in twentieth-century popular music. A good example was the German composer **Johann Crüger** (1598–1662), who composed music for such hymn writers as **Martin Rinkart** (1586–1649), **Paul Gerhardt** (1607–76), and **Johann Franck** (1618–77).

But many of the finest hymn writers provided the text only, written in a simple poetic fashion that easily lent itself to being set to congregation-style music. It is not unusual for a text created by Isaac Watts, for example, to be set to music again and again by different composers throughout the centuries. This is why your hymnbook often gives credit to both the writer of a hymn's words as well as the composer of its music.

A book about sacred music cannot ignore the vast contributions of the great hymn writers, even if their efforts were more poetic than musical. Later we will examine such hymn *composers* as **Lowell Mason** (1792–1872), who set the melodies to texts written by Isaac Watts and others.

Often we even have to give *triple* credit for a hymn's creation. A poet (that is, a hymn writer) writes the text. Then a musician notices that a certain melody—say by one of the great masters, such as Bach or Beethoven—fits very well (perhaps with some alterations) with the poetic text. And so a hymn is born—a joint creation of the hymn writer, the composer, and the arranger.

If this seems obscure, consider just three popular examples: the famous hymn "Joyful, Joyful, We Adore Thee" (text by Henry van Dyke, melody by Ludwig van Beethoven, arranged by Edward Hodges); "Joy to the World" (text by Issac Watts, melody by George Frideric Handel, arranged by Lowell Mason); and "Hark, the Herald Angels Sing" (text by Charles Wesley, melody by Felix Mendelssohn, arranged by William Cummings).

Why, then, when we think of the creator of a famous hymn, do we generally give credit to the writer of the text and hardly notice the writer of the music itself? Why, when we talk about a classic such as "Join All the Glorious Names," do we call it a hymn by Isaac Watts (who wrote the words) and never a hymn by John Darwall (who wrote the music)?

The answer lies in the very roots of Protestant theology. One of the principal emphases of the Reformation was the centrality of the Bible and the "ministry of the Word," that is, the sermon. One of the things that the reformers objected to was musical excesses, which tended to obscure the text in favor of the music itself. Protestants emphasized the vocal text over the music. Therefore, if a hymn was created by a poet and a composer, we give principal credit to the writer of the text; it is the poet and not the composer of the melody who is called the hymn writer.

To some extent this emphasis on the text is one of the overall differences between the music of the two streams. In the classical stream, the music and the composer are of supreme importance. In the

*QUICK*TAKES
Recommended Recording

Hymns through the Centuries
Cathedral Choir Society of Washington, D.C.
J. Reilly Lewis, conductor
(Aeolian Recordings ADR6J002D)

Compared to the great works from the nineteenth century—the golden age of hymnology—the earlier hymns sound somewhat plain. This fascinating CD overcomes the problem by cleverly inserting carillon and peal bells in the typical organ accompaniment. The result is a smooth balance of the old and the new, with such pieces as "A Mighty Fortress Is Our God," "O Sacred Head Now Wounded," "Come, Ye Thankful People, Come," and "All Glory, Laud, and Honor." J. Reilly Lewis has a well-deserved reputation for flawless choral preparation, and the chorus on *Hymns through the Centuries* has an expansive but well-controlled sound. Recorded in the National Cathedral in Washington, D.C., it is one of the few hymn collections where the early works sound as superb as the later ones.

popular stream, at least during the rise of hymn-ology, top billing is given to the creator of the text. The actual composer of this simple—but often very beautiful—music is less conspicuous.

CHARLES WESLEY

Born:
December 28, 1707
Epworth, England

Died:
March 29, 1788
London, England

Occupation:
preacher, composer, editor

Hobbies/Interests:
poetry, literature

Quotation:
"God buries His work-men but carries on His work."

Moravians and Methodists

Back in the sixteenth century, the reformer Jan Hus started a movement in Bohemia that would later produce a very musical group of zealous Christians known as the Moravians. This group was evangelistic in character and sent missionaries throughout the known world, spreading both the gospel message and their German hymns. Many of these hymns have been discovered in America—in North Carolina and Pennsylvania especially—and they reveal a remarkably high standard of musicianship.

It was on a ship crossing the Atlantic in 1735 that a group of Moravian missionaries met two equally fervent men from England, **John** (1703–91) and **Charles Wesley** (1707–88). A terrible storm threatened to sink the ship, and while the other passengers were crying out in terror, the Moravians sang their hymns and peacefully prayed. Their faith greatly inspired the Wesley brothers, and a lasting bond was established.

The Wesleys had already realized the importance of music in a spiritual revival. Indeed, their father, **Samuel Wesley** (1662–1735), was a clergyman and a hymn writer himself. The Moravian songs strongly confirmed their conviction. John Wesley began to translate some of the Moravian hymns into English and later traveled across Europe to meet the Moravian leader, Count Nicolaus Zinzendorf. The count was also a hymn writer, and the influence of his people is still heard in Methodist hymns today.

Even when the Wesley brothers were still in America, their evangelistic activities were coupled with music. John Wesley edited the first hymnal ever published in the New World, named simply *A Collection of Psalms and Hymns.* In their lifetimes, the brothers would publish more than fifty such collections.

But whereas John was the great preacher and the organizer of what would become the Methodist denomination, his brother Charles was the phenomenal hymn writer. He wrote more than six thousand hymns in all, of which some four thousand were published in his lifetime. His innumerable works include such renowned titles as "O, for a Thousand Tongues," "Jesus, Lover of My Soul," "Hark, the Herald Angels Sing," "Christ the Lord Is Risen Today," "Love Divine, All Loves Excelling," and many, many more.

One might say that the Wesleys created the first great "revivalist" hymns. Two centuries before Billy Graham revivals would end with the invitational hymn "Just as I Am without One Plea," the Wesleys were imploring the multitudes to

> Come, sinners, to the Gospel feast,
> Let every soul be Jesus' guest.

The Wesleys began by preaching in unassuming, open-air meetings. The music that accompanied their hymn texts was equally unpretentious. Often the melodies were culled from folk tunes or popular entertainment, such as the *Beggar's Opera,* a big hit in London. With such unadorned music,

JOHN NEWTON

Born:
July 24, 1725
London, England

Died:
December 21, 1807
London, England

Occupation:
sailor, preacher

Hobbies/Interests:
poetry, hymn writing

Quotation:
"My memory is nearly gone, but I remember two things, that I am a great sinner, and that Christ is a great Saviour."

the Wesleys created some of history's most moving hymns of praise, which are still sung around the world today.

The Hymn-Writing Mania Spreads

As mentioned earlier, English church music in the early eighteenth century was split between the Anglican Church and its various Dissenters. The latter group produced Issac Watts and many lesser followers, launching the English hymn-writing tradition. In the meantime, the Anglican Church prohibited hymn singing; only the Psalms were allowed to be sung.

But this attitude could not last forever. Soon Anglicans were permitted to sing hymns at meetings held outside the sanctuary itself. Eventually, they began writing their own hymns. Two men in particular—both of whom lived in the English town of Olney—were outstanding examples, publishing their work in a book called the *Olney Hymns.* They were **William Cowper** (1731–1800) and **John Newton** (1725–1807).

Virtually every Christian who speaks the English language has sung, or at least heard, Newton's autobiographical masterpiece, "Amazing Grace." This former slave trader gave his life to Christ after surviving a storm at sea. He described his experience in words that, even to this day, millions of people can still identify with. Although not as famous, his friend Cowper is best remembered for the hymns "There Is a Fountain Filled with Blood" and "O, for a Closer Walk with God."

Incidentally, an episode in Newton's life further illustrates the growing conflict between the two different streams of sacred music. After he had become a preacher, this great hymn writer railed against all "irreverent" sacred music that was performed outside of the church. Specifically, the writer of "Amazing Grace" preached every Sunday for more than a year against the "blasphemous" performance of Handel's *Messiah*!

Sacred music also existed in other parts of the British Isles. Ireland, Scotland, and Wales had long traditions of congregational singing that were quite distinct from that of their English neighbors. It is unfortunate that much of this musical wealth has been lost through the centuries. Scholars are still valiantly trying to put together the fragments of Scots, Gaelic, Irish, and Welsh early music, and some examples—such as the *plygain* singing service, sung in parts of Wales each Christmas for centuries— have survived to this day.

In Scotland, congregations inspired by the fiery sermons of John Knox began composing their own psalm tunes soon after the Reformation. A collection of these melodies with English text was published in Edinburgh as early as 1564. These tunes were sung antiphonally, and a clergy member or proxy (usually called a precentor) would introduce each line, which was then sung by the entire congregation. As these ornamental melodies grew increasingly complex, they evolved into the Long Tunes, a highly original form of sacred music that reached its artistic height in the Gaelic-speaking communities of the Western Isles and, in particular, on the Isle of Lewis. The Long Tunes music formed a centuries-old tradition of singing both in the home and in the church.

Hymn Singing Comes to America

What about the New World? Did America also experience a surge of congregational hymn singing? Yes, but since America was struggling with its basic survival, it was a bit slow in keeping up with all the new trends. There was neither time nor energy for such a luxury as music.

The earliest settlements of the New World had regular Christian worship services—as best they could in often primitive conditions—based on the religion of whichever European country founded the specific settlements. For instance, the Spanish settlements followed Catholic worship, while the English ones worshiped within the Anglican tradition. Most of these believers were working desperately just to subsist and had little time to ponder musical innovations and controversies.

The first book of any kind printed in America was a psalter put together by Puritans in Boston. This was in 1640, only twenty years after the Pilgrims had landed at Plymouth. Called *The Whole Booke of Psalms Faithfully Translated in English Metre,* it was generally known as the *Bay Psalm Book.*

Of course, the book contains only words, metered though they were, and no actual melodies. The vocal result wasn't always too edifying. One minister testified that "no two men in the congregation quaver alike or together. It sounds in the ears of a good judge like five hundred different tunes roared out at the same time, with perpetual interferings with one another."

Several distinct forces eventually ameliorated this cacophony. One was the rise of "singing schools" that emerged in America and England during the eighteenth century. Such efforts would produce a number of new hymnbooks, many with the tunes printed along with the notes. Another helpful influence was the music of the Moravians, whose settlements used a wide variety of more sophisticated sacred music.

Still another American movement added a new flavor to music in worship: the Shakers. These followers of Mother Ann Lee immigrated to the New World in the second half of the eighteenth century. In their self-sustaining towns they indulged in spontaneous displays of exuberant praise when they felt led to do so by the Holy Spirit. Most of their tunes were orally transmitted, but many were eventually written down and survive to this day. Such tunes as the well-known "'Tis a Gift to Be Simple" display the Shakers' unique and modest worship style.

Hymn singing grew immensely during the mid-eighteenth century, largely because of the Great Awakening, a far-reaching revival inspired by the dynamic preaching of George Whitefield (1714–70). This movement favored the hymns of Isaac Watts and other English hymn writers over the traditional psalm recitations. One of the thousands impressed by Whitefield's preaching was none other than Benjamin Franklin. Franklin also admired Watts, and he published Watts's extremely popular *Psalms and Hymns*.

In the urban centers of the East Coast, the beginnings of musical appreciation were stirring. A Boston tanner named **William Billings** (1746–1800) was the first important composer from the United States. In 1770 he published the *New-England Psalm Singer,* the first collection of original music by an American musician. Despite having a crippled arm and leg and being blind in one eye, Billings became famous throughout New England, especially after he established many singing schools in eastern towns.

No account of early American sacred music could be complete without mentioning Negro spirituals. These pearls of praise and worship were created in the midst of the cruelest states of slavery and affliction. Until 1770, African Americans were forbidden by law to form churches, and their first hymnbook did not appear until 1801. (The bulk of discussion on this subject will be presented in a later chapter.)

Nevertheless, it must be noted that the roots of Negro spirituals go far back into the seventeenth and eighteenth centuries. The melodies and "hollers" sustained the people through wretched slave ship

Other Listening Recommendations

William Cowper
"Hark, My Soul, It Is the Lord"

Nicolaus Decius
"All Glory Be to God on High"

Martin Luther
"A Mighty Fortress Is Our God"

John Newton
"Glorious Things of Thee Are Spoken"

Martin Rinkart
"Now Thank We All Our God"

Shaker melody
"'Tis a Gift to Be Simple"

Isaac Watts
"There Is a Land of Pure Delight"

Charles Wesley
"O, for a Thousand Tongues"

journeys and the never-ending work on the planta-
tions. Indeed, the genesis of the spirituals truly is
found not in the New World but in the musical traditions of the African continent.

CHAPTER 9

THE GROWTH OF HYMNOLOGY
(1750–1900)

This is my story, this is my song,
praising my Savior all the day long.

Fanny Jane Crosby

While it took America a long time to establish its own classical, or first-stream, traditions, it soon embraced the popular second stream. By the beginning of the nineteenth century, many variants of sacred music existed in America, from the camp meetings and wild revival services to the growing hymnology of the urban churches.

Since the original philosophy behind popular congregational music was to create sacred music for "everyman," it soon spread out in order to truly embrace the musical backgrounds of "everymen." For example, the popular worship music of affluent New England congregations would not be the same music as that of the rural South.

147

Throughout the nineteenth century the differences between various worship styles would become more noticeable. Eventually, these differences would lead to the formation of new streams of sacred music in the subsequent century. But the genesis of the many different styles we see today had its origins in the philosophy Martin Luther unleashed: that every Christian worshiper should be able to sing music to the glory of God.

Many of us might view such a philosophy as obvious and indisputable. Yet the classical composers of sacred music's first stream felt very differently. When Haydn wrote an oratorio or Mozart wrote a mass, they knew that not every Christian would have the ability to sing it. They were composing music for trained musicians to perform.

Of course, classical composers wanted everyone to be able to appreciate and enjoy *listening* to their sacred music. They desired that their sacred compositions would inspire their audiences to love God with greater fervency, which is quite different from writing music uncomplicated enough for the average person to be able to sing—to be able to fully enter into the expression of sacred music.

Let us now continue our discussion of the popular Christian music that grew so rapidly after the Reformation. The chorales and early hymn writers were followed by a long tradition of sacred song that spread far beyond the original boundaries of the Lutheran Church. It would soon encompass

Christians of every background, race, national
origin, and denomination.

The Spiritual

It should come as no surprise to readers of the New
Testament that some of history's most beautiful
and heartrending music should emerge from an oppressed group of people. Yet thousands of Africans
who were kidnapped from their homeland, sold into
slavery in America, and subjected to the cruelest
forms of servitude somehow managed to create an
entire class of sacred music that has inspired
Christians for over two centuries.

It is interesting that although the slaves accepted
the Christianity of their oppressors without doctrinal modification, their Christian music was quite
different from that of their masters. The Negro
spiritual, as it is now called, was a blend of African
rhythm and melodic inflection, folk songs of early
America, and the delirious ecstasy that characterized
the slaves' emotional Christian meetings. Above all,
the spirituals were metaphorical, containing veiled
criticisms of slavery and references to the journey to
the promised land couched in rich biblical imagery.

As one might expect, the earliest roots of the
spiritual are rather obscure. Although certainly
many naturally gifted musicians existed among the
slaves, few had musical training, and virtually all
were illiterate. Therefore, most of the famous Negro
spirituals are labeled "anonymous" or "traditional"
in hymnals today.

149

*QUICK*TAKES
Recommended Recording

*Wade in the Water: African American
Sacred Music Traditions* (Vols. I-IV)

Various Artists and Ensembles

(Smithsonian Folkways SF40072)

Focusing on a specific branch of hymnology, this four-CD recording
is a marvelous collection that examines four aspects of the sacred music
tradition within the black community: African American spirituals,
African American congregational singing, African American gospel music,
and African American community gospel. From the moving harmony
of "Swing Low, Sweet Chariot" by the Princely Players to the exhilaration
of "Sign of the Judgment" by the McIntosh Country Shouters, this anthol-
ogy captures both the joys and sorrows in the musical history of African
American faith.

When one hears a fine performance of such spirituals as "Sometimes I Feel like a Motherless Child,"
"Swing Low, Sweet Chariot," or "Were You There
When They Crucified My Lord?" it is not difficult to
imagine their humble beginnings. These simple
melodies of a subjugated people have had a major
impact on the sacred music of hundreds of Christian
churches. This musical richness has been observed
for two and a half centuries, as evidenced by a remark
made by the Reverend Samuel Davies in 1755:

"I cannot but observe that the Negroes, above all the species that I ever knew, have an ear for Musicke, and a kind of extatic Delight in Psalmody."

Music of the Camp Meetings

Another notable influence on popular worship in the nineteenth century was the camp meeting. Although often characterized as a southern phenomenon, these outdoor meetings were also found throughout much of America and England. They were emotional meetings of a "Holy Ghost revival," and their music was often unaccompanied and of a very rural flavor.

The American composer **Charles Ives** (1874–1954) writes of these meetings, which he often attended in his youth: "There was power and exaltation in these great concaves of sound, sung by thousands of 'let out' souls." Sometimes Ives accompanied the singers on the melodeon (a small reed organ), and he listened closely, intrigued as the fervor of the singing would often throw the key as much as a whole tone higher. His father, who usually led the outdoor congregations with his cornet, had a special sliding valve added to the instrument so he could rise with the singers and not hold them down!

Camp meeting music usually consisted of fast, foot-stomping hoedowns or slower, emotional choruses. Seldom did either type move musically beyond two or three harmonies, and the text was mostly organized around a repeated refrain. Sometimes a song leader would bellow out the many verses, and the congregation would join in on the well-known chorus.

Such old songs as "Shall We Gather at the River?" "Come to Jesus," "I Do Believe," and "Where Are the Hebrew Children?" were indicative of this unpretentious camp meeting spirit. Involving no musical innovations, the music nonetheless kindled a powerful excitement that would stimulate hymn writers in even the most sophisticated of churches. It would also serve as a catalyst for many of the revivalist hymns written for urban congregations on the East Coast and in England.

Shape Note and Sacred Harp Singing

We usually take musical notation for granted today, as if it has been with us in its present form for millennia. Actually, notation has evolved through the centuries (and continues to do so for modern composers). For example, some of the early psalters, such as the 1562 *Sternhold and Hopkins*, used letters to specify pitches, a throwback of almost two thousand years to the earliest notation of the Greeks!

Another notational development involved the use of differently shaped note heads—squares, circles, triangles—to denote pitch. Sometimes these note heads would be placed on a five-line stave; other times they were written without any lines at all. America's first hymnbook, the 1698 *Bay Psalm Book*, used various shaped notes, a practice that continued throughout the nineteenth century and flourished in southern and rural areas that had been subjected to a minimal amount of European musical influence.

One of the most important collections of shape note hymns was **Benjamin Franklin White's** *The Sacred Harp,* first published in 1844. The book was so popular that sacred harp singing became a huge movement throughout the South.

This musical tradition involved long singing sections, where the singers would usually face one another in a circle. The group would learn the notes first by carefully singing the indicated pitches. Then words were added, often using a large number of verses sung to the same tunes. Sacred harp singing was widespread in country churches, community meetings, and in many Christian homes throughout the country. Some of the original melodies such as "Come, All Christians, Be Committed," can still be found in modern hymnals.

Sacred harp singing is not simply an interesting bit of musical history. The late twentieth century has seen a revival of this tradition, and it continues to spread across both America and England. Hundreds of amateur singers are learning to read shaped notes and to participate in a sacred music tradition, bringing believers of many denominations together.

Great Hymn Writers of the Early Nineteenth Century

There are so many notable nineteenth-century hymn writers from both sides of the Atlantic that it is

153

difficult to know where to begin. Let's look at a few of the most important.

James Montgomery (1771–1854) was one of the first great hymn writers of the nineteenth century. Born in Scotland, he was the son of a Moravian minister. In his twenties he moved to London and then to Sheffield, where he became a poet and a newspaper editor. A man of strong conviction, his outspoken writing twice landed him in prison. This forthright soul gave us the hymns "Stand Up and Bless the Lord," "Prayer Is the Soul's Sincere Desire," "Hail to the Lord's Anointed," "God Is My Strong Salvation," "Be Known to Us in Breaking Bread," and the Christmas carol "Angels from the Realms of Glory."

Another hymn writer was **Reginald Heber** (1783–1826), who wrote the famous "Holy, Holy, Holy," which the poet Alfred, Lord Tennyson called the greatest hymn ever written. Born in Cheshire, England, Heber showed his poetic gift at an early age and soon became a scholar and lecturer. He later entered the ministry and went on to become the bishop of Calcutta in 1823. His best-known hymns include "Brightest and the Son of God Goes Forth to War," "Best of the Sons of the Morning," "Watchman, Tell Us of the Night," and the communion hymn "Bread of the World in Mercy Broken."

Charlotte Elliott (1789–1871) is best known for her guileless hymn "Just as I Am, without One Plea," immortalized in the twentieth century by its constant use in the Billy Graham crusades. An invalid, Elliott wrote the poem during a time of frustration in which her condition prevented her from helping her brother, a successful minister. He would later testify that "in the course of a long ministry, I hope I have been permitted to see some of the fruit of my labor, but I feel that far more has been done by a single hymn of my sister's." She is also known for her "O Holy Savior, Friend Unseen" and "My God, My Father, while I Stray."

An extremely prolific writer, **John Mason Neale** (1818–66) created the songbook collections *Hymns for Children, Hymns for the Young, Hymns for the Sick,* and his celebrated *Sequences, Hymns, and Other Ecclesiastical Verses.* Born in London, he became a brilliant scholar and translator, writing almost constantly while also working at a school and an orphanage. His greatest contributions to hymnology were the excellent translations made of ancient hymns, such as "All Glory, Laud, and Honor," "The Day Is Past and Over," "Come, Ye Faithful," "Raise the Strain," "The Day of Resurrection," "Jerusalem the Golden," and the Christmas carols "Good Christian Men Rejoice" and "O Come, O Come, Emmanuel."

Lowell Mason

When hymnology is surveyed, one principally examines the writers of the text rather than the often unknown composers of the music. Surely the greatest exception to this practice is the musician **Lowell Mason** (1792–1872). It has been said that

Mason did more for sacred music than any other writer of the nineteenth century.

Mason was born in Medfield, Massachusetts, and was a choir leader by the age of sixteen. Although he worked as a banker in Savannah, Georgia, for several years, his musical talent was such that Mason was soon conducting a number of choirs and was offered a salary of two thousand dollars to conduct in Boston—good money in those days. In 1835 he received a doctorate in music from New York University, the first American college to grant such a degree. This was at a time when the arts were almost unheard of in American colleges.

Mason was an innovator in music education and organized the Boston Academy of Music, giving free lessons to hundreds of talented students. Within a few years, he was also teaching in the Boston public schools. Two of his most important publications were *The Child's Introduction to Sacred Music* and *The Juvenile Psalmist.*

But his greatest legacy was hymnology. Mason composed or arranged the music for dozens of the hymns we still sing today. Much of the great poetry of Isaac Watts and Charles Wesley are best known to us in the musical settings Mason created. Among his many masterpieces are "My Faith Looks Up to Thee," "Come, Sinners, to the Gospel Feast," "A Charge to Keep I Have," "And Let Our Bodies Part," "Be Present at Our Table, Lord," and "Nearer My God to Thee."

William Bradbury and the Sunday School Hymn

One of Mason's Boston choirs was located in the Bowdoin Street Church. Among the many singers Mason taught there was a young man named **William Batchelder Bradbury** (1816–68). Bradbury would carry on the musical tradition of his mentor. He learned music so quickly that he was soon made the organist at a small church. After moving from one position to another, in 1841 he settled into the job that would make him famous: organist at New York City's Baptist Tabernacle.

Bradbury had a natural gift for working with children, and he formed a number of very successful children's choirs. He organized the Juvenile Music festivals that were known throughout the city. Following in the footsteps of Mason, Bradbury gave hundreds of free music classes to children and composed hymns specifically for children's Sunday schools. He was the composer of the well-known "Jesus Loves Me This I Know."

After leaving his post as an organist, Bradbury spent years composing and arranging hymns and compiling songbooks. These would eventually total fifty-nine collections. In addition, he and his brother founded the Bradbury Piano Company in 1854. He was also a great encouragement to other hymn writers, particularly Fanny Crosby (more on her later). **Thomas Hastings** (1784–1872), who composed the music for the hymn "Rock of Ages," and **George Frederick Root** (1820–95), who composed the music for the Isaac Watts hymn "There Is

157

a Land of Pure Delight," also counted among his friends.

Bradbury composed the music for some of the nineteenth century's finest hymns, including "He Leadeth Me," "Sweet Hour of Prayer," "Prince of Peace, Control My Will," "My Hope Is Built on Nothing Less," "Savior, Like a Shepherd Lead Us," "Never Further than Thy Cross," "Return, O Wanderer, Return," and the perennial favorite "Just as I Am, without One Plea."

Great Hymn Writers of the Mid-Nineteenth Century

Now that we've looked at two of the greatest hymn composers, let's again discuss some of the greatest writers of hymn texts.

The Irishman **John Samuel Bewley Monsell** (1811–75) was born in Londonderry, educated at Trinity College in Dublin, and spent most of his life as the rector of Saint Nicholas Church in Guildford, England. A prolific poet, he wrote eleven volumes of poems. His best known, *Hymns of Praise and Love,* was published in 1863. Monsell also wrote some three hundred hymns, the most famous being "Fight the Good Fight," "O Love, Divine and Golden," "Light of the World, We Hail Thee," and the missionary hymn "Lord of the Living Harvest."

A very different hymn writer was **Frederick William Faber** (1814–63), who was raised a Calvinist and later entered the Anglican ministry at Oxford. Influenced by the writings of John Henry

Cardinal Newman, Faber converted to Catholicism. Sensing that his fellow Catholics had few hymns to match those of the Protestants, he determined to rectify the situation and wrote 150 hymns, including "O How the Thought of God Attracts," "There's a Wideness in God's Mercy," "Hark, Hark, My Soul!" "O Come and Mourn with Me Awhile," and "I Worship Thee, Most Gracious God." His famed "Faith of Our Fathers" is now sung—with doctrinal modification—in more Protestant churches than Catholic ones.

How about a man who wrote both the words and the music to his hymns? **Philip Paul Bliss** (1838–76) was born in rural northern Pennsylvania and gave his life to Christ at the age of twelve while attending an outdoor revival meeting. Inspired by a William Bradbury music convention, Bliss began to teach music and distribute his own hymns, traveling by horse and accompanied by an old melodeon. He edited and published many songbooks and donated the royalties (almost thirty thousand dollars) to the evangelistic ministry of W. D. Whittle, with whom Bliss worked. Bliss gave us the words and music to "Hallelujah, What a Savior," "Jesus Loves Even Me," and "Wonderful Words of Life" in addition to the music to the celebrated "It Is Well with My Soul."

Frances Ridley Havergal (1836–79) was the youngest daughter of Reverend W. H. Havergal, who was himself a hymn writer. She was born in Worcestershire, England, and as a youth she showed

PHILIP PAUL BLISS

Born:
July 9, 1838
Rome, Pa.

Died:
December 29, 1876
Ashtabula, Ohio

Occupation:
teacher, composer, writer, singer

Hobbies/Interests:
poetry, humor

Quotation:
"Doubtless upon this, more than anything else, depends your future greatness: By all means, follow the star of empire!"

**FRANCES RIDLEY
HAVERGAL**

Born:
December 14, 1836
Worcestershire,
England

Died:
June 3, 1879
Caswell Bay, Wales

Occupation:
writer, composer

Hobbies/Interests:
poetry, Greek,
Hebrew

Quotation:
*"I am trusting Thee to
guide me; Thou alone
shalt lead. Every day
and hour supplying
all my need."*

enormous intelligence, learning many foreign languages and becoming a gifted musician. Later she would memorize the entire New Testament, all the Psalms, Isaiah, and the minor prophets! In her short life, she wrote many hymns, including "Lord, Speak to Me," "I Am Trusting Thee, Lord Jesus," "Like a River Glorious," "Who Is on the Lord's Side?" "I Gave My Life for Thee," and "Another Year Is Dawning," but she is best known for "Take My Life and Let It Be."

Revivalism and the Second Great Awakening

As we saw earlier, the camp meeting phenomenon used a great deal of music in its ministry as it spread across nineteenth-century America. Of course, the impact of such meetings was felt most in rural sections of the country. Nevertheless, the Second Great Awakening in the first part of the century had a profound effect on the cities of the Northeast. Its music played a significant part in nineteenth-century sacred music.

Charles Grandison Finney (1792–1875) was one of America's great revivalists. For over three decades he preached an uncompromised gospel and witnessed more than half a million conversions through his work. His principal musician was **Thomas Hastings**, who published fifty volumes of sacred song, including more than six hundred hymns and over a thousand hymn tunes.

Revivalism in the second half of the century was dominated by the team of Moody and Sankey. **Dwight Lyman Moody** (1837–99) was a powerful preacher who usually worked with **Ira David Sankey** (1840–1908). Sankey, whose beautiful voice was heard by millions in America, England, Scotland, and Ireland, composed the music for dozens of hymns in a straightforward and unpretentious style that complemented Moody's rather flamboyant preaching.

Once, during an evangelistic meeting in Edinburgh, Moody finished his sermon on the Good Shepherd and then turned to his partner for a song. Nothing appropriate had been prepared, but Sankey remembered a poem he had clipped from a local newspaper. He quickly laid the poem, entitled "The Ninety and Nine," in front of him, and before thousands he improvised the celebrated song. Such spontaneous and ingenious music seemed to flow from Sankey, almost like classical melodies had flowed from Mozart's pen.

Some of Sankey's other well-known hymns include "I Am Praying for You, Lord," "A Shelter in the Time of Storm," "Hiding in Thee," "Lay Some Soul upon My Heart," "Under His Wings," "Faith Is the Victory," and "Trusting Jesus." Sankey was one of the original compilers of the evangelistic songbook *Gospel Hymns.* His influence helped to create the genre of gospel hymns, which would continue in popularity and significance into the next century with the revivals of Billy Sunday and Billy Graham.

IRA DAVID SANKEY

Born:
August 28, 1840
Edinburg, Pa.

Died:
August 13, 1908
Brooklyn, N.Y.

Occupation:
chaplain, singer, composer

Hobbies/Interests:
business, counseling

Quotation:
"I never touch a song that does not speak to me in every word and phrase."

Fanny Crosby

We now come to the hymn writer of hymn writers, **Frances Jane Crosby** (1820–1915), better known as

FANNY CROSBY

Born:
March 24, 1820
Putnam County, N.Y.

Died:
February 12, 1915
Bridgeport, Conn.

Occupation:
writer, poet

Hobbies/Interests:
singing, knitting

Quotation:
"I seem to have been led little by little toward my work; and I believe that the same fact will appear in the life of anyone who will culti-vate such powers as God has given him, and then go on, bravely, quietly, but persistently, doing such work as comes to his hands."

Fanny. This remarkable woman holds the world record for writing the most hymns: over eight thousand! She did not begin to write hymns until she was forty-four, but she lived to be ninety-five and often wrote as many as eight hymns a day.

As a six-week-old baby, she was permanently blinded by an incompetent doctor. Yet she had no bitterness in her heart. A minister once said to her, "I think it is a great pity that the Master did not give you sight when He showered so many other gifts upon you." She exclaimed, "Do you know that if at birth I had been able to make one petition, it would have been that I should have been born blind?" When the astonished preacher asked why, she replied, "Because when I get to heaven, the first face that shall ever gladden my sight will be that of my Savior!"

Crosby attended the New York Institution for the Blind, but she neither mastered Braille nor ever tried to write down her hymns herself. She had a phenomenal memory and would simply dictate the finished texts to a friend. In her lifetime, she would use more than two hundred pen names for her work. She married Alexander Van Alstyne, a blind music teacher at the institution. Her first published book was called *The Blind Girl and Other Poems* (1844).

Attending a revival meeting in 1850, Crosby was profoundly moved by the Isaac Watts hymn "Alas, and Did My Savior Bleed?" Herself committed to the Lord, she eventually wrote hymns to bring others to Christ. In 1864 she met the Sunday school hymn writer William Bradbury, who was impressed with her talents and greatly encouraged her work. Crosby was soon under contract with the publisher Biglow and Main to submit three hymns each week for publication.

Her works were widely popularized during the Second Great Awakening in dozens of revival meetings led by Moody and Sankey. Crosby and Sankey became great friends, and he was often the first to sing her finished works. Her simple hymns were very Christ-centered, and her favorite topics included the joys of heaven and the certain return of Jesus to the earth. In both revivals and churches these hymns brought tears of repentance to thousands, and many are still sung today.

A list of Crosby's hymns would take up the rest of this book, but those named here are some of her most popular: "All the Way My Savior Leads Me," "Will Jesus Find Us Watching?" "Jesus Is Tenderly Calling," "Nearer the Cross," "Take the World, but Give Me Jesus," "'Tis the Blessed Hour of Prayer," "I Am Thine, O Lord," "Though Your Sins Be As Scarlet," "My Savior First of All," "Tell Me the Story of Jesus," "Jesus Keep Me Near the Cross," "Safe in the Arms of Jesus," "Rescue the Perishing," and her autobiographical favorite, "Blessed Assurance."

Great Hymn Writers of the Late Nineteenth Century

The great century of hymn writing continues! **Cecil Francis Alexander** (1818–95) was an Irish Sunday school teacher determined that her students would understand the basic tenets of the Christian faith, especially the Apostles' Creed. She published the collection *Hymns for Little Children,* which deals with rather weighty matters in the simple language of her young students. Thousands of children over the years have been enlightened by such hymns as "All Things Bright and Beautiful," "Once in Royal David's City," "There Is a Green Hill Far Away," and "Jesus Calls Us."

In a similar spirit, Scotsman **Horatius Bonar** (1808–89) wanted the children of his parish to play a more meaningful part in the worship service. To this end, he wrote "I Lay My Sins on Jesus" and many other hymns, including "Here, O My Lord," "I See Thee Face to Face," "Go, Labor On!" "Spend and Be Spent," "No, Not Despairingly," and his most popular, "I Heard the Voice of Jesus Say." Outside of his clerical duties, Bonar was also the editor of two church periodicals, *The Border Watch* and the *Journal of Prophecy.*

John Ellerton (1826–93) was one of the most important English hymnologists of his day. He not only wrote a number of fine hymns, but he also edited many hymnbooks, including the revered *Hymns, Ancient and Modern.* Some of his best-known works are "The Day Thou Gavest, Lord, Is Ended," "Now the Laborer's Task Is O'er," "The Lord Be with Us Every Day," "This Is the Day of Light," "Savior, Again to Thy Dear Name We Raise," and "Behold Us, Lord, a Little Space." He refused to copyright his work, stating that if these hymns were "counted worthy to contribute to

Christ's praise in the congregation, one ought to feel very thankful and humble."

And finally, we end the nineteenth century not with a hymn writer, but with someone with an equally important responsibility: translating great hymns. **Catherine Winkworth** (1829–78) was a brilliant scholar who did much to advance the cause of women's education in her native England. But she is remembered best for the excellent translations she made of German hymns. These include such favorites as "Praise to the Lord, the Almighty," "Now Thank We All Our God," "Blessed Jesus," "At Thy Word," "All My Heart This Night Rejoices," "If Thou but Suffer God to Guide Me," "Now God Be with Us," "Lift Up Your Heads, Ye Mighty Gates," and "Jesus, Priceless Treasure."

Obviously, this period was a busy, busy time for hymn writing, and many more hymn writers could have been mentioned here. Please be forgiving if your favorite was omitted!

The Stream Begins to Split

As we approach the twentieth century, the stream of popular sacred music is overflowing with the growing diversity of musical styles. The old-time camp meetings developed into a complete class that is usually called country music. The rapid growth of hymnology sparked a huge interest in church choir singing, while the revivalist movement led to the gospel song that in turn spawned an entire genre of gospel music.

As was pointed out at the beginning of the chapter, popular sacred music veered off into very specialized areas and continues to do so to this day. As people's lives become more dissimilar, it seems they desire music to fit their own situations. Some want to worship God with gospel hymns, others with a folk flavor, still others with the most contemporary approach possible.

A major factor that influenced all of these categories was the advent of recorded music. With the popularity of records, tapes, and CDs, sacred music has never been quite the same. Instead of taking place at the local level in churches and revival meetings, the creation of new sacred music has become available to "everyman" everywhere.

Technology at the end of the twentieth century has enabled composers and hymn writers to send their songs around the world only seconds after the works are completed. This is a far cry from the days of Gutenberg! But before we enter the bewildering world of twentieth-century sacred music, let us finish out the preceding century by once more returning to the first stream of sacred music.

Other Listening Recommendations

Cecil Francis Alexander
"There Is a Green Hill Far Away"

Philip Paul Bliss
"Hallelujah, What a Savior"

Fanny Crosby
"Blessed Assurance"

Charlotte Elliott
"Just as I Am, without One Plea"

Lowell Mason
"My Faith Looks Up to Thee"

Ira David Sankey
"The Ninety and Nine"

Traditional
"Come, All Christians, Be Committed"

Traditional
"Sometimes I Feel like a Motherless Child"

Traditional
"Where Are the Hebrew Children?"

THE TWENTIETH CENTURY AND
THE ADVENT OF RECORDED MUSIC

CHAPTER 10

MODERN CLASSICAL COMPOSERS
(1900–PRESENT)

The church knew what the Psalmist knew: music praises God. Music is as well or better able to praise Him than the building of the church and all its decorations; it is the church's greatest ornament.

Igor Stravinsky

M usic lovers express quite a diversity of opinions on the music of the twentieth century. Some readers may feel that after many chapters about ancient history, we have finally arrived at their favorite century. Others, especially those devotees of the baroque, classical, and romantic periods, may bemoan the advent of "weird" modern music.

It is true that much classical music of the twentieth century, particularly of the latter half, is very different from the loveliness of a Mozart aria. This is equally true of the period's sacred music. But as we study the music more closely, we find that the intent of composers is generally not to sound "weird," but to be innovative, to add something new to the realm of musical thought.

Innovation in music composition is not new. The previous chapters have been replete with countless examples of work sparked by genius. But as the twentieth century progresses, it seems that composers' love of innovation almost turns to madness, as if each composer wants to do something a little wilder than other composers. The results can get rather out of hand.

The Test of Time

Is this emphasis on innovation something new? Are we simply too close to it to appreciate it?

To answer such questions, we must examine the whole concept of time. We often hear that a composer is "ahead of his time." What this really means is that he is ahead of his audience, which is probably enjoying the music of an earlier era. Composers of the last two centuries, at least, have not been fully appreciated until long after their deaths. As composer Arthur Honegger once wryly observed, "It is clear that the first specification for a composer is to be dead."

Beethoven once asserted that "art demands that we not stand still." He, like many other composers throughout history, paid heavily for such a conviction. Although Beethoven is now universally admired, it was not always so. When Goethe heard Beethoven's famous Symphony no. 5, he declared, "How big it is—quite wild! Enough to bring the house about one's ears." Another of his contemporaries, Jean-François Le Sueur, noted that "one ought not to write music like that." Still another musician, after hearing Symphony no. 7, proclaimed that Beethoven "is quite ripe for the madhouse."

Be assured that this attitude was not just a problem for Beethoven; similar quotations are readily available for nearly every composer you can imagine. Many, many composers throughout history have struggled with audiences that could not understand or appreciate their music.

Why is this? For one thing, members of a typical audience may love music, but they do not spend all day studying it. They have many other things to do, like making a living! But composers generally devote most of their waking hours to creating music, and this understandably gets them a bit ahead of everyone else.

Furthermore, classical composers choose to push on into the unknown. This trailblazing technique may lead us into wonderful new musical vistas, but it pushes true recognition for a composer far into the future. There are composers today who deliberately write music for an audience of a future era. This future-audience awareness is one of the things that differentiates classical music from popular music, which is intended to be enjoyed immediately by a contemporary audience.

This situation is not completely new. When Beethoven was once upbraided for the complexity of his later string quartets, he replied, "Oh, they are not for you, they are for another age." He was right. In his day very few could make any sense of these ingenious pieces. Today they are performed everywhere and hailed as masterpieces.

Therefore, typical audiences of any given age, including our own, don't have the capability to determine what is great modern music and what is, shall we say, less than great. They may know what they like, but this somewhat arbitrary opinion is worth little.

So let us not be too hasty in dismissing all this "weird" modern music. Beethoven sounded rather weird to many of his contemporaries, but we eventually recognized him as a true master. Who knows? The very composer whose modern music so irritates you may someday be as popular as Mozart is today.

A Continuation of Nationalism

With all this as a backdrop, let's look at the sacred music of several twentieth-century composers. One of the things we examined in the chapter on the romantic period was the rise of national styles in music. This trend continued for many years, and you will notice that the composers of the first half of the century represent quite diverse nationalities.

The next batch of composers is not presented in any particular order. Although all were born before 1900, their compositions represent some of the best classical music of the first half of the twentieth century. Some are better known for their instrumental works, but all created at least one major sacred composition. Eastern Europe will be our starting point, with the composers **Leoš Janáček** (1854–1928) and **Zoltán Kodály** (1882–1967).

Janáček was a composer from Czechoslovakia and, like fellow Czech Antonín Dvořák, had a tremendous interest in its native folk music. (Many other twentieth-century composers shared this preoccupation with local folk music.) Janáček's principal sacred work is *Festival* Mass, which, like such predecessors as Bach's Mass in B Minor and Beethoven's *Missa Solemnis,* could never be used as a liturgical mass. Rather, it is a joyful celebration of the Christian faith, designed more for the common people than for a sophisticated concert audience.

The Hungarian Kodály also had an affinity for indigenous folk music. Many of these melodies are found in his works for unaccompanied chorus, as well as in his best-known sacred piece, the huge *Psalmus Hungaricus.* Written for tenor soloist, chorus, and orchestra, this composition does for sacred music what a work like Liszt's *Hungarian Dances* does for the orchestra: it totally incorporates native folk melodies into the classical setting, in this case creating a truly Hungarian sacred music.

In France, the first half of the twentieth century primarily involved the impressionist music of Claude Debussy and Maurice Ravel. Unfortunately, these masters left us with no sacred music except Debussy's mystical cantata, *L'Enfant Prodigue,* written when he was a student. But another composer, **Arthur Honegger** (1892–1955), created two French oratorios that are still popular today, *Le Roi David*

(1923) and *Jeanne d' Arc au bûcher* (1939). Both of these works are interesting in their dramatic sensationalism, combining the form of oratorio with the theatrics of opera.

If we allude to sensationalism, we must take note of the German composer **Carl Orff** (1895–1982) and his one well-known choral work, the infamous *Carmina Burana*. This bombastic piece is sometimes called sacred music, but this is a misnomer at best. The vulgar and sometimes lewd text was written by monks of the tenth through the thirteenth centuries, and their spirituality was rather overwhelmed by their sensuality.

Another work on the fringes of sacred music is the *Hymn of Jesus* by the English composer **Gustav Holst** (1874–1934). The seemingly Christian title is perplexing, since the entire text of the piece is taken from the apocryphal Acts of Saint John instead of the canonical Bible. Therefore, this peculiar work is virtually never peformed in a church; rather, it sounds more at home in secular concert halls. *Hymn of Jesus* is perhaps the only sacred music that is neither Christian nor non-Christian. Its text obviously concerns the founder of Christianity, but its words have been rejected by Catholics, Protestants, and Orthodox alike.

Ralph Vaughan Williams

We find ourselves again on solid ground with the sacred music of Holst's good friend, the composer **Ralph Vaughan Williams** (1872–1958), who became much more renowned than any of his countrymen of that day. Vaughan Williams (whose first name is pronounced "Raaf") is best known for his nine fascinating symphonies, but he also made a lasting impact on sacred music. In fact, he worked as an editor for a number of English hymnals, including the *Oxford Book of Carols* and the popular collection *Songs of Praise.* The latter contained two of his original songs, "At the Name of Jesus" and "Savior, Again to Thy Dear Name We Raise."

Vaughan Williams became an expert on hymnology at an early age. The son of a clergyman, he began his musical career as the organist at Saint Barnabus Church in London and was soon immersed in the world of choirs and choral music, directing the city's famed Bach Choir. Later in life he founded the Dorking Bach Choir, where he worked until his retirement in 1954. His work in hymnology was of the highest standard, and he deplored "the false sentimentality of many of our modern hymns as compared to the true feeling and dignity of earlier examples."

Vaughan Williams also became a leading authority on English folk music, which he incorporated into such genres as opera, orchestral music, and choral works. He collected folk melodies directly from the rural folk, spending weeks riding through the countryside with notebook and pencil in hand, knocking on doors, and asking total strangers if they knew any old folk songs. This painstaking method

RALPH VAUGHAN WILLIAMS

Born:
October 12, 1872
Down Ampney,
England

Died:
August 26, 1958
London, England

Occupation:
organist, composer,
conductor

Hobbies/Interests:
folk music,
hymnology

Quotation:
"If the roots of your art are firmly planted in your own soil and that soil has anything individually to give you, you may still gain the whole world and not lose your own soul."

led him to beautiful tunes that might have been forgotten except for his diligence.

His finest sacred music includes a powerful Te Deum composed for the installation of the archbishop of Canterbury, a Christmas cantata called *Hodie,* two motets entitled *The Souls of the Righteous* and *O vos omnes, Sancta Civitas* (a work for tenor, baritone, chorus, and orchestra), and the exquisite Mass in G Minor. This last work is interesting in its references to the music of the past, with its modal influences and open fifths sounding like an echo of the medieval period.

Vaughan Williams also composed a number of other pieces that may be considered sacred, including the fascinating opera *The Pilgrim's Progress,* the orchestral suite *Job (A Masque for Dancing),* and *Five Mystical Songs* for baritone, chorus, and orchestra. For the texts of the *Songs,* he selected poetry by **George Herbert** (1593–1633), one of England's greatest Christian poets. Vaughan Williams also wrote many smaller works, such as *O Taste and See,* Dona Nobis Pacem, *O Clap Your Hands,* and his well-known arrangement of *Old Hundredth.*

Perhaps the greatest reason for Vaughan Williams's profound influence on later composers of sacred music was his absolute standard of quality. He believed that the same expertise and diligent labor that great composers employ while writing symphonies should apply to even the simplest hymns for Christian worship. He asked the crucial question, "Why should we not enter into our inheritance in the church as well as the concert room?"

America's First Major Classical Composers

Most of America was still wilderness when Beethoven was writing symphonies, so it is not surprising that the United States was far behind Europe in producing composers of classical music. Actually, some of our founding fathers were gifted musicians, including Benjamin Franklin and Thomas Jefferson. And the music of other early American composers such as William Billings is now being brought to light. But the first truly great American in this field did not emerge until the early twentieth century, and even then his rise to the forefront was painfully slow.

Charles Ives (1874–1954) was born in Danbury, Connecticut, and educated by his father, who insisted on such outrageous musical exercises as playing the piano part of "Swanee River" in C major while singing it in the key of E-flat! Small wonder that Ives would later compose music of innovative complexity and hair-raising dissonance. His music was decades ahead of his time, and he might have starved as a composer had he not become a successful insurance executive who wrote on the side.

Ives was also a gifted organist, and even as a youth worked in that capacity in a number of churches. He developed a lifelong affinity for sacred choral music, composing numerous psalms and sacred songs, such as the noted "General William Booth Enters into Heaven." As a symphonist, Ives showed his proclivity

CHARLES IVES

Born:
October 20, 1874
Danbury, Conn.

Died:
May 19, 1954
New York, N.Y.

Occupation:
insurance executive, organist

Hobbies/Interests:
composing, literature

Quotation:
"Most of the forward movement of life in general and of pioneers in most of the great activities have been the work of essential religious-minded men."

for sacred themes by borrowing extensively from gospel-hymn tunes, often highlighting them in the most unusual musical circumstances. From his orchestral compositions to his multifaceted chamber music, more than fifty different hymn tunes are "quoted," such as "What a Friend We Have in Jesus," "Jesus, Lover of My Soul," and "Just as I Am, without One Plea."

Another of the first great American composers was **Aaron Copland** (1900–90). Born in Brooklyn, he established an "American style" that has had a profound influence on other American musicians. He is best known for his orchestral works and music for the ballet, yet he also composed sacred music, including settings of psalms and a fascinating piece for unaccompanied chorus and alto soloist entitled *In the Beginning.* Copland described himself as an agnostic, but his Jewish background is easily discernable in this work, which concerns the Genesis account of the Creation.

Leonard Bernstein (1918–90) was perhaps the most celebrated American musician of the twentieth century. Known principally as a dynamic conductor, he also excelled as a pianist, author, lecturer, educator, and composer. Many of his compositions were a mix of popular and classical styles, and this is certainly true of his well-known Mass, composed for the opening of the Kennedy Center in Washington, D.C. As we have seen over the centuries, many masses defy the rules of liturgical-mass structure, but none as blatantly as Bernstein's. Written in English, it is surely the only work of its kind that actually employs profanity. This is characteristic of the iconoclastic Bernstein and the rebellious 1960s in which he composed, but his Mass remains popular today.

Igor Stravinsky and Serious Wildness

Musical iconoclasm was practiced long before Bernstein, and perhaps its greatest exponent was **Igor Stravinsky** (1882–1971). While still in his thirties, he produced several of the most innovative musical pieces ever written with his three Russian ballets: the *Firebird, Petrushka,* and the *Rite of Spring.* If you have heard these ferocious pieces, you may be surprised to find that Stravinsky also composed a good deal of sacred music.

At the age of forty-four Stravinksy converted to Christianity, stating that "for some years before my conversion, a mood of acceptance had been cultivated in me by a reading of the Gospels and by other religious literature." His next composition was the famous *Symphony of Psalms,* which he dedicated to "the glory of God."

Symphony of Psalms is certainly one of the most important choral works of the twentieth century. It depicts an awakening sense of distance from God and the human choice to return to him. The first movement was written in "a state of religious and musical ebullience," Stravinsky explained. The second movement, "Psalm 40," is "a prayer that the new canticle may be put into our mouths. The Alleluia [third movement] is that canticle."

IGOR STRAVINSKY

Born:
June 17, 1882
Oranienbaum, Russia

Died:
April 6, 1971
New York, N.Y.

Occupation:
composer, pianist, conductor

Hobbies/Interests:
traveling, gymnastics, writing

Quotation:
"The church knew what the Psalmist knew: music praises God. Music is as well or better able to praise Him than the building of the church and all its decorations; it is the church's greatest ornament."

QUICKTAKES
Recommended Recording

Igor Stravinsky
Symphony of Psalms

City of London Sinfonia, Westminster Cathedral Choir
James O'Donnell, conductor

(Hyperion CDA66437)

Concerning the *Symphony of Psalms*, Stravinsky biographer Francis Routh wrote, "No composer could write such a work without a very secure, rock-like religious faith." Stravinsky's rocklike strength is very evident in James O'Donnell's recording of this work. Throughout the first movement, the persistent opening chords and percussive attacks are accentuated with vigor. And the rapidly paced passages of the last movement are performed with a vitality that borders on reckless abandon. The effect is stark, primitive, and thoroughly Stravinskian. Yet the final slow section is tenderly devotional and clearly shows the worshipful heart of the newly converted composer.

Stravinsky became an outspoken Christian with much to say about the use of music. When asked if one must be a believer to compose church music, Stravinsky asserted:

> Certainly, and not merely a believer in "symbolic figures," but in the person of the Lord, the person of the Devil, and the miracles of the church. . . . I regard my talents as

> God-given, and I have always prayed to Him
> for strength to use them.

Throughout his long life Stravinsky often turned to sacred music. His compositions include *Three Sacred Choruses; The Flood; The Tower of Babel; Abraham and Isaac; Requiem Canticles; A Sermon, a Narrative and a Prayer; Threni; Canticum Sacrum;* a Credo; an Ave Maria; a Pater Noster; and a Catholic Mass which, he believed, "appeals directly to the spirit." He remained a faithful member of the Russian Orthodox Church, though he could never quite appreciate the music he and his fellow worshipers sang. He once confessed to a friend that he wrote *Three Sacred Choruses* to be used in the liturgy and said that the work was "inspired by the bad music and worse singing in the Russian Church."

Names You Need to Know

Some twentieth-century sacred music has become part of the standard repertoire and cannot be ignored. Let's examine a few examples from around the globe.

Francis Poulenc (1899–1963) spent most of his life in Paris. His vocal writing is particularly excellent, and he composed many choral pieces and more than two hundred songs. His best-known works of sacred music are the invigorating Gloria, the more mystical Mass in G Major, the Stabat Mater, and his unique opera, *Les Dialogues des Carmelites.* This last work concerns a group of Carmelite nuns during the French Revolution and has many powerful moments of spiritual drama.

Few twentieth-century works in the English language have had the impact of the huge cantata *Belshazzar's Feast,* composed by **William Walton** (1902–83). Its theatrical depiction of Daniel's story at first shocked British audiences, but now the work is performed everywhere, even by college students and community groups. Indeed, it has become so popular that many of Walton's other great works, such as his two ballets and his chamber pieces, have been overshadowed by it.

The opposite is true of the American composer **Samuel Barber** (1910–81). His many secular works are performed today by orchestras and chamber groups around the world, yet his two primary pieces of sacred music are less known. The *Hermit Songs* are settings of medieval Irish poetry, and the devotion displayed in this song cycle is gripping, especially in the exquisite song "The Crucifixion." In the *Prayers of Kierkegaard* (for soprano soloist, chorus, and orchestra), the contrast between the unchanging God and fickle Man is examined, grappled with, and finally resolved.

Again, you may notice that modern sacred music does not always fall into traditional groupings. Consider the Italian composer **Gian-Carlo Menotti** (1911–93), known for his many operas. One of these, *Amahl and the Night Visitors,* has become such a perennial Christmas hit as to almost rival

Handel's *Messiah*. Composed for television and first
aired on Christmas Eve in 1951, it tells the story of
the Wise Men meeting a poor woman and her crippled boy, Amahl. The boy volunteers to give his
crutches as a gift to the baby Jesus and is miraculously
healed. Audiences find its wide-eyed innocence and
warm Christian spirit timelessly endearing.

This section ends with a composer who has
truly put England back on the compositional map,
Benjamin Britten (1913–76). His success can be
attributed to his wonderful talent for vocal writing,
as seen in his many operas and choral music.
Britten's massive *War* Requiem is another unorthodox example of the genre, since he mixed nine antiwar poems by Wilfred Owen with the Latin text. His
best-loved sacred works are for chorus and various
ensembles. These include the unaccompanied *Hymn
to Saint Cecilia,* the *Festival* Te Deum, *Rejoice in the
Lamb, Saint Nicolas,* and another Christmas favorite,
A Ceremony of Carols.

The Twentieth Century's Greatest
Catholic Composer

We now come to **Olivier Messiaen** (1908–92),
a French composer who seems to break all stereo-
types. A brilliant musician, he was known to be
nonetheless humble and friendly. A world-class
composer whose works are respected throughout
the esoteric world of modern classical music, he
was an outspoken believer in Christ and the simple
faith. Ironically, though he was a man who was

OLIVIER MESSIAEN

Born:
December 10, 1908
Avignon, France

Died:
April 28, 1992
Paris, France

Occupation:
composer, organist, teacher

Hobbies/Interests:
theology, ethno-musicology, birdsongs

Quotation:
"Through Christ, the wonderful knowledge has been bestowed on us that this God, who's beyond Time, to whom nothing out of time or space clings, that He who is completely different from everything and is contained in Himself—that He came in order to suffer with us."

determined that every piece he composed would reflect his religious beliefs, he wrote very little of what is typically considered sacred music.

Messiaen's many compositions are found in most every genre of classical music: orchestral, chamber, and opera. Yet the majority of his titles, even those in such "secular" and nonvocal categories as organ solos and orchestral works, refer to religious themes. Examples include *Nativité du Seigneur* for organ; *Couleurs de la Cite celeste,* an orchestral work that interprets the colors mentioned in the book of Revelation; *Le tombeau resplendissant* for orchestra; and the famous *The Quartet for the End of Time,* dedicated to the angel in the book of Revelation "who lifts his hand towards the heaven saying 'There shall be no more time.'"

Some of Messiaen's sacred music fits easily into the norm. His *Trois Petites Liturgies de la Présence Divine,* for women's voices and orchestra, created a fury of controversy at its premiere. Its spiritual text was little appreciated by the secular critics, and the Christians in the audience were offended by the dissonant music. He also composed a moving opera, *Saint François d'Assise,* whose central figure was chosen by Messiaen because he believed that François was the saint who "most resembles Christ."

Messiaen never demurred when asked about his faith. His biographer Claude Samuel once asked him what impressions he wanted to communicate to his listeners. Messiaen replied, "The first idea that I wished to express—and the most important because it stands above them all—is the existence of the truths of the Catholic faith. I've the good fortune to be a Catholic. I was born a believer, and it happens that the Scriptures struck me even as a child." He always insisted that he was "a composer because I love music, and a Christian because I believe."

The conflict between the timeless truths of the gospel and the innovation of modern music come together in this man. When commenting on the initial uproar over his *Trois Petites Liturgies de la Présence Divine,* Messiaen simply said, "I wished to accomplish a liturgical act—that is to say, to transfer a kind of divine office, a kind of communal praise to the concert hall." As we come to the end of the twentieth century, the distance between the modern classical composer and the typical Christian audience grows so great as to make such a "liturgical act" the ultimate challenge for the creator of sacred music.

Sacred Classical Music at the End of the Twentieth Century

When you first hear music by some of the composers mentioned in this chapter, you may be tempted to throw up your hands and exclaim, "How crazy can it get? How far can they go? What else can they possibly do?"

The answer, of course, remains to be seen. Certainly, sacred composers have come a long way since Gregorian chant. And unlike the composers of popular music, they have leaped far ahead of their audiences. It may be another century or two before we discover who the truly great ones are. But we can identify several directions that are currently being explored, some of which are having a greater influence on sacred music than others:

1. *Many composers with classical training have elected to turn to more popular genres.* These composers see the difficulties inherent in constantly "being ahead" of today's audiences and take pleasure in mixing classical, jazz, and popular styles. In the realm of sacred music, dozens of gifted composers have taken a cue from Charles Ives and cleverly arranged well-known hymns into contemporary settings. As one might expect, such arrangements generally please the younger crowd and enrage the seniors.

2. *Some composers have decided to turn back the clock.* Although they remain classical composers, they repudiate the complex language of the modernists. Instead, they compose beautifully rich romantic music that recalls the late nineteenth century. Many of these musicians are snatched up by Hollywood because they often create the most imaginative movie scores. In this way, they secure something that is rare among classical composers today: prosperity.

3. *A number of late-twentieth-century composers have moved toward minimalism.* With its incessant repetitions, minimalism brings some degree of order to the complexity of modern music and has, at times, become wildly popular. An example of someone who often writes excellent sacred music scores is the Polish composer **Henryk Gorecki** (1933–). A recording of his Symphony no. 3 sold 500,000 copies in 1993

alone, a feat unheard of in contemporary classical music. Many of his sacred compositions explore the music of the ancient Polish church, and Gorecki is often called a holy minimalist.

4. *Many composers continue to carry the banner of extreme aleatorism, or "chance music."* These composers are still pushing pianos out of seventh-story windows and setting violins on fire with microphones nearby to amplify the crackle of the burning wood. As you may imagine, these recalcitrant innovators are usually not found in the world of sacred music. Nevertheless, musicians and audiences might do well to cease mocking this crowd, since their novelties are often later picked up by the greatest of composers, as history has proven again and again.

5. *Many composers continue to advance the complexity of our musical systems, frequently with marvelous results.* **Krzysztof Penderecki,** another Polish composer born in 1933, has written numerous works, including much sacred music, using massive tone clusters, continuous string ornamentation, and microtones. Perhaps his greatest sacred work is the sublime *Saint Luke* Passion, which expresses the ageless Christian faith in a most contemporary setting.

6. *The advent of electronic music has given new musical tools to adventurous composers.* Often coupled with traditional instruments and ensembles, computer technologies offer an endless array of possibilities. One of America's most versatile composers, **Charles Wuorinen** (1938–), uses both electronic

and traditional instruments with great skill. He has written a number of significant sacred works, including *Missa Renovata,* the monumental *Genesis* for chorus and large orchestra, and *An Anthem for Epiphany,* based on fragments from the Gospels.

Clearly, we are a long way from the pleasant masses of Haydn and Mozart. Contemporary classical music may be an acquired taste, but the rewards are usually worth the struggle. The music of this genre brings us to the very edge of what is possible in the realm of sacred music. Who knows where it will end?

Other Listening Recommendations

Benjamin Britten
A Ceremony of Carols

Aaron Copland
In the Beginning

Charles Ives
"General William Booth Enters into Heaven"

Zoltán Kodály
Psalmus Hungaricus

Gian-Carlo Menotti
Amahl and the Night Visitors

Olivier Messiaen
Trois Petites Liturgies de la Présence Divine

Krzysztof Penderecki
Saint Luke Passion

Ralph Vaughan Williams
Five Mystical Songs

William Walton
Belshazzar's Feast

CHAPTER 11

CONGREGATIONAL MUSIC AND THE MODERN CHURCH CHOIR
(1900–PRESENT)

Shackled by a heavy burden,
'Neath a load of guilt and shame,
Then the hand of Jesus touched me,
And now I am no longer the same.

Bill Gaither

B y the end of the nineteenth century, we see the beginning of a new division within the second stream of sacred music. Since the days of Luther's Reformation, this stream had been the domain of the congregation, containing music that every Christian could sing, and standing in marked contrast to the performer-versus-audience dichotomy of classical sacred music.

But with the great revivals of the nineteenth century, a number of solo singers began to gain popularity. From **Philip Phillips** (1834–95) and **Charlie Alexander** (1867–1920) to **Homer Rodeheaver** (1880– 1955) and **George Beverly Shea** (1909–),

traveling evangelists have had their soloists, who performed for a listening—but not singing—audience.
This trend marked the beginning of the huge gospel
music revolution that would emerge in the twentieth
century.

As we have already seen, when a new stream
begins, the original stream continues to flow. In the
same way that Luther's chorales did not spell the end
of classical sacred music, so the rise of solo performers
in the second stream did not mean that congregations
no longer wanted to sing. In fact, they want to sing
more than ever.

The Importance of the Minister of Music

Until the twentieth century, the only churches that
employed full-time ministers of music were either
very large and urban or very classical in their music.
In thousands of churches across America and Europe,
the full-time staff consisted of the head pastor, perhaps a youth or other auxiliary pastor, and maybe a
secretary. Music leaders were recruited from among
the congregation and were seldom paid for their long
hours of work. Often only an organist was employed,
and the pastor led the singing, whether qualified
or not.

Therefore, those church congregations that sang
hymns rather than listened to Bach and Handel were
at a marked disadvantage in musical leadership. Not
only were their volunteers not paid for their efforts—
which cut back the hours and quality of their service—but these volunteers seldom had a thorough
musical education. Few seminaries gave sufficient

training in church music, and only classical sacred
music was taught.

With the rise of hymn singing in the nineteenth
century, a new field of study emerged: hymnology.
The first half of the twentieth century saw the creation
of many new Christian colleges and Bible schools,
which offered serious study of popular sacred music.
After World War II the growing prosperity in America
enabled hundreds of small churches to hire full-
time ministers of music, which greatly increased the
church's musical effectiveness.

In many small but growing churches today, the
second person hired (after the pastor) is the minister of music, and many larger churches hire more
than one. The musician's responsibility often goes
far beyond the training of a choir. With the exception of the actual sermon, the minister of music
controls the Sunday service, which has led to more
effectual services and allowed the pastor the time
to better convey the gospel message.

In many churches, both Protestant and Catholic,
the task of the musical leadership is twofold. Ministers of music must continue to provide appropriate
music for the congregation to sing each Sunday. In
addition, they must also work with select church
groups that have chosen to play an active part in the
music ministry. These groups include the choir(s)
as well as small vocal and instrumental ensembles
and sometimes even such nonmusical organizations
as drama groups.

The church choir is still king of most music ministry, however. It undergirds the Sunday morning worship in addition to working on long-term projects such as performing Handel's *Messiah* or other classical works within its ability. There has also developed a large "semiclassical" genre of choral music and arrangements for more advanced choirs. These pieces range from the dozens of popular cantatas produced annually by Nashville publishers to the more complex works by modern composers such as *The Peaceable Kingdom* by **Randall Thompson** (1899–1984), *Forsaken of Men* by **Leo Sowerby** (1895–1968), or the well-known Gloria by the English composer **John Rutter** (1945–).

The first half of the twentieth century saw the continuation of hymn writing for church choirs, now usually harmonized in "SATB" (soprano, alto, tenor, and bass) arrangements. Virtually every denomination printed its own hymnal, most of which contained many of the same songs, often with edited text to reflect the spiritual convictions of the specific denomination.

Certainly some of the finest hymn writers worked between 1900 and 1940. These include conventional hymn writers (those who composed the text only) such as **Elisha A. Hoffman** ("Leaning on the Everlasting Arms"), **Jessie Pound** ("I Know that My Redeemer Liveth"), and **Johnson Oatman** ("Count Your Blessings"). Yet also appearing on the horizon was a newer breed that composed both words and music: **James M. Black** ("When the Roll Is Called up

Yonder"), **George Bennard** ("The Old Rugged Cross"), **C. Austin Miles** ("In the Garden"), and **Alfred H. Ackley** ("He Lives").

The Rise of the Praise Chorus

By the 1940s, a new form of popular hymn arrived, the acceptance of which has made it a genre unto itself: the praise chorus. These simple melodies are often only four lines long or employ a refrain-verse alternation form. Their simplicity is reminiscent of the camp meetings of earlier days, and they are closely related to the gospel songs we will discuss in the next chapter.

One of the first successful composers of praise choruses was **John W. Peterson** (1921–). Sometimes he would write both the words and the music, as is the case with "No One Understands like Jesus," "Shepherd of Love," "Heaven Came Down," and "It Took a Miracle." Yet some of his best-known musical efforts used texts written by others, such as "Surely Goodness and Mercy Shall Follow Me" (text by **Alfred B. Smith**) and "So I Send You" (text by **Margaret Clarkson**).

By far the best-known creators of praise-oriented music are **Bill** and **Gloria Gaither.** This talented couple from the Midwest began to write choruses in the 1960s and were soon the most renowned composers in their field. Their style might be called middle-of-the-road—not too folksy, not too sophisticated. Some of their many songs include "Because He Lives," "He Touched Me," "Jesus, We Just Want to Thank You,"

BILL GAITHER

Born:
March 28, 1936
Alexandria, Ind.

Occupation:
composer, singer, pianist

Hobbies/Interests:
tennis, basketball

Quotation:
"Praise is a result of something that's happening in our lives, and when we stop to count our blessings, we realize we are truly blessed and can't help but praise him."

197

*QUICK*TAKES
Recommended Recording

Because He Lives
Bill and Gloria Gaither (and various artists)
(Spring House SPCN 7-474-05299-7)

Few people have had a greater impact on the praise movement than Bill and Gloria Gaither. They have spent decades writing popular songs of praise as well as recording and performing them around the world. In this pursuit, they have worked with some of the finest talent in the Christian music industry. This CD—almost a greatest-hits package—serves as a testimony to both their work and their collaboration with others. It includes such well-known songs as "Let's Just Praise the Lord," "There's Something about That Name," "I Just Feel like Something Good Is About to Happen," "Gentle Shepherd," and "Peace, Be Still." Guest artists joining the Gaithers include Gene McDonald, Reggie Smith, Danny Gaither, Mark Lowry, Donnie Sumner, and many more. The recording showcases the work of fine singers and fine songs, and the arrangements are especially well crafted.

"There's Something about That Name," "Let's Just Praise the Lord," "I Will Serve Thee," "His Name Is Life," "We Are So Blessed," "Gentle Shepherd," "The King Is Coming," "Come Holy Spirit," "Something Beautiful," and "The Family of God."

The last half of the twentieth century has produced hundreds of praise chorus composers who continue to produce thousands of songs. Some of the best known are **Jimmy Owens** ("Clap Your Hands"), **Kurt Kaiser** ("Pass It On"), **Ralph Carmichael** ("He's Everything to Me"), **Ken Medema** ("Lord, Listen to Your Children Praying"), **Jack Hayford** ("Majesty"), **Naida Hearn** ("Jesus, Name Above All Names"), **Michael O'Shields** ("I Will Call Upon the Lord"), and **Ken Lafferty** ("Seek Ye First").

Organ to Piano to Guitar to Synthesizer

If you listen to the songs listed above, you will immediately notice that we are a long way from Charles Wesley hymns. We're even a long way from Fanny Crosby hymns. Various musical subtleties define the actual differences in melody, harmony, and rhythm, but an easy way to analyze the growing differences is to trace the evolution of the principal accompanying instruments from organ to piano to guitar to synthesizer.

The earlier hymns were written to be accompanied on the organ (or its various relatives) because these instruments easily imitated and undergirded the human voice. But near the turn of the century, the piano began to gain popularity as the most appropriate instrument to accompany the more rhythmic music of the time. For decades many churches have compromised by having available both an organ and a piano.

By the middle of the century, the guitar (usually the steel-string guitar) began to appear in churches and youth meetings. Its portability was soon recognized as a marked advantage, although it was never

RALPH CARMICHAEL

Born:
May 27, 1927
Quincy, Ill.

Occupation:
composer, arranger, conductor

Hobbies/Interests:
horseback riding

Quotation:
"There is no limit, no particular kind of music that is unacceptable. God can use it all. We have such an incredible freedom. Now we have to put it to good use."

JACK HAYFORD

Born:
June 25, 1934
Los Angeles, Calif.

Occupation:
pastor, composer,
author

Hobbies/Interests:
collectibles, golf

Quotation:
*"When we assemble,
always keep Heaven's
Throne in view. Let
us come with joy and
humility, exalting
Jesus with our
worship in the under-
standing that He
is graciously ready
to dwell within it."*

completely satisfactory for accompanying the older hymns. Nevertheless, thousands of praise choruses were composed with the guitar in mind, both for Protestant and Catholic churches. Later, electronic instruments such as synthesizers and sequencers appeared in many contemporary worship services, delighting the youth while often distracting their parents.

Most large churches have solved the "which-instrument" riddle by simply incorporating all of them. In the more youthful churches, these ensembles are called praise bands, though more sophisticated churches generally refer to their "orchestra." The heterogeneous ensembles work very well for a variety of worship styles, especially in those fortunate churches where every musician does not insist on playing every song!

The Influence of Charismatic Worship Styles

The ecstatic musical practices of Pentecostalism have been with us for many years in such denominations as the Assemblies of God, the Pentecostal Holiness Church, and many smaller branches. Their traditions of worship—including spontaneous prophecy, speaking in tongues, "singing in the Spirit" (that is, singing in tongues), and the lifting of hands—have historically been ignored or even scorned by most mainline denominations.

Yet the 1960s saw a renewal of the charismatic movement, which has spread to many of the largest denominations. Charismatic music has had a major impact on worship styles, and it is not uncommon today to find charismatic groups within Episcopal, Methodist, Lutheran, Presbyterian, Anglican, and Catholic churches. Although the worship styles of these splinter groups often bear little resemblance to the traditional Sunday morning service, the musical influence of these groups is increasingly being felt. Furthermore, hundreds of new charismatic churches of various sizes have sprung up all over the Western world.

Compared to the reserve of typical denominational hymn singing, the music of Pentecostal and charismatic churches has always been rather boisterous and emotional. Newer songs range from the upbeat "Shine, Jesus, Shine" by **Graham Hendricks** to the simpler "I Will Bless the Lord" by **Frank Hernandez** to the sentimental "Let All that Is within Me" by **Melvin Harrell**. A virtual industry has emerged to distribute these new worship songs to thousands of ministers of music hungry for the latest material for their congregations to sing.

The popularity of charismatic music with youthful Christians has led many denominations who disagree with charismatic theology, such as the Baptist and Bible churches, to embrace its lively songs. Sometimes this even means adding the prerequisite drum set to their instrumental ensembles. It should be noted that the music created by the charismatic revival is regularly used in many of the mainline denominations, though usually without the more controversial aspects of Pentecostalism—tongues,

DAN SCHUTTE

Born:
December 28, 1947
Milwaukee, Wisc.

Occupation:
composer, priest, lecturer

Hobbies/Interests:
gardening, oil painting, weight training

Quotation:
"I have been privileged to put down on paper a few measures of the wondrous song that God sings to the world. It is such an honor to be able to help people raise their voices to God in jubilant praise."

prophecy, and the like. Other denominations use a blend of the older hymns and the newer praise services.

Catholicism since Vatican II

The tremendous musical revolution that has taken place within the Catholic Church since the Second Vatican Council (1962–65) can only be compared to the appearance of Luther's music following the Protestant Reformation. Just as the new Protestants had to work quickly to establish an entirely new genre of worship music, so have Catholic musicians created a new body of music for their congregations. But unlike the European Protestant Reformation, this new Catholic reformation is worldwide, particularly affecting English-, French-, and Spanish-speaking peoples.

The reforms of Vatican II allowed the centuries-old Latin services to be performed in the vernacular languages of the people. It also freed musicians to compose for the liturgy without the restraint of referring to chant and other older forms. Although Catholic composers from Palestrina to Messiaen had composed innovative masterpieces within the realm of classical music, the congregational worship had largely followed traditional molds. This loyalty to the music of the past had been emphasized by the Cecilian movement of the nineteenth century, which strove to elevate Gregorian chant while discouraging new innovative music. In marked contrast, contemporary Catholic musicians embrace everything from guitars and synthesizers to charismatic choruses.

One of the first popular results of these Vatican II reforms was the folk mass. From the late 1960s onward, thousands of guitar-oriented songs and full-scale liturgies have emerged. Some of the most well-known material came from a group of talented priests known as the **St. Louis Jesuits,** but soon this movement had as many composers and worship songs as that of the Protestant praise choruses. It became common for large Catholic churches to offer, in any given weekend, an array of choices: traditional masses, folk masses, organ masses, contemporary masses, even "silent" masses (without any music whatsoever).

Like the *missa brevis* of Mozart's time, many new and popular masses have been composed since Vatican II. The varieties are as plentiful as the different groups within the Catholic Church. From Peter Scholtes' *Missa Bossa Nova* and Richard Proulx's *Community* Mass to David Haas's *Mass of Light* and Marty Haugen's *Mass of Creation* to Alexander Peloquin's *Mass of the Bells* and Owen Alstot's *Heritage* Mass to Jeremy Young's *Bread of Life* Mass and Bob Hurd's Spanish-language *Missa de Americas,* these ventures into well-crafted popular music have had a wonderful effect on Catholic congregations, which now seem to sing with far more enthusiasm than they did a century ago.

It will be interesting to see how this musical revolution continues in the future. One of the movement's disadvantages is its sheer size and diversity. There is no authorized Catholic hymnal, for example, and the quality of new Catholic music being composed around the globe is somewhat uneven. The music for a given church is often left to whatever resources that particular parish may (or may not) have. Yet much has been done in ecumenical circles to bring Catholic and Protestant music closer together. It may be that music itself will have a profound effect on breaking down walls that have separated Christians for many centuries.

Congregational Music among Protestant Denominations

It would be virtually impossible to comment on the music of every Protestant denomination in the world today. To begin with, there are literally hundreds of them, not to mention the various splinter groups within each as well as the new ones that are being formed every year. Fortunately, many denominations have several musical elements in common (although their respective ministers of music will always argue to the contrary).

In order to examine the varieties of Protestant congregational music, a number of denominations that represent the majority of Protestants today have been selected. Please do not be offended if your denomination has been omitted. All are of inestimable value in Christ, but the ten church traditions

we will discuss were simply chosen to give some idea
of the various directions sacred music has taken in
Protestant churches in the twentieth century.

These comments are general and brief, and the
order in which the denominations are presented is
not meant to exalt one over another, but rather to
contrast the diverse styles of worship. No matter
what overall observations are made, it must be admitted that many exceptions exist. The music within
most denominations has become so varied that
commonalities are seldom universal. However, it is
useful to at least point out the major differences and
similarities that have developed in this century.

Lutheran

As we have seen in earlier chapters, the Lutheran
Church has a tremendous musical heritage. From
Luther himself to such notables as J. S. Bach, Lutherans have raised classical music and the entire spec-
trum of the fine arts to new heights. Their liturgies
still encompass some of the finest congregational
music, and their hymnals set the standard for many
other churches.

Although there is much variety within this
denomination, especially in such groups as the
Missouri Synod and the Evangelical Lutheran
Church in America, most Lutheran churches have
been hesitant to fully incorporate contemporary
music, rock music, or charismatic worship styles
into their musical services. Instead, they have exalted

the "art of the choir." Nevertheless, many congregations are beginning to use more gospel songs and popular music, and contemporary ensembles with drums and synthesizers are now emerging to challenge the traditional place of the organ.

Baptist

Again, it is difficult to make blanket statements about a denomination with so many diverse subdenominations. From the Baptist General Conference churches to those within the National Baptist Convention, there is a wide variance. But the majority of independent Baptist churches place a strong emphasis on the hymnal and on a thematic approach to Sunday services. The hymns and musical solos are carefully selected to underscore the topic of the sermon. Many Baptist choirs perform difficult modern arrangements, while congregational hymns generally date from the late nineteenth century and often have both an organ and a piano for accompaniment.

Few Baptist churches use contemporary music on Sunday morning, but many have established a Sunday evening service with a more modern approach. Often churches will use the hymnal in the morning and song slides (that is, the text of a song printed on a sheet of acetate) on an overhead projector in the evening. Although charismatic doctrines are generally rejected in Baptist churches, many praise choruses are now in use. Most Baptist churches are independent in their musical style, and the specific

blend of the old and the new is usually determined
by the local pastor and minister of music.

Assemblies of God

Another denomination that retains a high level of
autonomy is the Assemblies of God. These churches
have a different approach to music and worship
than most. Since the history of the Assemblies is relatively brief, its Pentecostal style of worship embraces
many contemporary trends. Upbeat gospel songs
with hand clapping are the norm, and the accompaniment ranges from a solo piano to an ensemble of
brass, guitars, electronic keyboards, and drums.

Larger "AG" churches have excellent choirs, but
these choirs usually sing contemporary arrangements instead of classical pieces or older hymns. In
smaller churches, the congregation sometimes
erupts in spontaneous song, and the instrumentalists then pick up the tune as best they can, which
requires musicians of a very high caliber. Many of
the Pentecostal and charismatic choruses were born
in the Assemblies of God tradition and have profoundly affected the music of other churches.

Presbyterian

Presbyterians have experienced a number of painful
divisions in the last half of the twentieth century, but
the overall musical tradition has roots that go back
several centuries. Like the Lutherans, most of these
churches have a distinguished standard for both
choirs and congregational hymn singing, though the

Presbyterians seldom use vestments and such. Their hymnbooks now include many modern choruses and gospel songs.

As is the case with many denominations, the smaller Presbyterian churches have no paid minister of music. Styles of worship are usually chosen by the local pastor or board of elders. Some charismatic groups within Presbyterian churches have influenced the music of the denomination, but nothing like Christian rock is to be found. Instead, Presbyterians still use the fine arts, classical music, and even dance to enhance their worship services.

Seventh-Day Adventist

The Seventh-Day Adventists are unique in Protestant churches in that their day of community worship is not Sunday, but Saturday. But they have much music in common with other churches, because their denomination was formed during the revivals of the nineteenth century and attracted many Christians who brought with them their traditions of worship. Adventist hymnals are very eclectic, and their services of hymns and gospel songs are often adorned with offerings of excellent classical music.

The organ has had a prominent place in the Adventist denomination—indeed, their larger churches contain some of the finest organs (and some of the best organists!) in the world. Although the Adventists began within a gospel and even camp meeting tradition, they have not assimilated much contemporary music or Christian rock into their services. They have, though, kept alive the great heritage of hymnody, with the denomination's larger churches adding many of the choral and orchestral masterpieces of the classical tradition.

African Methodist Episcopal

The African Methodist Episcopal Church is one of many black denominations in the United States that represent the finest Christian worship among African Americans. From its beginning in the early nineteenth century, this denomination has emphasized congregational singing, and its first hymnal was published in 1818. Although best known for its stirring spirituals, the AME repertoire contains a variety of gospel songs, hymns, and anthems.

In the late twentieth century, the AME has successfully incorporated music indigenous to the African American community into its repertoire. Liturgical dance and drama are increasingly used, and vestments and banners are often employed to enhance the worship. The music continues to vary between the older hymns and the latest gospel songs, with the traditional piano-organ combination increasingly giving way to a praise band of contemporary instruments.

Episcopal and Anglican

The Episcopal and Anglican musical traditions span many centuries, yet these churches are constantly aware of the need to stay contemporary. Therefore, their worship contains a huge variety of music, from responsorial psalms and even plainchant to the most contemporary of charismatic praise choruses. Most Sunday morning services are thematic—with the music reinforcing the sermon message—while Sunday or Saturday night services contain more contemporary music.

The charismatic movement has had a major impact on both sides of the Atlantic as well as in Australia, bringing in new songs and the use of the charismatic "gifts of the Spirit," augmented by the denominations' historical acceptance and support of the fine arts, including dance. Their choirs now sing a blend of standard hymns and the latest choruses. In larger churches, full orchestras are sometimes used, not only for modern arrangements but also for large classical works.

Church of Christ

One of the most musically unique of the Protestant denominations is the Church of Christ (which should not be confused with the many other smaller denominations with similar names). The music for its worship services is devoid of any instruments. The unaccompanied congregational singing is reminiscent of the early Christian church, which also objected to the use of instruments as having negative connotations and encouraging worldly practices.

Yet even with its absence of instruments, the music of the Church of Christ is diverse and vibrant. Its hymnals contain the oldest of hymns as well as many contemporary choruses. Most of these churches employ a conventional song leader, but some of the congregations are led by a vocal ensemble or chorus. These smaller groups differ from the traditional Protestant choir, which often performs separately from the rest of the church. The Church of Christ services conscientiously focus their attention on God and avoid anything that would encourage performer-audience interplay.

Methodist

The Methodist Church traces its roots to the Wesleys, who were known not only as powerful preachers but also as excellent hymn writers. Therefore, music has always played a large part in the denomination's worship services. Historically, the Methodists have nurtured the fine arts, and today their many accomplishments in this area are represented by the Fellowship of United Methodists in Worship, Music, and Other Arts.

There is quite a variance of "high church" and "low church" practices among Methodists. Some churches have large altar guilds, vestments, and banners, while others are more conservative. Still other Methodist churches sponsor charismatic meetings with many contemporary praise choruses. But all employ the incomparable Wesleyan tradition of hymnology, both in congregational singing and in choirs of a generally very high caliber.

Bible Churches

The most original "denominations" to emerge in large numbers during the twentieth century are the Bible churches. Most are completely independent, and the musical style used for worship is decided by the local pastor and staff members. The Bible churches are a kind of musical melting pot and seek to embrace the very best from a variety of different traditions.

Many of these churches use hymns, but most also sing contemporary music with praise band accompaniment. Although Bible churches are usually not in agreement with the charismatic "gifts of the Spirit," many of their favorite songs are taken directly from the charismatic movement. The Bible churches have created a dynamic new type of church service: the seeker service. By using a combination of upbeat music, drama, and low-key evangelism, these seeker-friendly meetings have brought many new unchurched people to Christ.

Interdenominational and Ecumenical Awakenings

Anyone reading the above observations about these various denominations will surely notice a number of commonalities. As a very general rule, most modern Protestant denominations are increasingly moving toward a more contemporary style of music without abandoning their respective traditions. In the process, they are inadvertently moving closer to one another.

At the beginning of the twentieth century, the walls separating different denominations seemed high and unscalable. Baptists only sang from the *Baptist Hymnal,* Presbyterians only sang from the *Presbyterian Hymnal,* and so on. Even if they sang the same song, it was often harmonized differently!

Throughout the second half of the century, attitudes have been slowly changing, which has had a major effect on sacred music within the various churches. A number of factors have contributed to this blending of worship styles:

1. *The last part of the century has seen the growth of huge, "parachurch" ministries with members and supporters from a multitude of denominational backgrounds.* From Campus Crusade for Christ to Youth with a Mission to Focus on the Family, these organizations have brought Christians from many different denominations together.

2. *The rise of the contemporary Christian music industry has provided music enjoyed by the young (and sometimes not-so-young) of virtually every denomination.* Since the vast finances of the recording industry cannot be derived from just a portion of modern Christendom, industry executives actively seek to cater to *all* Christian churches.

3. *Both Catholic and many Protestant churches have ventured into ecumenical dialogue.* Without losing their roots and identities, they have nonetheless realized that the commonalities among all Christians far outweigh the differences.

4. *This century has seen an expansive creation of nondenominational or interdenominational churches.* Many are led by pastors and laypeople alike who have rejected the limitations of ministering within only one tradition. These believers simply call themselves Christians and worship within a conglomeration of musical styles.

Where will it all end? God alone knows, but there is no doubt about the direction. As the different styles of musical worship come closer together, perhaps we will see a host of new Christians entering the church. Instead of the divisions within Christianity, sacred music may help bring us all closer together and closer to the God we praise.

Other Listening Recommendations

George Bennard
"The Old Rugged Cross"

Bill and Gloria Gaither
"There's Something about That Name"

Marty Haugen
Mass of Creation

Jack Hayford
"Majesty"

Graham Hendricks
"Shine, Jesus, Shine"

Elisha A. Hoffman
"Leaning on the Everlasting Arms"

Bob Hurd
Missa de Americas

Ken Lafferty
"Seek Ye First"

John W. Peterson
"Heaven Came Down"

John Rutter
Gloria

CHAPTER 12

GOSPEL MUSIC PERFORMERS AND COMPOSERS
(1900–PRESENT)

*When I realized how hard some folks were fighting the gospel
idea, I was determined to carry the banner.*

Thomas Dorsey

What exactly is the third stream of sacred
music? To answer that question, let us
first review the differences between the
first and second streams.

When Christian music was first organized
(after Constantine converted to Christianity), a large
body of chant was developed that congregations
of believers could sing to worship God. Later,
during the medieval and Renaissance periods, composers experimenting with new ideas created music
that became more and more complicated. Soon the
illiterate congregations found it difficult to cope
with the new music and became spectators at

church, while trained choirs did all the elaborate singing.

Enter Luther and the reformers. Among other things, Luther wanted everyone to be able to sing at church so that the congregation might be more than a mere audience. Tremendous amounts of new, uncomplicated music for congregations were developed, which we call the second stream of sacred music. Meanwhile, composers of the first stream continued to create music for professional performers, as has been the case throughout the history of classical music.

Thus, important differences between the two streams arose. To sum up:

- The first stream set up a performer-audience situation in which a soloist or an ensemble was "onstage," while an audience listened.
- The second stream obliterated this performer-audience condition, allowing everyone to participate so that no one remained a passive spectator.

Obviously, the music of the second stream had to remain simple enough to be sung by non-musicians. This popular type of sacred music gave rise to the wonderful heritage of hymnology and congregational singing.

But what happens when popular sacred music is sung by a soloist, with an "audience" listening? Answer: the third stream of sacred music.

The performer-audience situation was formerly reserved for classical music, but in the nineteenth and twentieth centuries, it entered the realm of popular sacred music. The format may have been classical, but the music was definitely popular and immediately accessible to everyone, regardless of their musical training.

Now we have arrived at the performer (solo or ensemble) tradition of popular sacred music. Although born in obscurity, this third stream has since grown into a multimillion-dollar entertainment industry. The next three chapters tell the story of its development.

What's in a Name?

Before we begin this journey, something must be said about the confusing terminology that has cropped up within popular music. In the beginning, gospel music was just that—gospel music. Each performer was expected to have his or her own style and to be versatile enough to perform different kinds of songs without difficulty.

But by the end of the twentieth century, so many subbranches of gospel music exist that almost every new song seems to inhabit a branch all its own. A performer might say, "I never do southern white gospel music, I only do northern urban commercial synthesis." Then he or she will write a new song—perhaps adding another chord—and an entirely new branch of music (complete with another name) has just been born.

At any given moment in music history, sub-branches may serve a purpose. But after the appropriate time has elapsed, they are soon forgotten. In the same way, many modern categories will not be remembered unless they expand, flourish, and later evolve into other, more substantial branches. In the meantime, who can tell?

The chapters concerning the third stream of sacred music will not split hairs regarding this or that definition or subdivision. Instead, we will focus on the broader directions that popular sacred music has taken in the twentieth century: gospel music; its largest subbranch, CCM (or contemporary Christian music); and several other subbranches. In this way, we can more clearly see the relationships between different musical styles.

Part of the problem lies in the wonderful practice of contemporary performers of creating music in many different styles. The same person might write a praise chorus for church congregations to sing while also giving performances of Christian rock in a performer-audience situation. In this book, that person will usually be found in the section where he or she has had the greatest impact.

The Gospel in Black and White

The birth of gospel music is a fascinating topic, since it evolved in the opposite way from most musical genres. Usually, a type of music emerges, gradually expands, and eventually splits into two or more smaller parts. But one might say that the birth of gospel music occurred in two different places, then gradually came together to form a larger whole.

In the nineteenth century, both white gospel and black gospel music appeared almost simultaneously, usually without knowledge of the other. Because of the deplorable prejudice and enmity between the races in America, few African Americans knew the music of the white church and even fewer whites knew the music of the black church.

Yet both were creating a new musical genre. Although some differences existed in the music itself, both sides essentially shared the same musical goal: to create popular music to be sung not just by the congregation in worship services but by soloists for the "spiritual entertainment" of a listening audience.

It was not until the twentieth century that members of the two races began to appreciate each other's musical genius. Through the decades, whites slowly began to listen and learn from black artists, and vice versa. By the end of the century, much of the musical prejudice had diminished; music written and performed by a member of one race is now routinely played in churches of the other race. Although heinous bigotry still exists in society, gospel music has often led the way in breaking down racial barriers.

It is interesting how the music of one race has influenced the other. Musicians have interacted with, borrowed from, and imitated one another, bringing the two sides closer together. In many ways, the music is now so intermingled that it is sometimes difficult to tell white gospel and black gospel apart. They have come together at last, and their combination has now matured to the point that it has spawned new and fascinating substreams.

Because of this synthesis and their many commonalties, white and black gospel music are not treated separately here. It seems more appropriate to track their dawning and development simultaneously, even if it means we sometimes bounce back and forth between the two styles. In this way we see them grow side by side, and their ensuing amalgamation will seem more natural, as, of course, it should.

Early Roots of Gospel Music

As we noted earlier, the original concept of popular sacred music was congregational: that is, music that everyone could sing in praise to God. But some people sing better than others. Obviously, those members of a congregation who were born with excellent voices will come to the forefront.

The Fisk Jubilee Singers, a group of very gifted singers from Fisk University in Nashville, Tennessee, was one of the first groups to organize. In an effort to raise money for the school, these superb African American singers toured the country in 1871, singing popular spirituals to admiring audiences everywhere. They were the first in a long line of gospel choirs that continue to attract crowds today.

The first national popular solo singer of gospel music was **Philip Phillips** (1834-95), who gave thousands of sacred song "services" (as he referred to his performances). Solo gospel performances may seem commonplace today, but it was such a novelty in 1875 that when Phillips sponsored an international singing tour, he wrote about it in his well-received book, *Song Pilgrimage Round the World.* How astonished this humble singer would be if he realized what he had started: hundreds of Christian entertainers now routinely tour around the globe.

Many traveling evangelists began to use vocal soloists to augment the congregational music that accompanied their meetings. In an earlier chapter we examined the hymn compositions by Dwight Moody's musical associate, Ira Sankey. But it must also be mentioned that Sankey's practice of occasionally singing solo was soon widely imitated.

When the great evangelist Billy Sunday conducted his huge meetings, he traveled with the singer **Homer Alvan Rodeheaver** (1880–1955). Rodeheaver would punctuate the congregational singing with his own solo songs. He later published gospel hymns and established one of the world's largest firms in the sacred music field, now known as Word Music.

This evangelist-soloist tradition continued throughout the second half of the twentieth century with the crusades of Billy Graham. Typically, Graham used one soloist to lead the congregational singing, usually the multitalented musician **Cliff Barrows**, and saved his star singer for the dramatic solo songs that preceded the sermon. For many years bass-baritone **George Beverly Shea** was the featured soloist, but Graham has also used **Ethel Waters** and dozens of other artists.

In the meantime, many other firsts were taking place in the world of gospel music, particularly within African American churches. **Charles Albert Tindley** (1851–1933), born of slave parents, wrote a number of gospel songs, including the well-known "We'll Understand It Better By and By." In 1919, **Lucy C. Campbell** wrote the first of her many gospel hymns, "Something within Me." And in 1923, Paramount Records recorded its first black gospel singer, **Hurd Fairfax**. *Gospel Pearls,* printed by the National Baptist Convention in 1921, was one of the first publications to feature the newer gospel songs.

Slowly moving from country churches into the large cities, gospel music was beginning to establish a presence most everywhere. Yet despite its initial success, efforts on behalf of gospel music were sporadic and disjointed at best because of its lack of effective musical leadership. This rather messy condition would soon change, though, with the arrival of a truly amazing musician, **Thomas A. Dorsey** (1899–1993), often called the father of black gospel music.

The Father of Black Gospel Music

Thomas Dorsey's long life spanned most of the twentieth century, and his contributions to the gospel music repertoire included more than eight hundred songs. The manner in which he became involved in gospel music is almost prophetic in that it foreshadowed the struggles of many future gospel musicians. While still in his teens, Dorsey was such a noted ragtime and blues musician that he would often accompany the famous singers of his day, including Ma Rainey and Bessie Smith.

Dorsey was deeply moved by the songs of Charles Tindley, which he heard while attending a meeting of the National Baptist Convention. Torn between secular and gospel music, Dorsey finally opted for the latter. But churches shunned his jazzy blues style, and his early days were rather discouraging. At one point Dorsey said he "borrowed five dollars and sent out five hundred copies of my song, "If You See My Savior," to churches throughout the country. . . . It was three years before I got a single order. I felt like going back to the blues."

But Dorsey never gave up. By 1929 he had devoted himself exclusively to gospel music, and in 1932 he organized the Gospel Singers Convention in Chicago. The next two decades were spent touring the United States with talented Christian singers and propagating his spirited gospel songs, which would eventually find acceptance and be widely imitated. Some of his best-known compositions are "There'll Be Peace in the Valley for Me" and "Precious Lord, Take My Hand."

Dorsey was one of the first of a long line of modern Christian musicians whose music was condemned as "the devil's music" by most of the church hierarchy. By blending sacred text with the secular style of blues and jazz, Dorsey was considered a renegade. His response to that charge has inspired

MAHALIA JACKSON

Born:
October 26, 1911
New Orleans, La.

Died:
June 27, 1972
Chicago, Ill.

Occupation:
singer

Hobbies/Interests:
business, civil rights

Quotation:
"Time is important to me because I want to sing long enough to leave a message. I'm used to singing in churches where no one would dare stop me until the Lord arrives!"

many musicians of later generations: "When I realized how hard some folks were fighting the gospel idea, I was determined to carry the banner."

Rise of the Great Soloists

By the 1930s gospel music was beginning to develop into a true entertainment medium. Those who had previously sung only in their local church now performed in more prestigious venues. The major singers and vocal groups started hiring managers and were able to make a good living. In 1938 **Rosetta Tharpe** recorded the first gospel record to sell one million copies.

Perhaps the greatest gospel singer of the time was **Mahalia Jackson** (1911–72). Born in New Orleans, she began singing in her hometown at a very early age. When only sixteen, she moved to Chicago and joined the Greater Salem Baptist Church Choir. Jackson's strong contralto voice soon singled her out as a soloist and thus jump-started her career—she made her first recording in 1934. Eight of her recordings sold more than one million copies, and her vocal sound was emulated by many blues and jazz artists. "I Can Put My Trust in Jesus," "Move on Up a Little Higher," "When I Wake Up in Glory," and "I Believe" were some of the songs she made famous.

If Thomas Dorsey was the father of black gospel music, then **James Cleveland** (1931–91) was its king. Indeed, young Cleveland got his first taste of the gospel style while at Chicago's Pilgrim Baptist

Church, where Dorsey was the music director. Although his was not the smooth sound of a typical soloist, Cleveland's rough voice nonetheless kept audiences' rapt attention. In his lifetime he recorded fifty-four albums, including such best-sellers as *Jesus Is the Best Thing, Lord Help Me, I Stood on the Banks,* and *Peace, Be Still.* Despite his hectic schedule, Cleveland still found time to serve as the pastor of several churches, including Detroit's Prayer Tabernacle and the Cornerstone Institutional Baptist Church in Los Angeles. He also founded the Gospel Music Workshop of America.

Another great name in gospel music was **Clara Ward** (1924–73). Like Mahalia Jackson, she began singing early, joining her first choir at the age of five. Although she had a wonderful voice and sang with her mother and sister as well as with huge choirs, her finest contributions were her compositions. She wrote more than two hundred songs, including such well-known pieces as "Come in the Prayer Room," "How I Got Over," "Prince of Peace," and "Packing Up."

While these outstanding black artists' careers flourished, southern gospel music was being advanced by **James D. Vaughn** (1864–1941). He published dozens of gospel songbooks and formed up to sixteen vocal quartets to tour the country. In 1921, several of these "Vaughn Quartets" made popular 78-RPM recordings, and Vaughn later founded a Christian radio station in Lawrenceburg, Tennessee, spreading the southern gospel sound.

JAMES CLEVELAND

Born:
December 5, 1931
Chicago, Ill.

Died:
February 9, 1991
Culver City, Calif.

Occupation:
singer, composer, pianist, arranger, pastor

Hobbies/Interests:
cooking, movies

Quotation:
"Jesus is the best thing that ever happened to me."

*QUICK*TAKES
Recommended Recording

Gospel's Greatest Hits
Various Artists
(CGI Records 5141610902)

Rather than focusing on one legend in gospel music, this CD show-cases solo artists, mass choirs, and current stars as well as the work of early gospel pioneers. For those who revel in the power of multiple voices, the recording includes such songs as "He That Believeth" by the Chicago Mass Choir and "Going Up Yonder" by Walter Hawkins and the Love Center Choir. And for those who prefer a more intimate experience, there is Andrae Crouch and the Disciples performing "It Won't Be Long." This wonderful CD has something for every gospel music fan; each composition has been carefully selected to present the music's broad panorama.

Composers or Performers or Both?

Most of this book, like any book concerning music history, is about composers and the music they wrote. Since their music was written down and has survived long after their deaths, we can still enjoy it today. Unfortunately, this is not the case with the performers of long ago. Franz Liszt may have been the greatest pianist of the nineteenth century, but our primary interest in him today concerns his compositions, which are still being performed.

In the second-stream chapters on hymnology, we expanded our study of composers and their music to include hymn writers—that is, those who wrote the words of hymns. With the arrival of recordings, the third stream gives us another new angle, the performers of sacred music. Some of the most important people in gospel music never wrote a song, neither the words nor the music. But their performances, recorded for posterity, enable us to appreciate their talent.

Even more so than classical music performers, the performer of popular sacred music adds a huge portion of personal material to the finished product. In gospel music in particular, much of the music is of an improvisatory style, with different performers taking great liberties to produce extremely diverse recordings of the same song. Thus, the performers themselves become an intricate part of our study.

Quartets, Ensembles, and Performing Choirs

As we have seen, the third stream of performed popular sacred music evolved from the second stream of congregational singing. It should not be surprising, then, that a large portion of gospel music's performers were not solo artists, but ensembles. From the smallest groups to the mass choirs, gospel music has often been a group art.

The Fisk Jubilee Singers has inspired many churches in the African American community to promote large gospel choirs. By the 1930s some of these groups were involved in making recordings. Two

of the best were the **Gospel Light Jubilee Singers**
and the **Roberta Martin Singers.** The latter group
recorded into the 1950s, producing such hits as
"Where Can I Go?" and "Only a Look." Other groups
included the Argo Singers, the Drinkard Singers, and
the Ward Singers, with Clara Ward as principal soloist.
By the end of the century, large mass gospel choirs
would be found in almost every major city in
America.

Another popular idiom in both black and white
gospel styles was the vocal quartet. In general, black
groups were more upbeat and unconventional,
whereas white quartets tended toward a more traditional approach. The names of these black groups
often demonstrate a rather flamboyant style: the
Swan Silvertones, the Sensational Nightingales, Wings
over Jordan, the Dixie Hummingbirds, the Soul
Stirrers, and the Mighty Clouds of Joy. Though most
of the famous quartets were exclusively male, a few
were exclusively female, such as the Caravans, the
Davis Sisters, and the Harmonettes.

Later in the century, especially within white
gospel categories, we find quartets becoming quin-
tets, sextets, septets, and so on. A few key examples
are the Florida Boys, the Kingsmen, the Celestials,
the Statesmen, and the Imperials. It is not uncommon to have a gospel music group from within a
single family (or with several members from the
same family) as in the case of the Speer Family, the
Thrasher Brothers, the Happy Goodman Family,
the Blackwood Brothers, and many others.

For each of the groups mentioned here, there were hundreds of lesser-known groups trying to "make it big" in the gospel music scene. Again, we see a major difference between the second and third streams of sacred music. Within the second stream of congregational music there is little competition. Most church choirs simply sang for their own church and no one else. Yet the performers of the third stream are much less parochial. Their impact was national and even international, so the competition between different groups and artists appealing to the same market could be considerable.

Relationships to Secular Music

Competition is just one of the similarities between gospel music and the secular music of today. Another is marketing. Just like in the secular music industry, when a gospel artist releases a new album, many thousands of dollars are spent on such nonmusical items as cover design, photography, news releases, and advance publicity.

One of the hallmarks of gospel music is touring. When the Fisk Jubilee Singers toured in 1871, they were trying to raise money for Fisk University. When a gospel artist tours today, much money is also raised, but it goes to cover a myriad of tour-related expenses. Unlike the free performances of musicians who traveled with big-name evangelists, ticket prices for the performances of today's gospel artists can be as high as those of any secular artist.

And why not? Professional gospel singers are making their living through their music, the same as any other professional musician. Since Sunday morning church doesn't charge admission, we can too often fall into the mentality that everything offered by Christians should also be free.

Finally, there have never been any major musical differences between sacred classical music and secular classical music. The same is true of the musical aspects of hymns and those of secular choruses.

These similarities help explain why so many artists have successfully bridged the gospel and secular worlds. Not only have many of the above-mentioned artists performed nongospel songs, but many secular artists have also worked in the gospel field with remarkable ease, such as Sam Cooke, Aretha Franklin, Ray Charles, and Elvis Presley. Presley recorded a number of very successful gospel albums.

An Explosion of Artists

In the last half of the twentieth century, two fundamental developments have transformed the gospel music genre into a huge industry: the fragmentation into many categories, especially CCM (more on that in the next chapter), and the explosion of new artists. Certainly only a fraction of these artists can be mentioned here, so we again ask the difficult question, Who should be selected? The answer depends not so much on who was the most popular (short-term impact) as on who was the most influential (long-term impact).

One of gospel music's most influential female vocalists has been **Shirley Caesar.** To some degree she followed in the traditions of Mahalia Jackson and Clara Ward, but she also found her own powerful style, which has been greatly imitated. Starting her career at the age of ten, she was known as "Baby Shirley" and toured the South before joining the Caravans, an exclusively female gospel group. Once she launched her solo career, she was awarded many honors and gold records, as well as becoming the first female black singer to win a Grammy.

An important last name to remember in the gospel music world is Hawkins. **Walter** and **Tramaine Hawkins** led a musical family that set many standards in soul gospel music. Their albums featured the musical skills of many different family members, and one in particular—**Edwin Hawkins**—became nationally known in secular music circles with his recording of "Oh, Happy Day."

We have already seen how prevalent musical families are in gospel music. The style of **Buck** and **Dottie Rambo,** and their daughter **Reba,** may be more country than gospel, but their many recordings share a fascinating distinction: all of their songs were written by Dottie. After singing for years with her parents, Reba launched her own successful career with a more contemporary sound, strongly influenced by a stint with Andrae Crouch.

Thus, we come to the musician who has had the most influence on late-twentieth-century gospel

SHIRLEY CAESAR

Born:
October 13, 1938
Durham, N.C.

Occupation:
singer, evangelist, pastor

Hobbies/Interests:
reading, cruises

Quotation:
"They've got a saying going around that God is dead. But if that's so, just answer me three questions: Who killed him? Who was the undertaker? And why wasn't I notified, because I'm his child and he's my father?"

ANDRAE CROUCH

Born:
June 1, 1950
Los Angeles, Calif.

Occupation:
singer, pianist,
composer, pastor

Hobbies/Interests:
drawing

Quotation:
*"I want to let them
know that there is
help in time of trouble
and that a brighter
day is coming."*

music, **Andrae Crouch.** His father was a "boot-leggin' street preacher" who started a church in Los Angeles. The church's youth choir became Andrae's musical laboratory. Like many popular artists, his life soon became a combination of writing gospel songs and performing them. For years he worked with a touring band, Andrae Crouch and the Disciples, but he also enjoyed an extensive solo career as well as becoming a pastor.

Perhaps the reason Crouch has had such an impact is his ability to appeal to both white and black audiences. More than any other musician, he has brought these two worlds of gospel music together, reaching out without any musical bias. He once said, "I have one question when I write a new song: 'Does it reach you?' I feel the feedback from an audience if the song is working. I know what is real. That's what I get from being raised in the church, before those congregations."

There continue to be many new and talented gospel singers who will doubtless have a powerful influence on future performers. From the sweet sounds of **Yolanda Adams** to the more upbeat music of **BeBe** and **CeCe Winans,** the gospel music industry is constantly reinventing itself without forgetting its roots. One thing is certain: gospel music is not a genre for just whites or just blacks; it has merged the two and appeals to most everyone.

Later Divisions of Gospel Music

As we have seen, in the early days of the music, gospel was simply a matter of black and white. Yet we now recognize many new subdivisions, and more are rapidly being added. One of the best indicators of this trend can be seen in the different categories of the Dove Awards, an annual event that recognizes the best achievements in gospel.

Let us examine the additions made to the Dove Awards from 1969 to the present day. (We will focus only on the purely musical categories and skip such nonmusical varieties as Disk Jockey of the Year and Record Album Cover Art). In 1969, the basic categories were

Gospel Song of the Year
Gospel Record Album of the Year
Gospel Songwriter of the Year
Male Gospel Group
Mixed Gospel Group
Male Gospel Soloist
Female Gospel Soloist
Gospel Instrumentalist

Thirty years later, the list has grown to include thirty-nine categories:

Song of the Year
Songwriter of the Year
Male Vocalist of the Year
Female Vocalist of the Year
Group of the Year
Artist of the Year
New Artist of the Year

Traditional Gospel Recorded Song

Contemporary Gospel Recorded Song

Pop/Contemporary Recorded Song

Inspirational Recorded Song

Southern Gospel Recorded Song

Country Recorded Song

Urban Recorded Song

Rap/Hip-Hop Song

Alternative/Modern Rock Recorded Song

Metal/Hard Rock Recorded Song

Rock Recorded Song

Traditional Gospel Recorded Album

Contemporary Gospel Recorded Album

Pop/Contemporary Recorded Album

Inspirational Recorded Album

Southern Gospel Recorded Album

Country Recorded Album

Urban Recorded Album

Rap/Hip-Hop Album

Alternative/Modern Rock Recorded Album

Metal/Hard Rock Recorded Album

Rock Recorded Album

Instrumental Album

Praise and Worship Album

Children's Music Album

Special Event Album

Musical

Youth Musical

Choral Collection

Producer

Short Form Music Video

Long Form Music Video

Much has occurred in the intervening three decades. What has happened? Several things.

Many of the additions can be easily explained. While choral collections, praise and worship, and producers were around in 1969, no one had thought to include them. Music videos were yet to be invented. Presumably, someone later thought to add Musical of the Year and then Youth Musical of the Year. These types of additions do not really concern us.

But so many other categories consist of subdivisions and subdivisions of subdivisions. Traditional gospel has evolved to inspirational gospel, which leads to contemporary gospel and pop/contemporary gospel. Some classifications, such as southern gospel and country gospel, are clearly related. But as soon as rock music is added, gospel expands to include metal/hard rock, alternative/modern rock, urban, and rap/hip-hop.

Of all the different genres within modern gospel music, CCM has had the most profound impact. Its repercussions will be examined in the next chapter.

Other Listening Recommendations

The Blackwood Brothers
Sheltered in the Arms of God (Camden CAS-2446)

Shirley Caesar
The Best of Shirley Caesar (Savoy 14202)

James Cleveland
Trust in God (Savoy 14302)

Andrae Crouch
Take Me Back (Light LS 5637)

Thomas Dorsey
"Precious Lord, Take My Hand"

The Imperials
Heed the Call (Dayspring DST 4011)

Mahalia Jackson
I Believe (Columbia CS-8349)

The Rambos
The Son Is Shining (HeartWarming R3398-C)

The Roberta Martin Singers
Only a Look (Apollo 214)

Charles Albert Tindley
"We'll Understand It Better By and By"

CHAPTER 13

CONTEMPORARY CHRISTIAN MUSIC
(1950–PRESENT)

I'm an outcast to those who think my music is devil music,
perhaps, but I'm part of the Body, even if the Body sees me as
an ingrown whisker or toenail.

Larry Norman

At the time of this writing, contemporary
Christian music (CCM) in its various forms
is so popular with such a huge audience that
a disclaimer may be needed. Simply put, if you are a
CCM fan and you immediately turned to this chapter, please read the earlier ones first! This is not a
book about CCM per se—it may even omit your
favorite artist. Rather, it is a book that attempts to
show the historical connections that enabled Christian
music to evolve into the many different expressions
we have of it today.

With that behind us, we can examine one of the
fastest growing—and perhaps the most unexpectedly

popular—forms of sacred music. As we begin, it is important to note the unexpected nature of CCM's remarkable development. For if you were alive in the 1950s, you would probably never have anticipated the tremendous success of Christian rock and roll. At best, you might have imagined a fringe movement, with its own band of devout and loyal followers.

Why is this? First, because the popular Christian music of the 1950s had been primarily conservative and adult-oriented. Second, rock and roll was decidedly youth-oriented and nonconservative.

Today CCM is so popular that secular recording companies are negotiating deals to purchase Christian labels in order to get a piece of the huge profits. What was at first shocking and then controversial became accepted and commonplace within mainstream Christianity. Although the twentieth century has produced artists within Christian country music, Christian jazz, and Christian folk music (see the next chapter), none of these genres has grown at the same rate as CCM.

The Jesus Music of the 1960s

As we have seen in previous chapters, the beginnings of musical genres are not easy to pinpoint. Some consider CCM to be an outgrowth of gospel music. Others argue that it is simply a Christian reworking of secular rock music. But most informed devotees agree that this movement emerged from that peculiar decade in America called the 1960s.

Many factors came together to make the 1960s one of the most tempestuous decades in modern history. The carnage of the Vietnam War, the "God-is-dead" movement, the political assassinations, the pressure of the space race, the spread of mind-bending drugs, the fear of nuclear war, the flowering of hippiedom, the rise of violent protests, and many other chaotic factors made it a time of great disillusionment among young people. Antiestablishment demonstrations occurred frequently on many college campuses, and suspicion of conventional institutions became the norm.

Two of the most significant phenomena that emerged from this seedbed of turbulence were the rapid growth of secular rock music, and the Jesus movement.

The popularity of secular rock had already begun with such performers as Buddy Holly, Elvis Presley, and dozens of other artists who appeared in the years following World War II. But in the 1960s, the unprecedented popularity of the Beatles accelerated the acceptance of many similar groups. The antiwar, antiestablishment mood offered abundant material and promised a willing market. By 1965 rock music was a billion-dollar industry that could not be ignored by the world. Nevertheless, most of it could not be understood, accepted, or appreciated by the Christian church, whether Catholic, Protestant, or Orthodox.

Yet at the same time as these worldly upheavals were occurring, a great spiritual revival was rapidly spreading, especially among young people. Thousands who had given up on both the establishment and the drug culture became hungry for something deeper. Many who had long since abandoned the "dead" churches of their parents now began to read the New Testament for themselves. Prayer groups dotted hundreds of college campuses, and it became cool for kids to "try Jesus."

What could these ex-druggies and flower children sing in their newfound Christianity? For those used to the driving beat of Steppenwolf or Cream, Fanny Crosby's "Blessed Assurance" must have sounded like music from another world, which, in a manner of speaking, it was.

What to do? The answer was obvious to many church leaders: have nothing to do with rock music, and learn the hymns. Like the early church fathers, they tried to draw a thick line between the music of the world and the music of the church. And like their predecessors, they would eventually see this line blurred as styles from both sides began to influence one another.

Larry Norman

One of the first innovators was **Larry Norman** (1947–), often called the father of contemporary Christian music. Although his musical contributions were considerable, he has modestly declined such a title. "I never invented Christian rock because the blacks invented it years ago," he explained. In this he was wisely aware of the ongoing development of popular Christian music.

Like many of his generation, Norman says he "walked out of church when I was nine years old. I didn't like the hymns and couldn't stand the hymns anymore." He soon began writing his own songs and formed a rock band called People. Norman's first record, *Upon This Rock,* is still considered by many to be the first recording of Christian rock music.

Perhaps it is appropriate that the leader of such a controversial genre of music should become so controversial himself. Like many artists who would follow in his footsteps, Norman sincerely loves God and desires to serve him through his music. Yet he often has been misunderstood, censured, and denounced by many church leaders. *Time* magazine once called Norman the "poet laureate of the Jesus movement," but his outspoken lyrics have earned him much less flattering names from his brothers in faith.

Nevertheless, Norman continues to have a profound influence on CCM artists. He is also well known for encouraging the talents of other performers through his founding of Solid Rock Records and the Street Level Artists Agency. Some of his many memorable songs are "One Way," "I Love You," "Moses," "I Wish We'd All Been Ready," "666," "I Am a Servant," and "UFO."

Early Hippies and Rockers for Jesus

Like its older cousins in traditional gospel music, CCM has as many performers as composers, both soloists (usually vocal soloists) and ensembles (that is, bands). The CCM world also includes everyone from record producers and booking agents, to publicists and tour roadies. But for the purposes of this book, we will concentrate on the most influential performers and songwriters. From CCM's earliest days, specific "stars" came to the forefront.

One of the first was **Randy Stonehill,** friend and colleague of Larry Norman. Stonehill aligned himself with more conservative Christian leaders such as Billy Graham (he even starred in the Billy Graham film *Born to Run*) and thus avoided much of the controversy of his comrade Norman. Stonehill's lyrics are nonetheless a thoughtful and honest exploration of faith. His best-known songs are "Gone Away" and "Born Twice."

Dallas Holm was among the first of the young artists to be accepted by many from the traditional gospel music world. In fact, in 1978 he became the first composer other than the celebrated Bill Gaither to win the coveted Songwriter of the Year award presented by the Gospel Music Association. That year he also won in the Male Vocalist category, and his band, **Praise,** won the Mixed Gospel Group award. His best-selling albums include *Rise Again, Nothing but Praise,* and *Tell 'Em Again.*

Conversion to Christianity by leading secular musicians has sometimes led to a career in the

Christian market. Early examples include **Barry McGuire** (1935–) and **B. J. Thomas** (1942–). Both men had secular hits ("Eve of Destruction" and "Raindrops Keep Falling on My Head," respectively) before they came to Christ, and their musical styles after conversion have not been greatly altered. Instead, their lyrics became powerfully Christ-centered. McGuire's best-known Christian albums are *Lighten Up* and *Seeds,* and Thomas's are *Home Where I Belong* and *You Gave Me Love.*

Phil Keaggy (1951–) also experienced a similar career change after his conversion to Christianity. He is one of CCM's finest instrumentalists and has inspired many other artists. Before finding Christ, Keaggy worked with a number of secular groups, including the popular band Glass Harp. But in 1972 he devoted himself full-time to Christian music, both as a soloist and a much sought-after collaborator. He regularly appears on many other artists' albums. His own efforts include *Emerging* and *The Master and the Musician.*

Many of these soloists started their own back-up groups, and Christian bands of all sorts became more and more popular in the 1970s. One of the first successful groups was a trio of singers (Nelly Greisen, Annie Herring, and Matthew Ward) with the original name **2nd Chapter of Acts**. They toured extensively throughout America and Europe and recorded a number of best-selling albums, including *Mansion Builder* and *To the Bride.*

245

The Devil's Music?

Before going any further, perhaps we should discuss the controversy surrounding CCM. Many Christians involved in more traditional forms of sacred music strongly oppose CCM, especially works by heavy metal practitioners, denouncing it as "the devil's music." Doubtless, many readers may find it shocking that CCM would be covered in a book entitled *The Music of Angels.* (Unless, in their imagination, it includes the music of fallen angels.)

So far, we have looked at a number of early artists and groups. By later standards of rock, the musicians already mentioned may seem rather tame. Yet even from its beginning, CCM has spawned controversy and has unfortunately caused tension among Christian churches, teachers, and families. Why?

There are as many answers to this question as there are parents and teenagers, and you've probably already heard them all. Rather than try to sort them all out—which could not be done in a short book anyway and, perhaps, not even in a long one—let us examine the principal objection.

When CCM (among other music) is condemned, it is often attacked on moral or spiritual grounds: it is called immoral, wrong, harmful, evil, or even demonic. Such accusations have much more weight than simply complaining that the music is crummy, inferior, substandard, mediocre, or just plain awful. Perhaps the most honest parent might say, "I hate it! I don't know if it's demonic or not, but I can't stand it!"

One could say the same about various types of music—including every one mentioned in this book—and be perfectly valid. We each have the right to our individual musical opinions without getting into the more sensitive area of spiritual judgments. But opinions come and go, and the corporate opinions of one age are seldom imitated by the next.

From the historical point of view, CCM is simply another branch of the third stream of Christian sacred music. It may be excellent CCM or dreadful CCM, and it may employ a beautiful soprano or a guitar smashed against a huge amplifier. But as it is a valid form of Christian music, it fits within the realm of this book.

The CCM Industry Arises

By the late 1970s many Christian recording labels and publishers had emerged. Every year brought new artists and bands with their own distinctive sounds. Some of the older ones changed with the times, but many more were left in the dust, not unlike their counterparts in secular music.

One must be flexible when categorizing these new artists. Some are clearly in the rock music vein, while others are lighter or middle-of-the-road. There are so many obscure new subbranches of CCM that to describe them all would be inappropriate here. The artists mentioned are among those who have made the greatest popular impact and influence on other artists.

Keith Green had a burning passion for Christ. Playing dozens of bars and clubs before he became a

*QUICK*TAKES
Recommended Recording

Amy Grant: The Collection
Amy Grant (and various artists)
(RCA 66258–2)

Contemporary Christian music covers a lot of ground, from early rockers to a wide variety of bands. Nevertheless, it would be difficult not to choose Amy Grant as its primary soloist, especially during her busy 1980s period. The combination of her captivating voice, excellent original compositions, and superb arrangements makes each of her albums top sellers. She lost some fans by crossing over to make secular records, but by doing so, she made thousands of new fans and continues to expand her base. This collection includes the biggest hits from recordings that span much of her meteoric career, from *Father's Eyes* (1979) and *Age to Age* (1982) to *Thy Word* (1984) and *Love Can Do* (1986).

Christian, he knew well the corruption of the world. After his dramatic conversion, he wrote and performed songs that implored Christians to turn away from worldliness and complacency. He was tragically killed in a plane crash, but not before forming the Last Days Ministries and creating such powerful albums as *No Compromise* and *For Him Who Has Ears to Hear*.

Another very charismatic CCM performer goes by the name of **Carman** (1956–)—he dropped his last name, Licciardello. He became a Christian while attending a concert by Andrae Crouch and the Disciples, and some of his musical styles reflect a modern rendering of Crouch's rhythm and blues. But Carman's lyrics, especially his dramatic brand of spiritual warfare, are very deliberately confrontational. His many albums include *Revival in the Land, Comin' On Strong, The Standard,* and *Carman Live . . . Radically Saved.* This last recording deserves special mention since Carman's live concerts are known for their wildness and exhilaration, including dancing both onstage and off.

A very different but equally convincing sound comes from singer-songwriter **Steven Curtis Chapman** (1962–). His youthful enthusiasm and thoughtful lyrics catapulted his career in a very short time. His debut album, *First Hand,* was released in 1987, and in less than a decade he went to the top of the CCM world, winning two dozen Dove and three Grammy awards. Chapman's style is often called pop rock.

Another collector of awards (thirty-three Doves and five Grammys) is the soprano **Sandi Patty** (1956–). Although she is best known in Christian circles, her powerful voice impresses all who hear it, as evidenced by the huge number of phone calls ABC received on July 4, 1986, after she sang "The Star Spangled Banner" on national television. Her many albums include *Songs from the Heart, Make His Praise Glorious,* and *Find It on the Wings.* An indication of the admiration that her vocal style warrants is the peculiar fact that she has sold more than one and a

STEVEN CURTIS CHAPMAN

Born:
November 21, 1962
Paducah, Ky.

Occupation:
singer, composer, guitarist

Hobbies/Interests:
collecting guitars, riding motorcycles

Quotation:
"If you turn the light on and throw open the doors and windows, the enemy can't do anything but run. He can't work when the light is shining there."

SANDI PATTY

Born:
July 14, 1956
Oklahoma City,
Okla.

Occupation:
singer

Hobbies/Interests:
reading, golf, volley-
ball, softball, cooking

Quotation:
*"When it is all said
and done, I want
someday to be re-
membered as a
woman who loved the
Lord, a woman who
loved her family, and
when she had the
chance, she sang
about it."*

half million instrumental accompaniment tracks with
which aspiring singers may sing along.

There are almost as many female soloists in
CCM as male soloists, and one of the most versatile is **Kathy Troccoli** (1958–). She is one of the few
artists whose songs make the top-ten lists in both
Christian and secular charts, such as her hit "Everything Changes." An outspoken advocate for many
pro-life ministries, Troccoli has been a national
spokesperson for Prison Fellowship Ministries and
the National Catholic Youth organization, LifeTeen.
Her many albums include *Stubborn Love, Pure
Attraction,* and *Love and Mercy.*

One of the top CCM artists of the 1980s and
1990s was **Michael W. Smith** (1957–). After pulling
himself out of the drug culture, he wrote many
songs for such artists as Sandi Patty, Larnelle Harris,
Kathy Troccoli, and Amy Grant. In fact, Smith was
one of the first CCM composers since Bill Gaither
to have his songs appear in many mainline hymnbooks. His upbeat, contemporary music is a blend
of smooth vocal lines and interesting harmonies, as
exemplified in his popular song "O Lord Our Lord,
How Majestic Is Your Name in All the Earth."

Another noted songwriter who has been embraced by both the CCM world and traditional
hymnbooks is **Twila Paris** (1958–). She comes from
a family immersed in music and ministry for several
generations, and her first piano teacher was her father. Her compositions are extremely versatile, and
her songs range from progressive innovation to

hymnlike adoration. She has recorded many albums and is best known for her solo songs, such as "We Will Glorify the King of Kings," "He Is Exalted," and "Hold On."

There are dozens of other excellent CCM soloists, and new ones emerge every year. Some are variations on those who have gone before, while others are quite original and imaginative. But few will have the overwhelming impact of that young girl from Nashville who wrote her first song at the age of fifteen and whose influence has grown every year since.

Amy Grant and the Challenge of Crossover

On November 25, 1960, a baby girl was born to Gloria and Burton Paine Grant who would later become a teenage sensation. The release of her first album in 1979, simply entitled *Amy Grant,* made her an overnight success. After the resounding sales of the 1982 *Age to Age,* with its megahit "El Shaddai," Amy Grant became the undisputed queen of CCM throughout the 1980s.

But Grant believed that God wanted her to expand into the secular world instead of just serving within Christian circles. She was not in any way renouncing her deep faith but simply felt called to reach out beyond the walls of the church. Although this simple concept, often called crossover, has been practiced by classical musicians for centuries, it was rather new to the CCM world. The criticism Grant received from Christian fans for crossing over caused her intense grief.

TWILA PARIS

Born:
December 28, 1958
Elm Springs, Ark.

Occupation:
singer, composer, pianist

Hobbies/Interests:
antiques, zoos, driving Land Cruisers

Quotation:
"We can have fun with the music; that's okay. But on another level, that respect should always be there—concern for the message, and concern for those to whom we deliver the message."

AMY GRANT

Born:
November 25, 1960
Augusta, Ga.

Occupation:
singer, composer,
guitarist

Hobbies/Interests:
gardening, skiing,
golfing

Quotation:
*"I see myself as a sort
of combination per-
former and evangelist.
I hope people enjoy
my singing, but at the
same time their lives
are affected by the
words."*

Unguarded, her 1985 release, was the first to be heavily promoted to a secular audience. Her fans still loved Grant's songs but were confused by the non-Christian interest. When she released the album *Lead Me On* three years later, many former loyalists were openly hostile. Her biggest "mainstream" (as secular ventures are called by the CCM world) success came in 1991 with the best-selling album *Heart in Motion.*

Some of the antagonistic reactions of the Christian public were almost combative, revealing the betrayal some of Grant's former fans felt. Others were outraged at what they considered a lowering of moral standards, and rumors began flying. She was once challenged by a well-meaning young father who gave her a bouquet of flowers with a note reading, "Turn back. You can still be saved if you repent what you've done." The artist was soon in tears. Yet she bravely continues to produce music from her heart that is loved by thousands of believers and unbelievers alike.

The entire issue of crossover remains a point of debate within CCM. At the beginning of the movement, Christian artists wanted to stand apart from the larger world and often tried to distance themselves from secular markets. But later, artists tried to bring their talents to the mainstream audience as well as to their brothers and sisters in the faith.

Why are they doing this? What is their motive? The answer depends on whom you ask. Some note that the church has always been called to seek the lost and should perpetually endeavor to bring the gospel message to unbelievers. Others murmur that the motivation may be less than spiritual, a desire only to make greater profits by appealing to larger secular markets.

It will be interesting to see how CCM resolves this divisive issue as the next century unfolds.

The Rise of Christian Rock Bands
Some of the most contentious controversies about CCM involve its many bands. The complaints are inevitable: these bands sound and often look very much like their secular counterparts, many of whom are known for some extremely anti-Christian music and behavior. Yet these Christian rock bands have created a loyal following so strong among young people that it might easily be envied by secular groups. And whatever you think about the music they create, it must be noted that the vast majority of the musicians have an extremely devout faith and a determination to use their music to glorify God.

It is quite impossible to mention more than a smattering of the Christian bands popular today. There are literally hundreds of them, categorizing themselves as rock, metal, alternative, punk, slam, grunge, rap, ska, and so on. As it is too early to discern which of these smaller categories might sustain itself long enough to become a new branch, we will not worry much about specific labels. The bands that are mentioned often perform in several categories on any given record. They were selected on

253

the basis of overall impact and influence on other like-minded musicians.

Surely the most enduring of all the Christian rock bands is **Petra** (from the Greek word for "rock.") When guitarist **Bob Hartman** (1949–) founded the band in 1972, probably no one, including the band members themselves, imagined that they would still be together more than twenty years later. They have not only recorded over twenty albums—including *More Power to Ya, Not of This World, This Means War!* and *Wake-Up Call*—but have also released four greatest-hits collections. In addition, they have created their own Bible studies, devotional books, and retreat materials. They have won every award possible in their genre and have sold more records than any other Christian band (over six million). Recognized by the secular music world as well, they were the first Christian group to be enshrined in London's Hard Rock Cafe.

Although the personnel and even the musical style of Petra may have changed over the years, their vision of ministry has remained constant. Petra's founder explains:

> [We] want to write our songs to make kids think, to make them see themselves as a Christian, as part of something very big, the Body of Christ. Kids have so many influences on their lives now, and probably the hardest thing for a young person is to gain a Christian perspective on the world. We want to help them do that.

This motive is echoed by hundreds of similar Christian bands.

Rap music has also found its exponents in CCM. One of the best-known Christian groups to incorporate rap into their style is **DC Talk.** Its three members (Kevin Smith, Toby McKeehan, and Michael Tait) created a national sensation with *Jesus Freak.* Its content was simple and straightforward: "I don't really care if they label me a Jesus freak." Many of DC Talk's songs, such as the popular "Colored People," creatively explore the problems within society, especially racism. Although the three members come from very different backgrounds, they have effectively forged a musical style that is truly their own.

DC Talk actually helped the next group get started. Three young musicians—Mark Stuart, Barry Blair, and Will McGinnis—were attending Kentucky Christian College in the 1980s when they were approached by a fourth, Bob Herdman, who had written "My God." Together they recorded the song and formed a new band called **Audio Adrenaline.** When DC Talk performed at the college, the tape recording was given to one of its members, who passed it on to their record label. Soon, Audio Adrenaline's heavy metal–rap sound, including the hit "Big House," was heard throughout the country. Their recordings include *Don't Censor Me, Bloom,* and *Some Kind of Zombie.*

Another band that started on a college campus is **Jars of Clay** (the name is a reference to 2 Cor. 4:7).

While in the campus recording studio, several students began a bit of experimentation. When they were satisfied with the results, they sent a few songs to a contest sponsored by the Gospel Music Association. In 1994 they won the association's Spotlight competition, and their song "Flood" was soon heard on Christian radio stations everywhere, in addition to many secular stations. Their albums, *Jars of Clay* and *Much Afraid,* feature many hit songs, including "Love Song for a Savior" and "Crazy Times." Their sound is one of the most original of the Christian bands, blending everything from pop rock to acoustic music.

America does not have a monopoly on popular Christian bands, though, as evidenced by the **Newsboys,** who hail from Australia. In the 1990s they became extremely successful with their theatrical performances, featuring an assortment of extravagant outfits. They've probably set world endurance records: in 1995 they gave almost 250 concerts, sometimes three in a single day. Their recordings capture the exuberance of their stage productions and include the albums *Take Me to Your Leader, Not Ashamed,* and *Going Public.*

In yet another substream of CCM, the **Supertones** became one of the most well-known Christian ska bands. Ska music, with its driving horns, distinctive drumbeat, and offbeat guitar emphasis, began in Jamaica in the 1960s and spread in several waves to Europe and America. Since it is usually associated with dance music, it might seem surprising to find it within

Christian circles. But the Supertones are leading this new trend with spirited songs such as "Resolution," "Tonight," and "Perseverance of the Saints."

How Grungy Can We Get?

There are differences between Christian rock bands and non-Christian rock bands. While some of the latter openly indulge in profanity, drugs, violence, and sexual perversion, Christian groups usually sing about Jesus and a biblical lifestyle, including many bold lyrics that strongly suggest the need for serious repentance. Furthermore, the vast majority of Christian rock musicians have been commended for living a life of holiness and selfless ministry. This in itself separates them from the bulk of most secular rock stars.

But note that these differences are not musical. Indeed, there are no apparent differences in their musical styles. Some Christian bands are as grungy and loud as any of their secular counterparts. It would seem that there is no limit to how far these groups can push traditional musical boundaries.

Such groups as The Crucified, Stavesacre, Blindside, Every Day Life, and Skillet try to outdo each other in wildness. Their styles are almost indescribable, but all emphasize a driving drumbeat, harmonic distortion, and very little melodic content. The vocal lines contain at least as much screaming as true singing, and the volume at concerts usually stays above one hundred decibels. Nevertheless, their lyrics examine real problems found in the life of young Christians and point to Christ and biblical teachings for solutions.

The majority of Christians either ignore or abhor their music. Many band members have been roundly condemned by their fellow Christians, not because of moral failings, but simply because of the type of music they play. Yet these very bands have been courageously bringing the message of Christ to thousands of youth who might not hear it from anyone else within the church. Time will tell whether CCM and its subbranches will last into the coming decades.

Other Listening Recommendations

2nd Chapter of Acts
To the Bride (Myrrh MSX 6548)

DC Talk
Jesus Freak (Forefront FFD 5140)

Amy Grant
Age to Age (Myrrh/Word MSB 6697)

Keith Green
No Compromise (Sparrow SPR 1024)

Dallas Holm
Nothing but Praise (Greentree R3354-C)

Larry Norman
Upon This Rock (Impact R3121-C)

Sandi Patty
Make His Praise Glorious (A&M Records R7586)

Petra
More Power to Ya (Sparrow CDSSD8045)

Skillet
Skillet (Chordant 25159)

The Supertones
Supertones Strike Back (Chordant 17401)

CHAPTER 14

COUNTRY, FOLK, JAZZ, AND MORE
(1950–PRESENT)

Behind all the foolishness I do there is nothing but Jesus.

Roy Clark

T hus far we have found quite a variety of sacred music styles within the twentieth century, from innovative classical compositions to the wildest of heavy metal music. Other streams exist that we have yet to examine, some of which represent a large part of the world's music and entertainment industries.

Before we delve into these streams, it would be wise to ponder the question, Has Christianity penetrated *all* styles of Western music? Perhaps some might ask if Christians should (or can) be involved in all musical styles. Or are there some types of music that by their very nature defy a Christian approach?

These are questions of tremendous controversy today. On the one hand, we have those who, echoing the Great Commission (Matt. 28:16–20, where Jesus commands his disciples to "go and make disciples of all nations"), assert that Christians should endeavor to be involved in every form of music for the sake of the gospel. On the other hand, some believe that certain types of music are inherently evil and that true Christians should have nothing to do with them.

The purpose of this book is not to answer these questions but simply to report on the historical growth of Christian music. Yet when one looks at the big picture revealed over the last two thousand years, certain trends are unmistakable. For example, musical styles that were once taboo for believers are usually invaded sooner or later by pioneering Christian musicians. Eventually, the new style is accepted by the general Christian populace. This has happened to everything from Luther's chorales to Christian rock.

Therefore, it is difficult to find any type of music that will not inevitably become part of the Christian culture. For instance, the coming century may witness a huge growth in Christian jazz that could possibly dwarf the CCM market. Who knows? In the meantime, let us examine some of the other branches of music that have a strong Christian element.

The Blending of Origins

A book about the origins of country music will almost certainly mention the early history of gospel music. A book about early folk music will examine both country and gospel. Books about the origins of jazz or rhythm and blues often begin with the religious music of the early nineteenth century.

Just as many streams can flow from the same source, so can many forms of popular music trace a common origin. For instance, we have seen how the music from the nineteenth century camp meetings led to the growth of congregational hymns as well as influenced early gospel performers. These rural meetings also were a part of the history of folk music and the origin of today's country music.

All these factors make it difficult to establish rigid boundaries between such genres as gospel, country, and folk. This difficulty is compounded because many country and folk singers have always performed Christian material that fits within their own styles. Furthermore, the same artist may move between various styles within a single performance or recording. This to-and-fro leads to the inevitable squabbling about whether such and such artist is a gospel singer or a country singer, and so on.

It should be noted that the genres of music discussed in this chapter are primarily found within mainstream secular music. The gospel and CCM categories that we have already examined are not. Thus, gospel singers and CCM bands are typically known as Christian artists and would have to cross over into secular music to be appreciated by the masses. Yet such genres as country, jazz, and folk are basically mainstream. We shall soon observe how they, too, have been influenced by Christian music.

Country Music

Next to traditional gospel music and CCM, country music has the greatest amount of Christian content of any popular twentieth-century music. From its earliest days, many of its performers were outspoken believers who sang Christian hymns and choruses. Even today, despite all the glittery songs about drinkin', gamblin', fightin', cheatin', and divorce, there are still many fervent Christians among country music stars.

The history of country music somewhat parallels gospel music's rise to prominence. Like gospel, most of its stars had their beginnings in small country churches. The principal city of country music, Nashville, is also called the "buckle of the Bible Belt" and is a world center of religious publishing. Its famous Ryman Auditorium, home of the Grand Ole Opry, was originally a nineteenth-century church built by reformed steamboat captain Thomas Greene Ryman for evangelistic services.

One of the earliest country music recording sensations was the **Carter Family,** which included A. P. Carter (1893–1960); his wife, Sara Carter (1899–1979); and her cousin Maybelle Carter (1909–78). Collectively they were known as the first family of country music. The Carter Family made more than three hundred recordings, including many religious songs. A story from A. P.'s childhood illustrates the conflict between the sacred and the secular in country music. A. P. was raised a Christian and loved the old hymns, but he also loved the fiddle, which his parents regarded as the "devil's instrument." He had to wait years until he could buy one.

Many of the early country music stars were "singing cowboys." Certainly one of the best known, often called the king of the cowboys, was **Roy Rogers** (1911–98). (His real name was Leonard Franklin Slye.) When he wasn't riding his horse Trigger in movies and on television, this wholesome cowboy was making recordings, including many Christian songs in a country-western style. He made a number of religious recordings with his wife and costar, **Dale Evans** (1912–), including "The Bible Tells Me So" and "In the Sweet By and By."

By midcentury country music had grown to the point of splitting into an important substream. **Bill Monroe** (1911–96), the father of bluegrass, began a music tradition that is still vibrant more than sixty years after his successful sacred song "What Would You Give in Exchange for Your Soul?" hit the charts. After he and his brother Charlie (1903–75) split up, Bill formed the **Blue Grass Boys,** which recorded such songs as "Wicked Path of Sin" and "Little Community Church."

The bluegrass tradition gained in popularity throughout the second half of the twentieth century. Although much of bluegrass music is instrumental, some of its vocals fit into sacred music categories, usually as a combination of country music and traditional gospel. Among its many adherents is the **Lewis Family,** known as the first family of gospel bluegrass.

Formed in 1951, this seven-member group from Lincoln County, Georgia, has recorded over a dozen best-selling albums, including *Gospel Special, Country Faith,* and *Shall We Gather at the River?*

Another seminal bluegrass group was the **Easter Brothers.** Their name, perfect for a group of country gospel singers, actually comes from the three brothers' last name: Russell Easter (1930–), James Easter (1932–), and Ed Easter (1934–). Equipped with the standard instruments—guitars, banjos, fiddles, and mandolins—the Easter Brothers recorded thirteen successful albums. The best known are *Country Hymn Time, From Earth to Gloryland,* and *He's the Rock I'm Leaning On.*

As with both CCM and gospel music, country music has also had its share of famous secular performers who became Christians and then devoted themselves to sacred versions of the genre. A highly publicized example of such a conversion was **Stuart Hamblen** (1908–89). This rough-and-tumble cowboy, a heavy drinker who played bad guys in Roy Rogers movies and recorded such songs as "But I'll Go Chasin' Women," committed himself to Christ at Billy Graham's celebrated 1949 crusade in Los Angeles. Hamblen was changed forever, gave up drinking, and for years hosted the popular radio show, *Cowboy Church of the Air.*

A vignette from his life serves to illustrate the simple origins of many country songs. After his conversion, Hamblen ran into his friend John Wayne, who asked, "What's this I hear about you,

Stuart?" Hamblen answered, "Well, John, I guess it's no secret what God can do." Wayne retorted, "Sounds like a song!" It soon was, and "It Is No Secret" became a country classic. Besides the album by that name, Hamblen is also known for *The Country Church* and *A Man and His Music.*

Around the time of Hamblen's conversion, another singing cowboy was becoming a true country music legend. During his short life, **Hank Williams** (1923–52) created an image of the country singer that is still being emulated today. Although he suffered from alcoholism and depression, Williams is remembered for performing many uplifting spirituals and gospel songs. His concert posters often stated that he would perform "if the good Lord's willin' and the creek don't rise." Williams's best-known sacred album is *I Saw the Light.*

The Late Twentieth Century

In the 1960s and 1970s country music began to dominate the music industry. Country music became increasingly slick, with sequined suits replacing cowboy hats and electric guitars replacing acoustic ones. Country lyrics reflected a pattern of drinking, fighting, and cheating. Yet there were still a large number of stars who held to Christian beliefs and many more who continued to sing sacred songs.

Surely the greatest example of the sacred-secular dichotomy in country music is **Johnny Cash** (1932–). A singer with an impressive bass voice and a tremendous presence, he had to overcome a reputation

BARBARA MANDRELL

Born:
December 25, 1948
Houston, Tex.

Occupation:
singer

Hobbies/Interests:
camping, target
shooting, traveling

Quotation:
*"If there's a decision to
be made, I simply put
it in God's hands, and
things just fall into
place."*

for dabbling in drugs and having a bad temper (once he smashed the footlights at the Grand Ole Opry in a fit of anger). Yet Cash's life was turned around when he married **June Carter** (daughter of Maybelle Carter). He became a steadfast Christian and a regular with the Billy Graham crusades. He recorded many sacred albums, including *The Holy Land, Hymns from the Heart,* and *The Gospel Road.* When his producer pointed out that the last of these albums did not sell as well as Cash's famous pair, *Johnny Cash at Folsom Prison* and *Johnny Cash at San Quentin,* the singer declared, "My record company would rather I'd be in prison than in church."

The outspoken Christian faith of **Barbara Mandrell** (1948–) has had a powerful impact on her fans. She says that she sings both secular and sacred songs in order to have a greater evangelistic effect: "When I sing the gospel songs, they see something in my eyes that I mean what I'm singing about." Mandrell has often paid a price for her beliefs. After banning drugs and alcohol from her tour bus, she was labeled "Nashville's Snow White." But her sincere faith shines through all her work, especially her gospel album, *He Set My Life to Music.*

Like his idol Hank Williams, the popular country singer **George Jones** (1931–) encountered many hard times. Drinking his way through three divorces and bankruptcy, he became known as "No-Show Jones" after missing dozens of concert dates. But his fourth wife, Nancy Sepulvada Jones, helped him begin again, and he soon quit both cocaine and alcohol. Many hits followed, and in 1990 Jones's gratitude overflowed in the gospel album *Gospel Weekend,* containing songs like "Jesus Saves Today."

Country star **Connie Smith** (1941–) has a similar story. She made it big with a number of major hits and began touring vigorously. But she soon became overwhelmed with the pressure and sought psychiatric help. Smith then decided to dedicate her life to following Christ and switched record companies (from RCA to Columbia) in order to record more religious music. She recorded many successful country-gospel albums, including *God Is Abundant, Connie Smith Sings Great Sacred Songs,* and *Joy to the World.* But her best-known work in this genre is *Connie Smith Sings Hank Williams Gospel.*

There are many other country stars who incorporate sacred songs into their repertoire. "Sunday Mornin' Country" is a popular semiannual Christian show from the Grand Ole Opry. In 1990 it celebrated its tenth anniversary featuring some of the greatest names in country music: Roy Clark, Jack Greene, Connie Smith, Roy Acuff, Skeeter Davis, Johnny Russell, Lulu Roman, Hoyt Axton, Paul Richey, George Hamilton IV, Billy Walker, the Fox Brothers, the Country Corral, and the Hee Haw Gospel Quartet.

Christian Folk Musicians

With its rather fluid boundaries, folk music is a genre that defies easy categorization. Certainly, folk music has existed for thousands of years in every culture. Some would say that for all practical purposes, early music of any culture, including Western culture, that was not sacred music might legitimately be called folk music—that is, music of the people, as opposed to music of the church.

We know that during the centuries of chant, medieval polyphony, the Renaissance, and beyond, there were hundreds of folk troubadours roaming Europe. Since they existed outside the control of the church and were mostly illiterate, their music was seldom notated. Consequently, most of the music has been completely lost to history.

Until the modern era, many peoples lived in virtual isolation, seldom visited by outsiders. Therefore, the music of each group or nation was distinctive. Italian folk songs sounded very different from English folk songs, which sounded different from Russian folk songs. Many classical composers used folk music in their compositions, helping to preserve the individual flavors of their countries. Anyone who hears Dvořák's *Slavonic Dances* or Vaughan Williams's *Norfolk Rhapsodies* can instantly hear the unique folk style of these composers' countries.

By the nineteenth century, much folk music had been written down and was becoming assimilated throughout Europe and America. But it was still considered a genre for secular topics—love, courtship, war, heroes, and so on—in contrast to the religious music sung at church. The difference was primarily textual. From a purely musical point of view, there was little dissimilarity between a popular folk song about two lovers and a popular new hymn about the Resurrection.

So it should not surprise us to find that many soloists sang both gospel music and secular folk songs. One of the first of these was **"Singin' Billy" Walker.** Walker not only performed as a soloist but also popularized much sacred folk music with the publication of his songbook, *The Southern Harmony.* The music was similar to shape-note singing common in the South, except that *The Southern Harmony* presented its songs in three-part harmony.

The first folk singer to record sacred songs was **Ernest Stoneman** (1893–1968). This pioneering musician recorded more than two hundred times before 1934 and included many gospel songs in his broad repertoire. He began quite a tradition; his children later formed a successful group called the **Stoneman Family.** Their folk-bluegrass sound is captured on many albums, including *Family Bible, Old Rugged Cross,* and *For God and Country.*

Again, it must be noted that the boundaries between such genres as folk, country, bluegrass, and gospel are difficult to define. Only after an appropriate length of time has elapsed and a degree of musical maturation has been established can we classify, with any certainty, just how a particular genre should sound. Such songs as "The Old Country Church" by the Georgia Pals, for example, show not only all of the above influences but also traces of the blues and a smattering of Tin Pan

Alley. But as the century progressed and increasing numbers of recordings were made, artists became more specialized and their styles more distinctive. There were soon well-defined folksingers and country singers, though when they sang anything with a sacred text, it was simply considered gospel music, whatever the musical style.

Christian Folk Music of the Late Twentieth Century

When the folksinger **Judy Collins** (1939–) released her a cappella version of the hymn "Amazing Grace" in the early 1970s, it was a huge international hit. Collins's rendition combined the sacred and the folk traditions in a popular fashion, and the song came out about the same time as a new category of soloist emerged: the Christian folk singer. Of course, Christian folk singers were around earlier in the century, but their impact tended to be local in scope. Now there existed solo singers of sacred folk music with an international following.

One of the first "Jesus folksingers" was **John Fischer**. Fischer became a prophet of sorts to the entire Christian music industry, encouraging fellow artists to see their work as true ministry rather than entertainment. His many albums include *Have You Seen Jesus My Lord*, *Still Life*, and *New Covenant*. Fischer has also written nine books and numerous articles that have challenged those involved with Christian music to stay focused on quality ministry and to avoid the trappings of the "star" business.

Don Francisco was another folk artist who spoke to the youth of America during the 1970s. Having tried various Eastern philosophies, Francisco turned to Christ and began writing songs from a biblical viewpoint. Although he recorded seventeen albums, his first, *Brother of the Sun,* remains his most popular. He was at his best in the storytelling song, explaining, "I try to follow the leading of the Spirit in presenting the Word of God in contemporary language and song."

As with many other contemporary artists, secular folksingers have also become believers and devoted themselves to Christian music. Perhaps the best example is **Noel Paul Stookey** (1937–), who was for years famous as the "Paul" in the folk group Peter, Paul, and Mary. His conversion was dramatic and permanent. "The old Noel was replaced with the new," he proclaimed. He went on to make several Christian albums, including *Something New and Fresh* and *Real to Reel.*

Surely the folk artist who has had the greatest success at appealing to both Catholic and Protestant audiences is **John Michael Talbot** (1954–). After recording his first two albums, *John Michael Talbot* and *The New Earth,* he underwent a period of spiritual searching. His next album, *The Lord's Supper,* was based on the Catholic mass and showed that Talbot's musical calling had become clear. He continued to make recordings as well as write books. He also founded a new record label, Troubadour for the Lord, and an ecumenical community, the Brothers

JOHN MICHAEL TALBOT

Born:
May 8, 1954
Oklahoma City, Okla.

Occupation:
singer, writer, guitarist, Franciscan monk

Hobbies/Interests:
theology, communal life, feeding the poor

Quotation:
"As Christians, we must address human need, which is to embrace the whole Gospel of Jesus Christ."

*QUICK*TAKES
Recommended Recording

Brother to Brother
Michael Card and John Michael Talbot
(Word/Epic Records EK 67684)

Since the final chapter of this book covers country, folk, and jazz, no one recording could do justice to all three musical genres. The closest example is probably this collaboration by Michael Card and John Michael Talbot. *Brother to Brother* is an extraordinary accomplishment, both musically and spiritually. These great folksingers are generally heard by two distinct audiences: Talbot's large Catholic following and Card's equally large evangelical constituency. Yet these men have much in common. Both have a deep appreciation for spiritual mystery ("Live the Mystery"), the Lord's Table ("Come to the Table"), and the importance of praise ("Come Worship the Lord"). Furthermore, their voices and musical styles blend beautifully. *Brother to Brother* is a wonderful example of musical ecumenicism. One can only hope that their work together will serve as an inspiration to others, and begin a musical trend that will find its way through the various streams of sacred music.

and Sisters of Charity, located near Eureka Springs, Arkansas.

We end this section with a versatile musician who is usually categorized as a CCM artist but whose roots and writings are in the folk music tradition. **Michael Card** (1957–) was working on a master's degree in biblical studies at Western Kentucky University when he wrote his first song. Much of his work presents the power of Scripture through music. He flatly asserts that his songs are "interpretations of the Bible." Card has recorded almost twenty albums, including *The Final Word, Coram Deo, Unveiled Hope,* and a children's album, *Come to the Cradle.* Furthermore, he has composed well-known songs for other Christian artists, such as the moving "El Shaddai," made famous by Amy Grant.

Christians in Jazz

The fascinating world of jazz has yet to be fully embraced by the Christian culture. To be sure, jazz has had a profound musical impact on many of the singers and groups mentioned in the last two chapters. Numerous Christian colleges have jazz-studies classes and excellent jazz bands. Furthermore, jazz styles are often combined with other Christian music genres—many bands bill themselves as jazz-rock, jazz-fusion, and so on.

Still, at the end of the twentieth century only a small portion of jazz can be classified as distinctively Christian. This is in part because the jazz idiom has placed such emphasis on instrumental music, which believers specifically seeking a Christian message often find difficult to appreciate. It is also because jazz is rooted in the New Orleans, blues, swing, and bebop traditions that developed concurrently—and in contrast to—gospel music.

MICHAEL CARD

Born:
April 11, 1957
Nashville, Tenn.

Occupation:
singer, composer, guitarist, pianist

Hobbies/Interests:
theology, astronomy, Celtic music

Quotation:
"Biblical humility is, in truth, realizing who you are in Christ."

DUKE ELLINGTON

Born:
April 28, 1899
Washington, D.C.

Died:
May 24, 1974
New York, N.Y.

Occupation:
composer, singer, pianist

Hobbies/Interests:
poetry, art

Quotation:
"Every man prays in his own language, and there is no language He does not understand."

Nevertheless, there are moments in jazz history that reflect sacred concerns. Perhaps the greatest examples are the three "sacred concerts" produced by **Edward Kennedy "Duke" Ellington** (1899–1974). A devout, if unorthodox, Christian, Ellington used these performances and the songs he wrote for them as an expression of his faith. After the second sacred concert, he asserted that this concert was "the most important thing I have ever done."

Ellington had composed sacred songs earlier in his career (such as "Come Sunday" and "David Danced Before the Lord"), but the many compositions he wrote for the three sacred concerts represent his best in the genre. The first sacred concert took place on September 16, 1965, and opened with the powerful "In the Beginning, God." The production was performed more than fifty times and had a profound impact on the jazz world. Less than three years later, Ellington gave a second series of sacred concerts, which contained the well-known "Something about Believin'" and "Supreme God." His last sacred concert was on October 24, 1973, only seven months before his death. Although very ill, Ellington gave inspiring renditions of such classics as "Ain't Nobody Nowhere Nothin' without God."

The spiritual aspects of another jazz pioneer, **John Coltrane** (1926–67), are more difficult to define. This great instrumentalist was born into a devout family—both his grandfathers were African Methodist Episcopal Zion pastors—but the pressures of his early career led him into heroin and heavy drinking. Yet he tells how in 1957 he "experienced, by the grace of God, a spiritual awakening that was to lead me to a richer, fuller, more productive life." Coltrane abandoned drugs and alcohol, later claiming that his goal was to "live a truly religious life and express it in my music." His faith was always unorthodox, but he used many traditional religious titles in his compositions, including "The Father and the Son and the Holy Ghost."

Another interesting example concerns the career of jazz pianist **Dave Brubeck** (1920–). The versatile musician received an education in classical music and composed for orchestra, ballet, chorus, and chamber ensemble. But he is best known for his many jazz contributions. After converting to Catholicism, he wrote several effective works of sacred jazz music, including *The Voice of the Holy Spirit; The Gate of Justice; To Hope, a Celebration;* and his very popular *The Light in the Wilderness,* which contains a remarkably jazzy "Sermon on the Mount."

By the end of the twentieth century, more and more Christians have become interested in jazz. Certainly the greatest exponent to date is a six-man vocal group known as **Take 6.** This incredibly talented ensemble (with a combined range of more than four octaves!) usually performs unaccompanied and is known for their virtuoso vocal skills and creative arrangements. The secular music world has not been slow to notice the abilities of Take 6: their debut album, *Spread Love,* won the Grammy Award in 1988 for Best Jazz Vocal Performance (Duo or Group).

They have since won many other awards and recorded four more albums, including *So Much 2 Say* and their best-selling Christmas album, *He Is Christmas.*

Other Possibilities

The twentieth century has seen many other styles of popular music come to the forefront, from rhythm and blues to world music. Every year new variations and modifications are being used by a growing multitude of performers. These budding stars mean more competition, which, in effect, raises the standards of the musicians. The end result is increasingly sophisticated audiences.

As the century closes, Christian audiences appear more open to musical styles that they would have avoided only a few decades ago. CCM artists often employ blues, Latin, fusion, ska, hip-hop, and jazz in their quest for a new and unique sound. Many albums (and even individual songs) contain various combinations of the above genres, which demands more and more versatility from today's performers.

Startling advancements in technology have also had a profound effect on the music world, both on secular and Christian artists. Not only have recording techniques progressed dramatically, but synthesizers and computers are now used in virtually every style of music. Even the most old-fashioned country or folk music uses synthesis and digital editing techniques.

If we could take a time machine to a future century and listen to historians describing the various music of the late twentieth century, what would our reaction be? Would we be irritated by their cerebral analysis of the songs that are so close to our hearts? Would we be offended by their impartial judgment of what lasted and what did not?

Or would we see that the music of the twentieth century was truly a preparation for the music that would follow? Might we then acknowledge that all of the styles to date were only the catalyst for the explosion of new music that the twenty-first century will surely create?

Other Listening Recommendations

Michael Card
Unveiled Hope (Song 68175)

Johnny Cash
The Gospel Road (Columbia KG-32253)

Don Francisco
Brother of the Sun (Newpax NP 33010)

Stuart Hamblen
It Is No Secret (RCA Victor LPM-3265)

The Lewis Family
Country Faith (Canaan CAS 9820)

Barbara Mandrell
He Set My Life to Music (MCA 1492)

The Stoneman Family
Family Bible (Rutabaga 3012)

Take 6
So Much 2 Say (Warner/Alliance 2-25892)

John Michael Talbot
The Lord's Supper (Sparrow SPD-1183)

Hank Williams
I Saw the Light (Mercury 422-811900-2)

AFTERWORD

Thoughts on the Future of Sacred Music

I know of no way of judging of the future but by the past," asserted the great American partriot Patrick Henry in 1775. He may not have been a professional musician, but his statement certainly says something portentous about music history.

In this book, we have examined the principal types of Christian sacred music of the last two thousand years. We have witnessed evidence of increasing complexity, from simple plainchant to the complicated electronic music of today. We have also learned how one generation's music often rebels against that of the former generation, often creating a kind of pendulum effect as we bounce between competing musical ideals.

Yet there are overall patterns that can be discerned, some of which may indicate future trends. Three in particular are worthy of discussion. Of course, all predictions can fool us, and whatever general trends we identify today may only be recognizable in tomorrow's disguise. Nevertheless, as we enter the third millennium of sacred music, it is worth examining what we might expect to hear.

The Combination of Musical Styles

Although the various types of music explored in this book are continually expanding, they are also coming closer together. To again use the stream analogy, imagine three rivers running parallel to one another. If each begins to spread out, deltalike, they will soon run together. As this occurs, the combined flow of all three will create a single river containing elements of the three original rivers.

To a remarkable degree, this is what is happening in sacred music—and perhaps in all Western music—today. Classical composers borrow from jazz, country musicians perform with rock stars, and large orchestras accompany the "simple" songs of folksingers. No longer can one genre remain exclusively independent; they each borrow freely from one another.

Modern communications bring all musical styles into our collective living room. Most of Western civilization can now view—via cable television—entire channels devoted entirely to one musical genre. Thus, audiences have learned to appreciate many different styles, and musicians have learned to incorporate music far removed from their area of expertise. The growth of the Internet and the Web have allowed composers to communicate new music to other composers, performers, and audiences almost instantaneously.

It is my opinion that the struggle to create new and unique music will actually fan the flames of a growing revival of interest in the music of the past. Musicians will rediscover the wealth of musical styles from chant to early gospel and how it can speak to the music they are developing. The most successful contemporary musicians will often be those who have been influenced by the masters of the past. A corollary to this is the great interest Western musicians (especially composers) are already taking in Eastern musicians, and vice versa, which again will accelerate the mingling of musical techniques.

The end result will be a massive blending of styles. This does not mean that all divisions will cease. There will always be people who demand the purist approach to any given musical genre, and there will always be musicians available to meet these demands. Yet most audiences will certainly expect more and more performers to be able to produce a wide variety of music. Recordings will contain many styles, and even a single song might exhibit elements of jazz, classical, country, and heavy metal.

Music will become less categorized. Perhaps the only real boundaries in sacred music will eventually be the text itself. When artists say they perform Christian music, they will mean they perform any kind of music with Christian words. And what better designation could one desire?

The Flowering of Excellence

As more and more musicians enter the marketplace, the competition will allow audiences to choose only the very best music. This will mean a greater emphasis on musical excellence and virtuosity among performers, as well as those throughout the music industry. Audiences will have so many artists from which to choose that none who have musical flaws will survive for long.

This has been clearly demonstrated throughout the twentieth century in classical music. Performance standards rose every decade, as more and more young performers wanted the few available jobs in symphony orchestras. When you compare the older recordings—even of the great conductor Toscanini—with those of the late twentieth century, the differences are remarkable. As good as they were, the players in Toscanini's orchestras could not compete with the flawless performers of today.

This continued emphasis on excellence will pervade every form of sacred music. Only the best hymns will be used frequently, only the best rock groups will draw large crowds, only the best choral and solo recordings will be purchased in huge quantities. In the same way, audiences will demand the finest musical arrangements, the best studio recording techniques, even the most sophisticated CD artwork. Like an auditioner who listens to hundreds of hopefuls all trying for one part, tomorrow's audiences can afford to be choosy. Obviously, in such a large genre, mediocrity will occasionally occur, but it will be the exception, not the norm.

Heightened musical standards will necessitate more formal training of future musicians. Unlike the early days of popular music, more artists will have degrees in music, often graduate degrees. As the price for recording-studio time skyrockets, only the musicians who can learn quickly and perform faultlessly will be employed. Rare will be the folksy musician who never found time to learn how to read music. Even pop songwriters will be expected to know a good deal about music theory, analysis, and orchestration. In the future, lack of such experience and education will often banish inferior musicians to the realm of amateurs.

If such predictions alarm secular musicians, they should only inspire Christian artists. Future believers will be motivated by the biblical mandate to excel from King David's command to "play skillfully" (Ps. 33:3) to Saint Paul's admonition to think about things that are "excellent and praiseworthy" (Phil. 4:8). Surely, those who offer their musical gifts to God should endeavor to offer nothing but their very best.

The Human Element

With all the advancements in technology, another component of sacred music will undoubtedly be magnified. The most successful Christian musicians in the future will be those who can effectively communicate the human element. As our society becomes increasingly isolated and separated by the technology that brings music to our homes, we will desire Christian musicians with whom we can relate on a very human and personal level.

This is particularly true with regard to singers, especially popular singers. Within the jumble of electronic complexities, we will long for a voice that will move us in an emotional, noncerebral manner. This is a natural reaction to the invasion of the horrific overabundance of nonemotional data. The more our brains deal with an ongoing explosion of information, the more we thirst for that which is purely human—that which touches our hearts.

One of the many musical consequences of our need to be connected with other human beings will affect live performances. As we have every form of recorded music at our fingertips, including video performances, music lovers will find a greater need to experience music in person again. Live concerts will actually soar in popularity, though the audiences will again be very choosy in whom they seek to hear. This will result in fewer stars and more megastars—those who successfully integrate musical excellence and the human element in all their music.

As Christian music enters its third millennium, the possibilities are endless. Instead of being pigeonholed into one or two categories, musicians will embrace many new techniques and mix them to create entirely new musical concepts. Looking back a few centuries from now, it may seem that the first two thousand years of sacred music were but a prelude, a preparation for the greatest of true Christian music and worship.

The sacred music of the future will doubtless inspire our children and their children as they, in their time, continue to "sing to the LORD a new song" (Ps. 96:1).

FURTHER READING

Part 1: From Hebrew Psalms to the Renaissance

1. The Origins of Sacred Music

Barker, Andrew, ed. *Greek Musical Writings: The Musician and His Art.* New York: Cambridge University Press, 1989.

Crocker, Richard. *A History of Musical Style.* New York: McGraw-Hill, 1966. Reprint, New York: Dover, 1991.

Duffield, Samuel Willoughby. *The Latin Hymn-Writers and Their Hymns.* New York: Funk and Wagnalls, 1889.

Edersheim, Alfred. *The Life and Times of Jesus the Messiah.* Vol. 2. Grand Rapids, Mich.: Eerdmans, n.d.

Fellerer, Karl Gustav. *The History of Catholic Church Music.* Translated by Francis A. Brunner. Baltimore: Helicon Press, 1961.

Foley, Edward. *Foundations of Christian Music.* Chicago: Liturgical Press, 1996.

Haike-Vantoura, Suzanne. *The Music of the Bible Revealed.* New York: Bibal Press, 1991.

Harris, Rendel, and Alphonse Mingana. *The Odes and Psalms of Solomon 1, Text 2.* Manchester: University Press, 1916–20.

Karris, Robert Jr. *A Symphony of New Testament Hymns.* Chicago: Liturgical Press, 1996.

Larrick, Geary. *Music References and Song Texts in the Bible.* New York: Edwin Mellen Press, 1990.

Maas, Martha. *Stringed Instruments of Ancient Greece.* Boston: Yale University Press, 1989.

Manniche, Lise. *Musical Instruments for the Tomb of Tutankhamen.* New York: David Brown, 1976.

McKinnon, James. *Music in Early Christian Literature.* New York: Cambridge University Press, 1987.

Quasten, J. *Music and Worship in Pagan and Christian Antiquity.* Washington, D.C.: Catholic University Press, 1983.

Sachs, Curt. *The Rise of Music in the Ancient World.* New York: Norton, 1943.

———. *The Wellsprings of Music.* New York: Da Capo Press, 1977.

Schueller, Herbert M. *The Idea of Music: An Introduction to Musical Aesthetics in Antiquity and the Middle Ages.* Kalamazoo, Mich.: Medieval Institute Publications, 1988.

Stamer, John. *The Music of the Bible.* New York: Da Capo Press, 1970.

Walpole, Arthur Sumner. *Early Latin Hymns.* Cambridge: Olms Publishing, 1922.

Wellesz, Egon. *A History of Byzantine Music and Hymnography.* Oxford: Oxford University Press, 1961.

Werner, Eric. *The Sacred Bridge: The Interdependence of Liturgy and Music in Synagogue and Church during the First Millennium.* New York: Dobson, 1959.

2. Chant

Apel, Will. *Gregorian Chant.* Bloomington: Indiana University Press, 1966.

Bailey, Terence. *Antiphon and Psalm in the Ambrosian Office.* London: Institute of Medieval Music, 1994.

Bobko, Jane, Barbara Newman, and Michael Fox. *Vision, The Life and Music of Hildegard Von Bingen.* New York: Viking, 1995.

Cavadini, John C. *Gregory the Great: A Symposium.* Notre Dame, Ind.: University of Notre Dame Press, 1996.

Douglas, Charles Winfred. *Church Music in History and Practice.* Irvine, Calif.: Reprint Services, 1992.

Dudden, Frederick Homes. *Gregory the Great: His Place in History and Thought.* 2 vols. New York: Longmans, 1905.

———. *The Life and Times of Saint Ambrose.* 2 vols. Oxford: Clarendon Press, 1935.

Hozeski, Bruce, trans. *Hildegarde von Bingen's Mystical Visions.* New York: Bear, 1995.

Jeffrey, Peter. *Ethnomusicology in the Study of Gregorian Chant.* Chicago: University of Chicago Press, 1995.

Kark, Theodore. *Aspects of Orality and Formularity in Gregorian Chant.* Evanston, Ill.: Northwestern University Press, 1998.

Kelley, Thomas Forrest. *The Beneventan Chant.* New York: Cambridge University Press, 1989.

LaCrois, Richard. *Augustine on Music.* New York: Edwin Mellen Press, 1988.

LeMee, Katherine. *The Origins, Form, Practice, and Healing Power of Gregorian Chant.* New York: Bell Tower, 1995.

Lerry, Kenneth. *Gregorian Chant and the Carolingians.* Princeton, N.J.: Princeton University Press, 1998.

Markus, R. A. *Gregory the Great and His World.* New York: Cambridge University Press, 1997.

Nemmers, Erwin Esser. *Twenty Centuries of Catholic Church Music.* Westport, Conn.: Greenwood, 1978.

Page, Christopher. *Discarding Images: Reflections on Music and Culture in Medieval France.* Oxford: Clarendon Press, 1997.

Pierik, Marie. *The Spirit of Gregorian Chant.* Boston: McLaughlin and Reilly, 1989.

Robertson, Alec. *The Interpretation of Plainchant.* Westport, Conn.: Greenwood, 1970.

Smith, Huston, ed. *Gregorian Chant: Songs of the Spirit.* New York: KQED, 1996.

Squires, Russel N. *Church Music: Musical and Hymnological Developments in Western Christianity.* St. Louis: Bethany Press, 1962.

Weber, Jerome. *A Gregorian Chant Discography.* New York: Jerome Weber, 1990.

Weinandt, Elwin A. *Choral Music of the Church.* New York: Free Press, 1965.

3. Medieval Polyphony

Aubrey, Elizabeth. *The Music of the Troubadours.* Indianapolis: Indiana University Press, 1996.

Boone, Braeme, ed. *Essays on Medieval Music.* Boston: Harvard University Press, 1995.

Further Reading

Brothers, Thomas. *Chromatic Beauty in the Late Medieval Chanson.* New York: Cambridge University Press, 1997.

Crocker, Richard. *The Early Medieval Sequence.* Berkeley: University of California Press, 1977.

Davies, Horton. *Christian Worship: Its History and Meaning.* New York: Abingdon Press, 1957.

Donington, Robert. *The Interpretation of Early Music.* New York: Norton, 1992.

Everist, Mark. *French Motets in the Thirteenth Century.* Cambridge: Cambridge University Press, 1994.

Fallows, David. *Dufay.* London: J. M. Dent and Sons, 1982.

Fux, J. J. *Study of Counterpoint.* New York: Norton, 1965.

Gallo, F. Alberto. *Music in the Castle.* Chicago: University of Chicago Press, 1996.

Hoppin, Richard. *Medieval Music.* New York: Norton, 1978.

Hughes, Andrew. *Medieval Music.* Toronto: University of Toronto Press, 1980.

Huot, Sylvia. *The Sacred and Profane in Thirteenth Century Polyphony.* Stanford, Calif.: Stanford University Press, 1997.

Mayard, Winifred. *Elizabethan Lyric Poetry and Its Music.* Oxford: Clarendon Press, 1986.

McKinnon, James W. *Antiquity and the Middle Ages.* Englewood Cliffs, N.J.: Prentice Hall, 1991.

Mearns, James. *Canticles of the Christian Church Eastern and Western in Early and Medieval Times.* Cambridge: University Press, 1914.

Owst, Gerald Robert. *Preaching in Medieval England.* New York: Barnes and Noble, 1966.

Page, Christopher. *Music and Instruments of the Middle Ages.* London: Ashgate Publishing, 1997.

Pesce, Dolores. *The Affinities and Medieval Transposition.* Indianapolis: Indiana University Press, 1996.

Plumley, Yolanda. *The Grammar of Fourteenth Century Music.* New York: Garland, 1996.

———. *The Music of the Medieval Liturgical Drama in France and England.* New York: Garland, 1989.

Rankin, Susan, ed. *Music in Medieval English Liturgy.* Oxford: Oxford University Press, 1993.

Reese, Gustave. *Music in the Middle Ages.* New York: Norton, 1940.

Rosenberg, Samuel. *Chanter M'Estuet: Songs of the Trouveres.* Indianapolis: Indiana University Press, 1981.

Seay, Albert. *Music in the Medieval World.* New York: Waveland Press, 1991.

Southwood, John. *The English Medieval Minstrel.* New York: Boydell and Brewer, 1989.

Strohm, Reinhard. *Music in Late Medieval Brugges.* Oxford: Clarendon Press, 1990.

Switten, Margaret. *Music and Poetry of the Middle Ages.* New York: Garland, 1995.

VanDeusen, Nancy. *The Harp and the Soul: Essays in Medieval Music.* New York: Edwin Mellen Press, 1990.

Wilkins, Nigel. *Music in the Age of Chaucer.* Rochester, N.Y.: University of Rochester Press, 1995.

Wright, Craig. *Music and Ceremony at Notre Dame of Paris, 500–1500.* New York: Cambridge University Press, 1991.

4. The Renaissance

Bainton, Roland H. *The Reformation of the Sixteenth Century.* Boston: Beacon Press, 1985.

Best, Harold. *Music through the Eyes of Faith.* San Francisco: Harper San Francisco, 1993.

Bray, Gerald. *Documents of the English Reformation.* New York: Fortress Publishers, 1993.

Brown, Howard M. *Music in the Renaissance.* New York: Prentice Hall, 1976.

Charteris, Richard. *Giovanni Gabrieli.* New York: Pendragon Press, 1996.

Coates, Henry. *Palestrina.* London: J. M. Dent and Sons, 1948.

Comberiati, Carmelo Peter. *Late Renaissance Music at the Hapsburg Court.* New York: Gordon and Breach Science Publishers, 1987.

Crook, David. *Orlando DiLasso's Imitation Magnificats for Counter-Reformation Munich.* Princeton, N.J.: Princeton University Press, 1994.

Dearnley, Christopher. *English Church Music, 1650–1750.* New York: Oxford University Press, 1970.

Eisenbechler, Konrad, ed. *Crossing the Boundaries: Christian Piety and the Arts in Italian Renaissance Confraternities.* Lansing: Western Michigan University Press, 1991.

Fisher, Leonard E. *Gutenberg.* New York: Simon and Schuster, 1993.

Gangwere, Blanche M. *Music History in the Renaisssance Period.* New York: Greenwood Publishers Group, 1991.

Gleason, Harold. *Music in the Middle Ages and the Renaissance.* New York: Alfred Publishing, 1981.

Hagopian, Viola. *Italian Ars Nova Music.* Irvine: University of California Press, 1981.

Harran, Don. *In Defense of Music.* Lincoln: University of Nebraska Press, 1989.

Hillerbrand, Hans J. *Protestant Reformation.* New York: HarperCollins, 1984.

Knighten, Tess, ed. *Companion to Medieval and Renaissance Music.* Irvine: University of California Press, 1998.

Le Huray, Peter. *Music and the Reformation in England, 1549–1649.* Oxford: Gimell, 1991.

Long, Kenneth. *The Music of the English Church.* London: Hodder and Stoughton, 1991.

McGee, Timothy. *Medieval and Renaissance Music: A Performer's Guide.* Toronto: University of Toronto Press, 1988.

McGrath, Alister E. *A Life of John Calvin.* New York: Blackwell Publishers, 1990.

———. *Reformation Thought: An Introduction.* New York: Blackwell Publishers, 1993.

Meyer, Ernst Hermann. *Early English Chamber Music.* New York: Marion Boyars, 1983.

Pesce, Dolores. *Hearing the Motet.* Oxford: Oxford University Press, 1996.

Planchert, Alejandro. *Repertoire of Tropes at Winchester.* Princeton, N.J.: Princeton University Press, 1976.

Reese, Gustav. *Music in the Renaissance.* New York: Norton, 1954.

Reynolds, Christopher A. *Papal Patronage and the Music of St. Peters, 1380–1513.* Irvine: University of California Press, 1995.

Roche, Jerome. *Palestrina.* London: Oxford University Press, 1971.

Routley, Erik. *A Short History of English Church Music.* London: Mowbrays, 1977.

Spitz, Lewis W. *The Protestant Reformation.* St. Louis: Concordia, 1997.

Stevens, Denis. *Tudor Church Music.* New York: Norton, 1961.

Temperley, Nicholas. *The Music of the English Parish Church.* New York: Cambridge University Press, 1983.

Wegman, Robert C. *Born for the Muses: The Life and Masses of Jacob Obrecht.* Oxford: Clarendon Press, 1996.

Wells, Robin Headlam. *Elizabethan Mythologies: Studies in Poetry, Drama, and Music.* Cambridge: Cambridge University Press, 1994.

Williams, Peter. *The Organ in Western Culture.* New York: Cambridge University Press, 1993.

Part 2: From Baroque to Hymnology

5. The Baroque Period

Abraham, Gerald. *Handel: A Symposium.* London: Oxford University Press, 1954.

Arnold, Denis. *Monteverdi.* New York: Farrar, Straus, and Giroux, 1963.

———. and Nigel Fortune, eds. *The Monteverdi Companion.* London: Faber and Faber, 1968.

David, Hans Theodore, and Mendel Arthur. *The Bach Reader.* New York: Norton, 1966.

Deutsch, Otto Erich. *Handel: A Documentary Biography.* London: Adam and Charles Black, 1955.

Further Reading

Flower, Norman. *Handel: His Personality and His Times.* London: Panther Books, 1919.

Foelber, Paul Frederick. *Bach's Treatment of the Subject of Death in his Choral Music.* St. Louis: Concordia, 1961.

Forkel, Johann Nikolaus. *Johann Sebastian Bach: His Life, Art, and Work.* New York: Da Capo Press, 1970.

Geiringer, Karl. *Johann Sebastian Bach: The Culmination of an Era.* New York: Oxford University Press, 1966.

Grew, E. M., and S. Grew. *Bach.* New York: Collier, 1962.

Gurlitt, Wilibald. *Johann Sebastian Bach: The Master and His Work.* St. Louis: Concordia, 1957.

Heller, Karl, and David Marinelli. *Antonio Vivaldi: The Red Priest of Venice.* New York: Amadeus Press, 1997.

Kolneder, Walter. *Antonio Vivaldi: His Life and Work.* Berkeley: University of California Press, 1970.

Lang, Paul Henry. *George Frideric Handel.* New York: Norton, 1966.

Leaver, Robin. *J. S. Bach as Preacher.* St. Louis: Concordia, 1982.

Moser, Hans Joachim. *Heinrich Schutz: His Life and Work.* St. Louis: Concordia, 1959.

Muller, Erich H. *The Letters and Writings of George Frideric Handel.* Freeport, Mass.: Books for Libraries Press, 1970.

Myers, Robert Manson. *Handel's Messiah: A Touchstone of Taste.* New York: Octagon, 1971.

Perry, Charles, and Hubert Hasting. *J. S. Bach: The Story of the Development of a Great Personality.* Westport, Conn.: Greenwood, 1970.

Pincherle, Marc. *Vivaldi: Genius of the Baroque.* New York: Norton, 1962.

Schrade, Leo. *The Conflict between the Sacred and the Secular.* 1955. Reprint, New York: Da Capo Press, 1973.

Schweitzer, Albert. *J. S. Bach.* Trans. Ernest Newman. 2 vols. Boston: Humphries, 1964.

Spitta, Philipp. *Johann Sebastian Bach: His Work and Influence on the Music of Germany.* Trans. Clara Bell and J. A. Fuller-Maitl. New York: Dover, 1951.

Terry, Charles Sanford. *Bach, Cantatas, Oratorio, Passion, Magnificat, and Motets.* Oxford: Oxford University Press, 1923.

Tobin, John. *Handel's Messiah: A Critical Account of the Manuscript Sources and Printed Editions.* New York: St. Martin's Press, 1969.

Westrup, J. A. *Purcell.* New York: Collier, 1962.

Young, Percy M. *Handel.* New York: Farrar, Straus, and Giroux, 1965.

Zimmerman, Franklin B. *Henry Purcell, 1659–95: His Life and Times.* New York: St. Martin's Press, 1967.

6. The Classical Period

Anderson, Emily, ed. *The Letters of Mozart and His Family.* New York: St. Martin's Press, 1966.

Blom, Eric. *Mozart.* New York: Collier, 1962.

Brenet, Michel. *Haydn.* New York: Benjamin Blom, 1972.

Brophy, Brigid. *Mozart, the Dramatist.* New York: Harcourt, Brace and World, 1964.

Burnett, James. *Beethoven and Human Destiny.* New York: Roy Publishing, 1966.

Butterworth, Neil. *Haydn: His Life and Times.* Kent, Ohio: Midas Books, 1977.

Deutsch, Otto Erich. *Mozart: A Documentary Biography.* Stanford, Calif.: Stanford University Press, 1965.

Dies, Albert Christoph. *Biographical Accounts of Joseph Haydn.* Madison: University of Wisconsin Press, 1963.

Einstein, Alfred. *Mozart: His Character, His Work.* Trans. Arthur Mendel and Nathan Broder. New York: Oxford University Press, 1945.

Geiringer, Karl, and Irene Geiringer (contributor). *Haydn: A Creative Life in Music.* Berkeley: University of California Press, 1968.

Griesinger, George August. *Biographical Notes concerning Joseph Haydn.* Madison: University of Wisconsin Press, 1963.

Hadden, James Cuthbert. *Haydn.* New York: AMS Press, 1977.

Hughes, Rosemary. *Haydn.* New York: Collier, 1962.

Further Reading

Hutchings, Arthur. *Mozart, the Man, the Musician.* London: Thames and Hudson, 1976.

Jacob, Heinrich Edward. *Joseph Haydn: His Art, Times, and Glory.* Westport, Conn.: Greenwood, 1950.

King, A. Hyatt. *Mozart in Retrospect.* 3d ed. London: Oxford University Press, 1970.

Knight, Frida. *Beethoven and the Age of Revolution.* London: Lawrence and Wishart, 1973.

Landon, Howard Chandler Robbins. *Beethoven: A Documentary Study.* New York: Macmillan Co., 1970.

————. *The Collected Correspondence and London Notebooks of Joseph Haydn.* Fairlawn, N.J.: Essential Books, 1959.

————. *Haydn: Chronicle and Works.* Bloomington: Indiana University Press, 1977.

————. *Mozart Companion.* London: Oxford University Press, 1956.

Levey, Michael. *The Life and Death of Mozart.* London: Cardinal Publishers, 1971.

Marek, George. *Beethoven: Biography of a Genius.* New York: Funk and Wagnalls, 1969.

Nemetschek, Franz. *The Mozart Handbook.* Ed. Louis Bianciolli. Westport, Conn.: Greenwood, 1954.

Orga, Ates. *Beethoven: His Life and Times.* Neptune City, N.J.: Paganiniana Publications, 1980.

Peyser, Herbert F. *Joseph Haydn: Servant and Master.* New York: Philharmonic Symphony Society of New York, 1950.

Redfern, Brian. *Haydn: A Biography.* Hamden, Conn.: Archon Books, 1970.

Robertson, Alec. *Requiem: Music of Mourning and Consolation.* New York: F. A. Praeger, 1968.

Rolland, Romain. *Beethoven the Creator.* New York: Dover, 1964.

Rosen, Charles. *The Classical Style: Haydn, Mozart, and Beethoven.* New York: Norton, 1997.

Schindler, Anton Felix. *Beethoven as I Knew Him*. London: Faber and Faber, 1966.

Scott, Marion. *Beethoven*. New York: Farrar, Straus, and Giroux, 1960.

Solomon, Maynard. *Beethoven Essays*. Cambridge, Mass.: Harvard University Press, 1988.

Stadtlaender, Christina. *Joseph Haydn of Eisenstadt*. London: Dennis Dobson, 1968.

Sullivan, J. W. N. *Beethoven: His Spiritual Development*. New York: New American Library, Mentor Books, 1954.

Thayer, Alexander Wheelock. *The Life of Beethoven*. Ed. Elliott Forbes. 2 vols. Princeton, N.J.: Princeton University Press, 1964.

Tovey, Donald F. *Beethoven*. Ed. H. J. Foss. New York: Oxford University Press, 1965.

Turner, Walter J. *Mozart: The Man and His Works*. Ed. Christopher Raeburn. New York: Barnes and Noble, 1966.

7. The Romantic Period

Abraham, Gerald. *The Music of Tchaikowsky*. New York: Norton, 1974.

———, ed. *The Music of Schubert*. Port Washington, N.Y.: Kennikat Press, 1969.

Butterworth, Neil. *Dvorak: His Life and Times*. Kent, Ohio: Midas Books, 1980.

Capell, Richard. *Schubert's Songs*. 3d ed. London: Gerald Duckworth, 1973.

Chissell, Joan. *Brahms*. London: Faber and Faber, 1977.

Clapham, John. *Antonin Dvorak*. London: St. Martin's Press, 1966.

Demuth, Norman. *Cesar Franck*. London: Dennis Dobson, 1964.

———. *Introduction to the Music of Gounod*. London: Dennis Dobson, 1950.

Deutsch, Otto Erich. *Schubert: A Documentary Biography*. New York: Da Capo Press, 1977.

Edwards, Frederick George. *The History of Mendelssohn's Oratorio "Elijah."* London: Novello, Ewer, 1896.

Evans, Edwin. *Handbook to the Works of Johannes Brahms.* New York: Lenox Hill, 1970.

Gounod, Charles. *Autobiographical Reminiscences.* Trans. W. Hely Hutchinson. New York: Da Capo Press, 1970.

Harding, James. *Gounod.* New York: Stein and Day, 1973.

Hervey, Arthur. *Masters of French Music.* Plainview, N.Y.: Books for Libraries Press, 1976.

Hiller, Ferdinand. *Mendelssohn: Letters and Recollections.* New York: Vienna House, 1972.

Hoffmeister, Karel. *Antonin Dvorak.* Trans. Rosa Newmarch. Westport, Conn.: Greenwood, 1970.

Hughes, Gervase. *Dvorak: His Life and Music.* New York: Dodd, Mead, 1967.

Hurd, Michael. *Elgar.* London: Faber and Faber, 1969.

Hussey, Dyneley. *Verdi.* London: J. M. Dent and Sons, 1974.

Hutchings, Arthur. *Schubert.* New York: Octagon, 1973.

Jacob, Heinrich E. *Felix Mendelssohn and His Times.* Westport, Conn.: Greenwood, 1973.

Jacobs, Robert L. *Wagner.* Rev. ed. New York: Collier, 1965.

James, Burnett. *Brahms: A Critical Study.* New York: Praeger Publications, 1972.

Kaufman, Schima. *Mendelssohn: "A Second Elijah."* Westport, Conn.: Greenwood, l962.

McVeagh, Diana M. *Edward Elgar: His Life and Music.* London: J. M. Dent and Sons, 1955.

Redlich, Hans Ferdinand. *Bruckner and Mahler.* London: J. M. Dent and Sons, 1955.

Robertson, Alec. *Dvorak.* New York: Collier, 1962.

Suckling, Norman. *Faure.* London: J. M. Dent and Sons, 1951.

Werner, Eric. *Mendelssohn: A New Image of the Composer and His Age.* New York: Free Press, 1963.

White, Chappell. *An Introduction to the Life and Works of Richard Wagner.* Englewood Cliffs, N.J.: Prentice Hall, 1967.

Young, Percy M. *Elgar, O. M.: A Study of a Musician.* London: White Lion, 1973.

8. Chorales and Congregations

Bainton, Roland H. *Here I Stand: A Life of Martin Luther.* Nashville: Abingdon, 1950.

Blume, F. *Protestant Church Music.* New York: Norton, 1974.

Chase, Gilbert. *America's Music: From the Pilgrims to the Present.* Urbana: University of Illinois Press, 1987.

Dallimore, Arnold A. *A Heart Set Free: The Life of Charles Wesley.* Wheaton, Ill.: Crossway Books, 1988.

Daniel, Ralph T. *The Anthem in New England before 1800.* Evanston, Ill.: Northwestern University Press, 1966.

Davis, Paul. *Isaac Watts: His Life and Works.* New York: Dryden, 1943.

Douglas, W., and L. Ellinwood. *Church Music in America.* Boston: E. C. Schirmer, 1962.

Ellinwood, Leonard. *The History of American Church Music.* New York: De Capo Press, 1970.

Frost, Maurice. *English and Scottish Psalm and Hymn Tunes.* London: Oxford University Press, 1953.

Garside, Charles. *Zwingli and the Arts.* New Haven, Conn.: Yale University Press, 1966.

Hoetty-Nickel, Theodore. *Luther and Culture.* Martin Luther Lectures, vol. 4. Decorah, Iowa: Luther College Press, 1960.

Leaver, Robin A., *Goostly Psalmes and Spiritual Songes: English and Dutch Metrical Psalms from Coverdale to Utenhove, 1535–1600.* Oxford: Clarendon Press, 1991.

Leaver, Robin A., David Mann, and David Parkes, eds. *Ways of Singing the Psalms.* London: Collins, 1984.

Liemohn, Edwin. *The Chorale through Four Hundred Years.* Philadelphia: Muhlenberg Press, 1953.

————. *The Organ and Choir in Protestant Worship.* Philadelphia: Fortress, 1968.

Litton, James, ed. *The Plainsong Psalter.* New York: Church Hymnal Corp., 1988.

Lowens, Irving. *Music and Musicians in Early America.* New York: Norton, 1964.

Nettl, Paul. *Luther and Music.* Trans. Frida Best and Ralph Wood. Philadelphia: Muhlenberg Press, 1948.

Park, Edna. *The Hymns and Hymn Tunes Found in the English Metrical Psalters.* New York: Coleman Ross, 1966.

Patrick, Millar. *Four Centuries of Scottish Psalmody.* London: Oxford University Press, 1949.

Riedel, Johannes. *The Lutheran Chorale: Its Basic Traditions.* Minneapolis: Augsburg Publishing House, 1967.

Scholes, Percy. *The Puritans and Music in England and New England.* London: Oxford University Press, 1934.

Shaw, H. Watkins. *Eighteenth Century Cathedral Music.* London: Hodder and Stoughton, 1970.

Stevenson, Robert. *Protestant Church Music in America.* New York: Norton, 1970.

Wyton, Alec, ed. *Anglican Chant Psalter.* New York: Church Hymnal Corp., 1987.

Zim, Rikvah. *English Metrical Psalms: Poetry as Praise and Prayer, 1535–1601.* Cambridge: Cambridge University Press, 1987.

9. The Growth of Hymnology

Benson, Louis F. *The English Hymn.* Richmond, Va.: John Knox, 1962.

Bruce, Dickson, Jr. *And They All Sang Hallelujah: Plain-Folk Camp Meeting Religion, 1800–1845.* Knoxville: University of Tennessee Press, 1974.

Christ-Janer, Albert, Charles W. Hughes, and Carleton Sprague Smith. *American Hymns, Old and New.* New York: Columbia University Press, 1980.

Clarke, W. K. Lowther. *A Hundred Years of Hymns, Ancient and Modern.* London: Clowes, 1961.

Cobb, Buell E., Jr. *The Sacred Harp: A Tradition and Its Music.* Athens: University of Georgia Press, 1989.

Eskew, Harry, and Hugh T. McElroth. *Sing with Understanding: An Introduction to Christian Hymnody.* Nashville: Broadman, 1991.

Gatens, William J. *Victorian Cathedral Music in Theory and Practice.* Cambridge, Mass.: Cambridge University Press, 1986.

Hall, T. H. *Biography of Gospel Song and Hymn Writers.* New York: AMS Press, 1971.

Higginson, J. Vincent. *A Handbook for American Catholic Hymnals.* Springfield, Tex.: Hymn Society of America, 1976.

Hitchcock, H. Wiley. *Music in the United States: A Historical Introduction.* Englewood Cliffs, N.J.: Prentice Hall, 1988.

Hutchings, Arthur. *Church Music in the Nineteenth Century.* London: Herbert Jenkins, 1967.

Jackson, George Pullen. *The Story of the Sacred Harp.* Nashville: Vanderbilt University Press, 1944.

———. *White Spirituals in the Southern Uplands.* Chapel Hill: University of North Carolina Press, 1933.

Jefferson, H. A. L. *Hymns in Christian Worship.* New York: Macmillan, 1950.

Julian, J. *Dictionary of Hymnology.* 2d ed. London: John Murray, 1907. Reprint, Grand Rapids, Mich.: Kregel Publications, 1985.

Kingman, Daniel. *American Music: A Panorama.* New York: Schirmer, 1990.

Lovelace, Austin. *The Anatomy of Hymnody.* Chicago: GIA Publications, 1965.

———. *The Organist and Hymn-Playing.* Rev. ed. Carol Stream, Ill.: Hope Publishing, 1981.

Parker, Alice. *Creative Hymn Singing.* Chapel Hill, N.C.: Hinshaw, 1976.

Rainbow, Bernard. *The Choral Revival in the Anglican Church, 1839–1872.* New York: Oxford University Press, 1970.

Reynolds, William J. *Companion to Baptist Hymnal.* Nashville: Broadman, 1976.

———. *Songs of Glory.* Grand Rapids, Mich.: Zondervan Publishing, 1990.

———, and Milburn Price. *A Survey of Christian Hymnody.* Carol Stream, Ill.: Hope Publishing, 1987.

Routley, Erik. *The Music of Christian Hymns.* Chicago: GIA Publications, 1981.

———. *A Panorama of Christian Hymnody.* Chicago: GIA Publications, 1979.

Sallee, James. *A History of Evangelistic Hymnody.* Grand Rapids, Mich.: Baker Book House, 1978.

Sankey, Ira D. *My Life and the Story of the Gospel Hymns.* New York: Harper and Brothers, 1907.

Shorney, George H. *The Hymnal Explosion.* Carol Stream, Ill.: Hope Publishing, 1987.

Sizer, Sandra. *Gospel Hymns and Social Religion: The Rhetoric of Nineteenth-Century Revivalism.* Philadelphia: Temple University Press, 1978.

Spencer, Jon Michael. *Black Hymnody: A Hymnological History of the African-American Church.* Knoxville, Tenn.: University of Tennessee Press, 1992.

Stanislaw, Richard J. *A Checklist of Four-Shape Shape-Note Tunebooks.* Brooklyn, N.Y.: Institute for Studies in American Music, 1978.

Syndor, James Rawlings. *The Hymn and Congregational Singing.* Richmond, Va.: John Knox, 1960.

———. *Hymns and Their Uses: A Guide to Improved Congregational Singing.* Carol Stream, Ill.: Hope Publishing, 1982.

Tamke, Susan S. *Make a Joyful Noise unto the Lord: Hymns as a Reflection of Victorian Social Attitudes.* Athens: Ohio University Press, 1978.

Wilson, John. *Looking at Hymn Tunes: The Objective Factors.* Croydon, England: Hymn Society of Great Britain and Ireland, 1985.

Part 3: The Twentieth Century and the Advent of Recorded Music

10. Modern Classical Composers

Berger, Arthur. *Aaron Copland.* New York: Oxford University Press, 1953.

Bertensson, Sergei, and Jay Leyda. *Sergei Rachmaninoff: A Lifetime in Music.* New York: New York University Press, 1956.

Burkholder, James Peter. *Charles Ives: The Man behind the Ideas.* New Haven, Conn.: Yale University Press, 1985.

Copland, Aaron. *What to Listen for in Music.* New York: McGraw-Hill, 1957.

Cowell, Henry, and Sydney Cowell. *Charles Ives and His Music.* New York: Oxford University Press, 1955.

Craft, Robert, and Andre Marion. *The Message of Igor Stravinsky.* New York: Boosey and Hawkes, 1953.

Day, James. *Vaughan Williams.* London: J. M. Dent and Sons, 1972.

Dickinson, A. E. F. *Vaughan Williams.* London: Faber and Faber, 1963.

Foss, Hubert. *Ralph Vaughan Williams: A Study.* London: Harrap, 1950.

Hell, Henri. *Francis Poulenc.* New York: Grove Press, 1959.

Hurd, Michael. *Vaughan Williams.* London: Faber and Faber, 1970.

Ives, Charles. *Memos.* Ed. John Kirkpatrick. New York: Norton, 1972.

Kendall, Alan. *Benjamin Britten.* London: Macmillan, 1973.

Kennedy, Michael. *The Works of Ralph Vaughan Williams.* London: Oxford University Press, 1964.

Lockspeiser, Edward. *Debussy.* New York: Collier, 1962.

Mitchell, Donald, and Hans Keller, eds. *Britten: A Commentary on His Works from a Group of Specialists.* New York: Philosophical Library, 1950.

Morgan, Robert P. *Twentieth Century Music.* New York: Norton, 1991.

Newlin, Dika. *Bruckner, Mahler, Schoenberg.* New York: Columbia University Press, 1947.

Pakenham, Simona. *Ralph Vaughan Williams: A Discovery of His Music.* London: Macmillan, 1957.

Payne, Anthony. *Schoenberg.* New York: Oxford University Press, 1968.

Perlis, Vivian, ed. *Charles Ives Remembered: An Oral History.* New York: Norton, 1974.

Perry, Rosalie S. *Charles Ives and the American Mind.* Kent, Ohio: Kent State University Press, 1974.

Rochberg, George. *The Aesthetics of Survival: A Composer's View of Twentieth Century Music.* Ann Arbor: University of Michigan Press, 1984.

Rockwell, John. *All American Music: Composition in the Late Twentieth Century.* New York: Vintage Press, 1984.

Rossiter, Frank R. *Charles Ives and His America.* New York: Liveright Publishers, 1975.

Routh, Francis. *Stravinsky.* London: J. M. Dent and Sons, 1975.

Schaeffer, John. *New Sounds: A Listener's Guide to New Music.* New York: Harper and Row, 1987.

Sessions, Roger. *The Musical Experience of Composer, Performer, Listener.* Princeton, N.J.: Princeton University Press, 1987.

Stravinksy, Igor. *Expositions and Developments.* Garden City, N.J.: Doubleday, 1962.

———. *Poetics of Music in the Form of Six Lessons.* New York: Vintage Books, 1956.

———, and Robert Craft. *Dialogues and a Diary.* Garden City, N.J.: Doubleday, 1962.

Strobel, Heinrich. *Stravinsky: Classic Humanist.* New York: Da Capo Press, 1973.

Tansman, Alexandre. *Igor Stravinsky: The Man and His Music.* New York: G. P. Putnam's Sons, 1949.

Thretfall, Robert. *Sergei Rachmaninoff: His Life and Music.* London: Boosey and Hawkes, 1973.

Tierney, Neil. *The Unknown Country (Life of Igor Stravinsky).* London: Robert Hale, 1977.

Vallas, Leon. *Claude Debussy: His Life and Works.* Trans. Marie O'Brien. New York: Dover, 1973.

Vlad, Roman. *Stravinsky.* Trans. Frederick Fuller and Ann Fuller. 2d ed. New York: Oxford University Press, 1967.

White, Eric Walter. *Benjamin Britten: A Sketch of His Life and Works.* London: Boosey and Hawkes, 1954.

———. *Stravinsky: The Composer and His Works.* Berkeley: University of California Press, 1966.

Williams, Ralph Vaughan. *Heirs and Rebels.* New York: Cooper Square Publishers, 1974.

———. *National Music and Other Essays.* London: Oxford University Press, 1963.

Williams, Ursula Vaughan. *R. V. W.: A Biography of Ralph Vaughan Williams.* London: Oxford University Press, 1964.

Wooldridge, David. *From the Steeples and Mountains: A Study of Charles Ives.* New York: Knopf, 1974.

11. Congregational Music and the Modern Church Choir

Abbott, Walter M., ed. *The Documents of Vatican II.* New York: Guild Press, 1966.

Allen, J. P. *Reality in Worship.* Nashville: Convention Press, 1965.

Allen, Ronald, and Gordon Borror. *Worship: Rediscovering the Missing Jewel.* Portland, Oreg.: Multnomah Press, 1982.

Bauman, William A. *The Ministry of Music: A Guide for the Practicing Church Musician.* Washington, D.C.: Liturgical Conference, 1979.

Berglund, Robert. *A Philosophy of Church Music.* Chicago: Moody Press, 1985.

Blackwood, Andrew W. *The Fine Art of Public Worship.* Nashville: Abingdon-Cokesbury, 1939.

Boschman, Lamar. *The Prophetic Song.* Shippensburg, Tex.: Destiny Image, 1990.

———. *The Rebirth of Music.* Shippensburg, Tex.: Destiny Image, 1986.

Day, Thomas. *Why Catholics Can't Sing: The Culture of Catholicism and the Triumph of Bad Taste.* New York: Crossroad, 1992.

Dean, Talmage. *The History of Protestant Church Music in America in the Twentieth Century.* Nashville: Broadman, 1988.

Deiss, Lucien. *Spirit and Song of the New Liturgy.* Cincinnati: World Library Publications, 1976.

Further Reading

Dorgan, Howard. *Giving Glory to God in Appalachia: Worship Practices of Six Baptist Subdenominations.* Knoxville: University of Tennessee Press, 1987.

Erickson, J. Irving. *Sing It Again: A Handbook on the Covenant Hymnal.* Chicago: Covenant Press, 1985.

Evanson, Charles J. *Evangelicalism and the Liturgical Movement and Their Effects on Lutheran Worship.* St. Louis: Morning Star Publications, n.d.

Funk, Virgil C. *The Pastoral Musician.* Washington, D.C.: Pastoral Press, 1900.

Gelineau, Joseph. *Learning to Celebrate: The Mass and Its Music.* New York: Paulist Press, 1985.

Glover, Raymond F. *A Commentary on New Hymns.* New York: Church Hymnal Corp., 1985.

Hannum, Harold B. *Music and Worship.* Nashville: Southern Publishers Assn., 1969.

Hatchett, M. J. *A Manual for Clergy and Church Musicians.* New York: Church Hymnal Corp., 1980.

Hoelty-Nickel, Theodore, ed. *The Musical Heritage of the Church.* St. Louis: Concordia, 1944–81.

Hoffman, Lawrence, and Janet R. Walton, eds. *Sacred Sound and Social Change: Liturgical Music in Jewish and Christian Experience.* Notre Dame, Ind.: Univeristy of Notre Dame Press, 1993.

Huijbers, Bernard. *The Performing Audience.* Phoenix: North American Liturgical Resources, 1974.

Johansson, Calvin M. *Music and Ministry: A Biblical Counterpoint.* Peabody, Mass.: Hendrickson Publishers, 1984.

Mitchell, Robert H. *Ministry and Music.* Philadelphia: Westminster John Knox, 1978.

Montell, William Lynwood. *Singing the Glory Down: Amateur Gospel Music in South Central Kentucky, 1900–90.* Lexington: University of Kentucky Press, 1991.

Orr, N. Lee. *The Church Music Handbook.* Nashville: Abingdon, 1991.

Pass, David B. *Music and the Church.* Nashville: Broadman, 1989.

Peterson, John W. *The Miracle Goes On.* Grand Rapids, Mich.: Zondervan, 1976.

Poultney, David. *Dictionary of Western Church Music.* Chicago: American Library Assn., 1991.

Routley, Erik. *Twentieth Century Church Music.* New York: Oxford University Press, 1964.

———. *Words, Music, and the Church.* Nashville: Abingdon, 1968.

Sanchez, Diana, ed. *Introduction to the Hymns, Canticles, and Acts of Worship.* Nashville: Abingdon, 1989.

Schalk, Carl, and Carl Halter, eds. *A Handbook of Church Music.* St. Louis: Concordia, 1978.

Topp, Dale. *Music in the Christian Community.* Grand Rapids, Mich.: Eerdmans, 1976.

Underhill, Evelyn. *Worship.* New York: Crossroad, 1989.

Van Olst, E. H. *The Bible and Liturgy.* 3d ed. Grand Rapids, Mich.: Eerdmans, 1991.

Webber, Robert E. *Worship Old and New.* Grand Rapids, Mich.: Zondervan, 1982.

Westermeyer, Paul. *The Church Musician.* San Francisco: Harper and Row, 1988.

Winter, Miriam Therese. *Why Sing? Toward a Theology of Catholic Church Music.* Washington, D.C.: Pastoral Press, 1984.

Wohlgemuth, Paul W. *Rethinking Church Music.* Chicago: Moody Press, 1973.

12. Gospel Music Performers and Composers

Becker, Paula. *Let the Song Go On: 50 Years of Gospel Singing in the Speer Family.* Nashville: Impact Books, 1971.

Blackwood, James. *The James Blackwood Story.* Monroeville, Tenn.: Whitaker House, 1975.

Boyer, Horace Clarence. *How Sweet the Sound: The Golden Age of Gospel.* New York: Elliott and Clark Publishers, 1995.

Broughton, Vic. *Black Gospel: An Illustrated History of the Gospel Sound.* Dorset, England: Blandford Press, 1985.

Buckingham, Jamie. *O Happy Day: The Happy Goodman Story.* Waco, Tex.: Word Books, 1973.

Clower, Jerry. *Ain't God Good!* Waco, Tex.: Word Books, 1975.

Collins, Lisa. *The Gospel Music Industry Round-Up.* Culver City, Calif.: Eye on Gospel Publishing, 1994.

Crouch, Andrae. *Through It All.* Waco, Tex.: Word Books, 1974.

Cusic, Don. *Hank Williams: The Complete Lyrics.* New York: St. Martin's Press, 1993.

———. *Reba McEntire: Country Music's Queen.* New York: St. Martin's Press, 1991.

———. *The Sound of Light: A History of Gospel Music.* Bowling Green, Ohio: Bowling Green State University Popular Press, 1990.

Gaither, Bill, and Jerry Jenkins. *Homecoming: The Story of Southern Gospel Music.* Grand Rapids, Mich.: Zondervan, 1997.

Goreau, Laurraine. *Just Mahalia, Baby.* Waco, Tex.: Word Books, 1975.

Hagan, Chet. *Gospel Legends.* Nashville: Avon Publishers, 1995.

Hall, J. H. *Biography of Gospel Song and Hymn Writers.* New York: AMS Press, 1971.

Hall, Sammy. *Hooked on a Good Thing.* Old Tappan, N.J.: Fleming H. Revell, 1966.

Harris, Michael W. *Thomas A. Dorsey and the Rise of Gospel Blues.* New York: Oxford University Press, 1991.

Heilbut, Anthony. *The Gospel Sound: Good News and Bad Times.* New York: Anchor Books, 1975.

Hemphill, La Breesha Rogers. *La Breesha.* Nashville: Hemphill Music, 1976.

Hicks, Darryl. *Marijohn: Lord, Let Me Leave a Song.* Waco, Tex.: Word Books, 1978.

Hillsman, Joan R. *Gospel Music.* Washington, D.C.: Middle Atlantic Regional Press, 1990.

Hively, Kay, and Albert Brumley, Jr. *I'll Fly Away: The Life Story of Albert E. Bromley.* Branson, Mo.: Mountaineer Books, 1990.

Horn, Dorothy D. *Sing to Me of Heaven.* Gainesville: University of Florida Press, 1970.

Hustad, Donald. *Jubilate! Church Music in the Evangelical Tradition.* Carol Stream, Ill.: Hope Publishing, 1981.

Jackson, George Pullen. *White Spirituals in the Southern Uplands.* Hatboro, Pa.: Folklore Associates, 1964.

Jackson, Irene V. *Afro-American Religious Music.* New York: Greenwood Publishers, 1979.

Knaack, Twila. *Ethel Waters: I Touched a Sparrow.* Minneapolis: World Wide Publishing, 1978.

Liesch, Barry. *People in the Presence of God.* Grand Rapids, Mich.: Zondervan, 1988.

Montell, Lynwood. *Singing the Glory Down.* Lexington: University of Kentucky Press, 1991.

Mopson, J. Wendell, Jr. *The Ministry of Music in the Black Church.* Valley Forge, Pa.: Judson Press, 1984.

Oldham, Doug. *I Don't Live There Anymore.* Nashville: Impact Books, 1973.

Racine, Kree Jack. *Above All: The Blackwood Brothers.* Memphis, Tenn.: Jarodoce Publishing, 1967.

Rambo, Dottie. *It's the Soul of Me.* Nashville: Impact Books, 1969.

Schwerm, Jules. *Got to Tell It: Mahalia Jackson, Queen of Gospel.* Oxford: Oxford University Press, 1992.

Sego, James. *Sego: The Life of the Gospel Singer.* Plainfield, N.J.: Logos Interwall, 1977.

Shaw, Arnold. *Black Popular Music in America.* New York: Schirmer, 1986.

Spencer, Jon Michel. *Protest and Praise: Sacred Music of Black Religion.* Minneapolis: Fortress Press, 1991.

Stoller, Lee. *Christy Lane: One Day at a Time.* Madison, Wis.: LS Records, 1983.

Terrell, Bob. *J. D. Sumner: Gospel Music Is My Life.* Nashville: Impact Books, 1971.

———. *The Music Men: The Story of Professional Gospel Quartet Singing in America.* Nashville: Bob Terrell Publishers, 1990.

Young, Alan. *Wake Me Up This Morning: Black Gospel Singers and the Gospel Life.* Jackson: University Press of Mississippi, 1997.

13. Contemporary Christian Music

Atkins, Tim. *Music Worth Talking About.* Chicago: Baker Book House, 1995.

Bachman, John W. *The Church in the World of Radio-Television.* New York: Association Press, 1960.

Baker, Paul. *Paul Baker's Topical Index of Contemporary Christian Music.* Nashville: Music Helps, 1987.

Cua, Rick. *Songs to Live By.* Chicago: Honor Books, 1994.

Darden, Bob. *The Young Messiah.* Nashville: Chordant Publishers, 1995.

Ellsworth, Donald Paul. *Christian Music in Contemporary Witness.* Grand Rapids, Mich.: Baker Book House, 1979.

Frame, John. *Contemporary Worship Music: A Biblical Defense.* New York: Presbyterian and Reformed Publishing, 1997.

Green, Melody. *No Compromise: The Life Story of Keith Green.* Nashville: Sparrow Press, 1986.

Hart, Dave. *Staying in Tune: A Sane Response to Your Child's Music.* Nashville: Standard Publishers, 1996.

Hartman, Bob. *More Power to Ya: The Petra Devotional.* Nashville: Standard Publishers, 1997.

Haynes, Michael K. *The God of Rock.* Lindale, Tex.: Priority Ministries and Publications, 1982.

Hoge, Dean R., Benton Johnson, and Donald A. Luidens. *Vanishing Boundaries: The Religion of Mainline Protestant Baby Boomers.* Westminster, Ohio: John Knox, 1994.

Holm, Dallas. *This Is My Story.* Nashville: Impact Books, 1980.

Italia, Bob. *Amy Grant: Reaching for the Stars.* Nashville: Abdo and Daughters Publishers, 1992.

Keaggy, Bernadette. *A Deeper Shade of Grace.* Nashville: Sparrow Press, 1993.

Key, Dana. *Don't Stop the Music.* Grand Rapids, Mich.: Zondervan, 1989.

Licciardello, Carman. *Raising the Standard.* Nashville: Sparrow Press, 1993.

Littauer, Fred. *National Directory of Christian Artists.* Eugene, Oreg.: Harvest House Publishing, 1986.

Lloyd, James. *The Christian Media Directory.* Ashland, Calif.: James Lloyd Group, 1990.

Menconi, Al, and Dave Hart. *Today's Music: A Window to Your Child's Soul.* Nashville: Standard Publishers, 1989.

Millard, Bob. *Amy Grant.* Garden City, N.J.: Doubleday, 1986.

Miller, Steve. *The Contemporary Christian Music Debate: Wordly Compromise or Agent of Renewal?* Wheaton, Ill.: Tyndale House, 1993.

Mitchell, Robert. *I Don't Like That Music.* Nashville: Hope Music, 1992.

Peters, Dan, Steve Peters, and Cher Merrill. *What about Christian Rock?* Minneapolis: Bethany House Publishers, 1986.

Scott, Steve. *The Responsibilities of the Christian Musician.* Chicago: Cornerstone Press, 1995.

Seay, Davin, and Point of Grace. *Life, Love, and Other Mysteries.* Nashville: Pocket Books, 1997.

Smith, Michael W. *Friends Are Friends Forever.* Nashville: Thomas Nelson, 1997.

Stepleton, Sharon, and Lee Stepleton, eds. *The Christian Music Industry Directory.* Baton Rouge, La.: Sunshine Publishing, 1991.

Thomsen, Marilyn. *Wedgewood: Their Music, Their Journey.* Los Angeles: Pacific Press Publishers, 1996.

Turner, Steve. *Hungry for Heaven: Rock and Roll and the Search for Redemption.* London: Virgin Books, 1988.

14. Country, Folk, Jazz, and More

Card, Michael. *Immanuel: Thoughts on the Life of Christ.* Nashville: Thomas Nelson Publishers, 1993.

———. *Joy in the Journey.* Nashville: Thomas Nelson, 1996.

———. *The Parable of Joy.* Nashville: Thomas Nelson, 1995.

Carr, Roy. *A Century of Jazz.* New York: Da Capo Press, 1997.

Cash, Johnny, and Patrick Carr. *Cash: The Autobiography.* San Francisco: Harper San Francisco, 1997.

Eichenlaub, Frank. *All American Guide to Country Music.* Nashville: Country Roads Press, 1992.

Eiland, William U. *Nashville's Mother Church: The History of the Ryman Auditorium.* Old Hickory, Tenn.: Opryland USA, 1992.

Ellison, Curtis W. *Country Music Culture: From Hard Times to Heaven.* Jackson: University Press of Mississippi, 1995.

Epstein, Dena. *Sinful Tunes and Spirituals.* Urbana: University of Illinois Press, 1977.

Faragher, Scott. *Music City Babylon.* New York: Birch Lane Press, 1992.

Fischer, John. *Making Real What I Already Believe.* Chicago: Bethany House Publishers, 1991.

———. *Real Christians Don't Dance!* Chicago: Bethany House Publishers, 1994.

———. *True Believers Don't Ask Why.* Chicago: Bethany House Publishers, 1989.

———. *What on Earth Are We Doing? Finding Our Place as Christians in the World.* Ann Arbor, Mich.: Vine Books, 1997.

Gioia, Ted. *The History of Jazz.* Oxford: Oxford University Press, 1997.

Graham, David. *He Walks with Me: The Religious Experiences of Country Music Stars.* New York: Simon and Schuster, 1977.

Green, Douglas B. *Country Roots: The Origins of Country Music.* New York: Hawthorne Books, 1976.

Gridley, Mark C. *Concise Guide to Jazz.* New York: Prentice Hall, 1997.

Lambert, George Edmund. *Duke Ellington.* New York: A. S. Barnes, 1959.

Leonard, Neil. *Jazz: Myth and Religion.* New York: Oxford University Press, 1987.

Lomax, John, III. *Nashville: Music City USA.* New York: Abrams, 1985.

Malone, Bill C. *Singing Cowboys and Muscial Mountaineers: Southern Culture and the Roots of Country Music.* Athens: University of Georgia Press, 1993.

Maxwell, Will N. *The Country Music Guide to Life.* New York: Signet Publishers, 1994.

Millard, Bob. *Country Music.* New York: HarperCollins, 1993.

Owens, Thomas. *Bebop: The Music and Its Players.* Oxford: Oxford University Press, 1996.

Peretti, Burton W. *The Creation of Jazz.* Urbana: University of Illinois Press, 1992.

Rattenbury, Ken. *Duke Ellington: Jazz Composer.* New Haven, Conn.: Yale University Press, 1990.

Richards, Tad, and Melvin B. Shestack. *The New Country Music Encyclopedia.* New York: Fireside/Simon and Schuster, 1993.

Rosenberg, Neil V. *Bluegrass: A History.* Urbana: University of Illinois Press, 1993.

Smith, Huston, ed. *Gregorian Chant: Songs of the Spirit.* San Francisco: KQED, 1996.

Talbot, John Michael. *A Passion for God: Reflections on the Gospels.* Ann Arbor, Mich.: Servant Publishers, 1991.

———. *Simplicity.* Ann Arbor, Mich.: Servant Publishers, 1989.

———, and Steve Rabey. *The Lessons of St. Francis.* Chicago: E. P. Dalton Publishers, 1997.

Ulanov, Barry. *Duke Ellington.* New York: Da Capo Press, 1976.

Wilson-Dickson, Andrew. *The Story of Christian Music: From Gregorian Chant to Black Gospel.* Minneapolis: Fortress Press, 1996.

Wolfe, Charles, and Mark O'Connor. *The Devil's Box: Masters of Southern Fiddling.* Nashville: Vanderbilt University Press, 1997.

INDEX

Abraham and Isaac, Stravinsky, 183

Ackley, Alfred H., 197

Acuff, Roy, 269

Ad organum faciendum, 35

Adams, Yolanda, 234

Aelred, abbot of Rievaulx, 22, 41

African Methodist Episcopal (AME) churches, 209

Age to Age, Grant, 248, 251, 259

"Ain't Nobody Nowhere Nothin' without God," Ellington, 276

"Alas and Did My Savior Bleed," Watts, 134, 162

aleatory music, 189

Alexander, Cecil Francis, 163–64, 167

Alexander, Charlie, 193

"All Creatures of Our God and King," Francis of Assisi, 128

"All Glory Be to God on High," Decius, 145

"All Glory, Laud, and Honor," Neale, 155

"All My Heart This Night Rejoices," Winkworth, 165

"All Things Bright and Beautiful," Alexander, 164

"All the Way My Savior Leads Me," Crosby, 163

Alstot, Owen, 203

"Am I a Soldier of the Cross," Watts, 134

Amahl and the Night Visitors, Menotti, 184–85, 191

"Amazing Grace," Newton, 140, 141

Ambrose, bishop of Milan, 15, 18, 20, 30

Amy Grant: The Collection, 248

Amy Grant, 251

An Anthem for Epiphany, Wuorinen, 190

"And Let Our Bodies Part," Mason, 156

Andrae Crouch and the Disciples, 228, 234

"Angels from the Realms of Glory," Montgomery, 154

Anglican Church, 131, 201, 209–10

Annees de pelerinage, Liszt, 119

"Another Year Is Dawning," Havergal, 160

antiphonal singing, 6

Apostles, The, Elgar, 123

Argo Singers, 230

ars antiqua, 42

Ars cantus mensurabilis, 41, 42

ars nova, 42–43, 44

Assemblies of God churches, 200, 207

"At the Name of Jesus," Vaughan Williams, 177

"At Thy Word," Winkworth, 165

Athanasius, 21

Audio Adrenaline, 255

Augustine, bishop of Hippo, 20

"Ave Maria," Bach-Gounod, 118

Ave Maria, Stravinsky, 183

Axton, Hoyt, 269

Bach, Carl Philipp Emanuel, 81, 89, 90

Bach, Johann Christian, 81, 89

Bach, Johann Sebastian, 58, 59, 69, 87, 133

   cantatas of, 75, 76

   comparing the lives of Handel and, 77–86

   musical passions of, 75, 77

   oratorios of, 75

Balbulus, Notker, 29

Baptist churches, 206–7

Barber, Samuel, 184

Index

baroque period, 63–66, 69
    comparing the lives of Handel and Bach, 77–86
    composers, 69–73, 74–75
    oratorios, cantatas, and passions, 75–77
    vocal parts and their accompaniment, 73–74
Barrows, Cliff, 223
Bay Psalm Book, 142–43, 152
"Be Known to Us in Breaking Bread," Montgomery, 154
"Be Present at Our Table, Lord," Mason, 156
Beati omnes qui timent Dominum, Purcell, 72
Beatitudes, The, Franck, 122
Beatles, the, 241
"Because He Lives," Gaither, 197, 198
Beethoven, Ludwig van, 90–91, 99, 100, 101–5, 106, 107, 136, 172–74
Beggar's Opera, 139
"Behold Us, Lord, a Little Space," Ellerton, 164
Belshazzar, Handel, 80
Belshazzar's Feast, Walton, 184, 191
Bennard, George, 197, 215
Berlioz, Hector, 109, 117–18
Bernard of Clairvaux, 128
Bernstein, Leonard, 93, 180–81
Best of Shirley Caesar, The, 238
"Best of the Sons of the Morning," Heber, 154
Bible churches, 212
"Bible Tells Me So, The," Rogers, 265
Biblical Songs, Dvořák, 120–21
"Big House," Audio Adrenaline, 255
Billings, William, 144, 179
Black, James M., 196

Blackwood Brothers, 230, 238
Blair, Barry, 255
"Blessed Assurance," Crosby, 163, 167
"Blessed Jesus," Winkworth, 165
Blindside, 257
Bliss, Philip Paul, 159, 167
Blochwitz, Hans Peter, 79
Bloom, Audio Adrenaline, 255
Blue Grass Boys, 265
blues, 278
Bonar, Horatius, 164
Book of Common Prayer, 131
"Born Twice," Stonehill, 244
Bradbury, William Batchelder, 157, 158, 162–63
Brahms, Johannes, 113–15
Brandenburg Concertos, Bach, J.S., 69, 85
Bread of Life Mass, Young, 203
"Bread of the World in Mercy Broken," Heber, 154
"Brightest and the Son of God Goes Forth to War," Heber, 154
Britten, Benjamin, 185, 191
Brother of the Sun, Francisco, 273, 280
Brother to Brother, Card and Talbot, 274
Brothers and Sisters of Charity, The, 273–74
Brubeck, Dave, 277
Bruckner, Anton, 119, 125
Burgundy, music of, 47
"But I'll Go Chasin' Women," Hamblen, 266
Byrd, William, 62–63, 66

Caesar, Shirley, 233, 238
Calvin, John, 131, 132
camp meeting music, 151–52

Campbell, Lucy C., 224

cantatas, 76

Canticle of the Sun, Francis of Assisi, 39

Canticum Sacrum, Stravinsky, 183

cantus firmus, 36–37

canzone, 61

Caravans, the, 230, 233

Card, Michael, 274–75, 280

Carman, 248–49

Carman Live . . . Radically Saved, 249

Carmichael, Ralph, 199

Carmina Burana, Orff, 176

Carter, A. P., 264–65

Carter Family, 264–65

Carter, June, 268

Carter, Maybelle, 264

Carter, Sara, 264

Cash, Johnny, 267–68, 280

Catholic Church

    Anglican Church and, 131–32, 201

    Catholic composers, 58, 59, 62, 185–87

    Catholicism since Vatican II, 202–4

    the mass, 26–28

Celestials, the, 230

Ceremony of Carols, A, Britten, 185, 191

chance music, 189

chansons, 55

chant, 15–16

    anonymous composers, 28–29

    the church fathers and sacred music, 20–22

    classical age of, 16–17

    different types of, 18

    instrumental music, 22–24

    the mass, 26–28

    musical missionaries, 29–30

    notation technology, 19–20

    the offices, 24–25

Chapman, Steven Curtis, 249

"Charge to Keep I Have, A," Mason, 156

charismatic music, 200–202, 210

Charlemagne, 30

Charles, Ray, 232

Chicago Mass Choir, 228

Chicago Symphony Orchestra and Chorus, 79

children, hymns for, 163–64

Child's Introduction to Sacred Music, Mason, 156

Choir of Westminster Cathedral, 57

chorales and congregations, 127–28

    congregational music in the early reformation, 130–31

    hymn singing in America, 142–45

    hymn writers/writing, 133–37, 140–42

    Moravians and Methodists, 138–40

    more controversies, 131–33

chords, 39

"Christ the Lord Is Risen Today," Wesley, C., 139

Christ on the Mount of Olives, Beethoven, 103, 106

Christian music

    the earliest, 8–11

    music in the persecuted church, 11–13

Christian rock bands, 253–57

Christus, Liszt, 119, 125

Chrysostom, Saint John, 24

church choir. See Congregational music and the modern church choir

Church of Christ churches, 210–11

Index

City of London Sinfonia, 182

"Clap Your Hands," Owens, 199

Clark, Roy, 261, 269

Clarkson, Margaret, 197

classical period, 89–90

    the classical mass, 90–91

    composers, 92–100

Clement of Alexandria, 23

Cleveland, James, 226–27, 238

Coffee Cantata, Bach, J.S., 76

Collection of Psalms and Hymns, A, Wesley, J., 139

Collins, Judy, 272

"Colored People," DC Talk, 255

Coltrane, John, 276–77

"Come, All Christians, Be Committed," 153, 167

"Come Holy Spirit," Gaither, 198

"Come in the Prayer Room," Ward, 227

"Come, Sinners, to the Gospel Feast," Mason, 15

"Come Sunday," Ellington, 276

Come to the Cradle, Card, 275

"Come to Jesus," 152

"Come to the Table," Card and Talbot, 274

"Come Worship the Lord," Card and Talbot, 274

"Come, Ye Faithful," Neale, 155

Comin' On Strong, Carman, 249

Community Mass, Proulx, 203

conductus, 39

Confessions, Augustine, 20

congregational music and the modern church choir, 193–94

    Catholicism since Vatican II, 202–4

congregational music among Protestant denominations, 204–12

    influence of charismatic worship styles, 200–2

    interdenominational and ecumenical awakenings, 212–14

    ministers of music, 194–97

    rise of the praise chorus, 197–99

Connie Smith Sings Great Sacred Songs, 269

Connie Smith Sings Hank Williams Gospel, 269

Constantine, 13, 16

Contemporary Christian music (CCM), 213, 220, 232, 239–40

    Amy Grant and the challenge of crossover, 251–53

    the CCM industry arises, 247–51

    father of, 242–43

    Jesus music of the 1960s, 240–42

    rise of Christian rock bands, 253–57

Cooke, Sam, 232

Copland, Aaron, 180, 191

Coram Deo, Card, 275

Coronation Mass K. 317, Mozart, 97, 98–99, 106

Couleurs de la Cite celeste, Messiaen, 186

Council of Trent, 60

"Count Your Blessings," Oatman, 196

Counter-Reformation, 59–60

Country Church, The, Hamblen, 267

Country Corral, 269

Country Faith, Lewis Family, 266, 280

country, folk, jazz, and more, 261–62, 278–79

    the blending of origins, 262–63

    Christian folk music of the late 20th century, 272–75

Christian folk musicians, 269–72

Christians in jazz, 275–78

country music, 264–67

the late 20th century, 267–69

Country Hymn Time, Easter Brothers, 266

Cowboy Church of the Air, 266

Cowper, William, 140–41, 145

"Crazy Times," Jars of Clay, 256

Cream, 242

Creation, The, Haydn, 58, 93, 94–96, 106

Credo, Stravinsky, 183

Crosby, Frances "Fanny" Jane, 147, 157, 161–63, 167

crossover, 251–53

Crouch, Andrae, 233–34, 238

Crucified, The, 257

"Crucifixion, The," Barber, 184

Crüger, Johann, 135

Cummings, William, 136

"David Danced Before the Lord," Ellington, 276

Davidde Penitente, Mozart, 97

Davies, Samuel Rev., 150–51

Davis Sisters, 230

Davis, Skeeter, 269

"Day Is Past and Over, The," Neale, 155

"Day of Resurrection, The," Neale, 155

"Day Thou Gavest, Lord, Is Ended, The," Ellerton, 164

DC Talk, 255, 259

Debussy, Claude, 124, 175

Decius, Nicolaus, 130, 145

Deutsches Requiem, Brahms, 114–15

Dido and Aeneas, Purcell, 72

Dixie Hummingbirds, 230

dominant pitch, 64

Domingo, Placido, 91

Dona Nobis Pacem, Vaughan Williams, 178

Don't Censor Me, Audio Adrenaline, 255

Dorian mode, 64

Dorsey, Thomas A., 217, 224–26, 238

Dove Awards, 235–37, 249

Dream of Gerontius, The, Elgar, 122–23, 125

Drinkard Singers, 230

Dufay, Guillaume, 47

Dunstable, John, 46

Dvořák, Antonín, 107, 117, 120–21, 125, 175

Easter Brothers, 266

Easter, Ed, 266

Easter, James, 266

Easter, Russell, 266

Edict of Milan, 13, 16

Ein Deutsches Requiem, Brahms, 114, 115

"El Shaddai," Grant, 251, 275

electronic music, 189–90, 200

Elgar, Sir Edward, 122–23, 125

Elijah, Mendelssohn, 112–13, 125

Elizabeth I, 132

Ellerton, John, 164–65

Ellington, Edward Kennedy "Duke," 276

Elliott, Charlotte, 154–55, 167

Emerging, Keaggy, 245

Episcopal churches, 201, 209–10

Erasmus, Desiderius, 51

Esther, Handel, 80, 87

Evans, Dale, 265

"Eve of Destruction," McGuire, 245

Every Day Life, 257

Index

"Everything Changes," Troccoli, 250

Faber, Frederick William, 158–59
Fairfax, Hurd, 224
"Faith Is the Victory," Sankey, 161
"Faith of Our Fathers," Faber, 159
Family Bible, Stoneman Family, 271, 280
"Family of God, The," Gaither, 198
"Father and the Son and the Holy Ghost, The," Coltrane, 277
Father's Eyes, Grant, 248
Fauré, Gabriel, 116, 125
Faust, Gounod, 118
Festival Mass, Janácek, 175
Festival Te Deum, Britten, 185
Fifty Sacred Songs and Psalms, 131
"Fight the Good Fight," Monsell, 158
figured song, 22
Final Word, The, Card, 275
Find It on the Wings, Patty, 249
Finney, Charles Grandison, 160
Firebird, Stravinsky, 181
First Hand, Chapman, 249
Fischer, John, 272
Fisk Jubilee Singers, 222, 231
Five Mystical Songs, Vaughan Williams, 178, 191
flats, sharps and, 43–44
"Flood," Jars of Clay, 256
Flood, The, Stravinsky, 183
florid organum, 35–36
Florida Boys, 230
folk mass, 203
For God and Country, Stoneman Family, 271
For Him Who Has Ears to Hear, Green, 248

Forsaken of Men, Sowerby, 196
Fox Brothers, 269
Francis of Assisi, 39, 128
Francisco, Don, 273, 280
Franck, César, 121–22
Franck, Johann, 135
Franco of Cologne, 41–42
Franklin, Aretha, 232
Franklin, Benjamin, 144, 179
From Earth to Gloryland, Easter Brothers, 266
frottola, 61
fusion music, 278

Gabrieli, Giovanni, 63, 66
Gaither, Bill, 193, 197–98, 215, 244
Gaither, Danny, 198
Gaither, Gloria, 197–98, 215
Gate of Justice, The, Brubeck, 277
"General William Booth Enters into Heaven," Ives, 179, 191
"Gentle Shepherd," Gaither, 198
Gerhardt, Paul, 135
Glass Harp, 245
Gloria, Poulenc, 183
Gloria, Rutter, 196, 215
Gloria, Vivaldi, 75, 87
"Glorious Things of Thee Are Spoken," Newton, 145
"Go, Labor On!" Bonar, 164
God Is Abundant, Smith, C., 269
"God-is-dead" movement, 241
"God Is My Strong Salvation," Montgomery, 154
Goethe, Johann Wolfgang von, 172
Going Public, Newsboys, 256

"Going Up Yonder," Hawkins, 228

"Gone Away," Stonehill, 244

"Good Christian Men Rejoice," Neale, 155

Gorecki, Henryk, 188–89

Gospel Hymns, Sankey, 161

Gospel Light Jubilee Singers, 230

gospel music, 217–19

    an explosion of artists, 232–34

    birth of, 220–22

    early roots of, 222–24

    father of, 224–26

    later divisions of, 234–37

    quartets, ensembles, and performing choirs, 229–31

    relationships to secular music, 231–32

    rise of the great soloists, 226–27

    subbranches of, 219–20

Gospel Music Association, 244, 256

Gospel Music Workshop of America, 227

Gospel Pearls, 224

Gospel Road, The, Cash, 268, 280

Gospel Singers Convention, 225

Gospel Special, Lewis Family, 266

Gospel Weekend, Jones, 269

Gospel's Greatest Hits, 228

Gounod, Charles, 100, 118

Graham, Billy, 154, 161, 223, 224, 244, 268

Grammy Awards, 233, 249, 277

Grand Ole Opry, 264, 269

Grant, Amy, 248, 250, 251–53, 259

Great Awakening, the, 143–44

    revivalism and the Second Great Awakening, 160–61

Greek Evening Hymn, 13

Greek Morning Hymn, 12–13

Greek music, 4–5, 7–8

Green, Keith, 247–48, 259

Greene, Jack, 269

Gregorian Chant: Salve Regina, Benedictine Monks of the Abbey of Saint Maurice and Saint Maur, 23

Gregory the Great, 21–22

Greisen, Nelly, 245

Gutenberg, Johannes, 54

Haas, David, 203

"Hail to the Lord's Anointed," Montgomery, 154

"Hallelujah Chorus," Handel, 69, 81

"Hallelujah, What a Savior," Bliss, 159, 167

Hamblen, Stuart, 266–67, 280

Hamilton, George, IV, 269

Handel, George Frideric, 87, 136

    comparing the lives of Bach and, 77–86

    oratorios of, 75, 76

Happy Goodman Family, 230

"Hark, Hark, My Soul!" Faber, 159

"Hark, the Herald Angels Sing," Wesley, C., 136, 139

"Hark, My Soul, It Is the Lord," Cowper, 145

Harmonettes, the, 230

Harmonies poetiques et religieuses, Liszt, 119

harmony, 47

Harrell, Melvin, 201

Harris, Larnelle, 250

Hartman, Bob, 254

Hassler, Hans Leo, 130

Hastings, Thomas, 157, 160

Haugen, Marty, 203, 215

Have You Seen Jesus My Lord, Fischer, 272

Havergal, Frances Ridley, 159–60

Index

Hawkins, Edwin, 233

Hawkins, Walter, 228

Hawkins, Walter and Tramaine, 233

Haydn, Franz Joseph, 58, 89, 90, 92–96, 106

Hayford, Jack, 199, 200, 215

He Is Christmas, Take 6, 278

"He Is Exalted," Paris, 251

"He Leadeth Me," Bradbury, 158

"He Lives," Ackley, 197

He Set My Life to Music, Mandrell, 268, 280

"He That Believeth," Chicago Mass Choir, 228

"He Touched Me," Gaither, 197

Hearn, Naida, 199

Heart in Motion, Grant, 252

"Heaven Came Down," Peterson, 197, 215

Heber, Reginald, 154

Hee Haw Gospel Quartet, 269

Heed the Call, The Imperials, 238

Heiligenstadt Testament, Beethoven, 102

Hendricks, Graham, 201, 215

Henry VIII, 131

Herbert, George, 178

Herdman, Bob, 255

"Here, O My Lord," Bonar, 164

Heritage Mass, Alstot, 203

Hermit Songs, Barber, 184

Hernandez, Frank, 201

Herring, Annie, 245

"He's Everything to Me," Carmichael, 199

He's the Rock I'm Leaning On, Easter Brothers, 266

"Hiding in Thee," Sankey, 161

Hildegarde von Bingen, 28

Hill, David, 57

hip-hop music, 278

"His Name Is Life," Gaither, 198

hocket, 40–41

Hodges, Edward, 136

Hodie, Vaughan Williams, 178

Hoffman, Elisha A., 196, 215

"Hold On," Paris, 251

Holly, Buddy, 241

Holm, Dallas, 244, 259

Holst, Gustav, 176

"Holy, Holy, Holy," Heber, 154

Holy Land, The, Cash, 268

Home Where I Belong, Thomas, 245

Honegger, Arthur, 172, 175–76

"How I Got Over," Ward, 227

human voice, use of the, 65–66

Hungarian Dances, Liszt, 175

Hurd, Bob, 203, 215

Hus, Jan, 138

Hymn of Jesus, Holst, 176

Hymn of Praise, Mendelssohn, 112

Hymn to Faith, Hope, and Charity, Schubert, 110

Hymn to the Holy Spirit, Schubert, 110

Hymn to Saint Cecilia, Britten, 185

hymnology, growth of, 147–49, 165–66

    camp meeting music, 151–52

    great hymn writers of the 19th century, 153–65

    revivalism and the Second Great Awakening, 160–61

    shape note and sacred harp singing, 152–53

    the spiritual, 149–51

    William Bradbury and the Sunday school hymn, 157–58

hymns
> hymn singing in America, 142–45
> hymn writers/writing, 130–31, 133–37, 140–42

Hymns, Ancient and Modern, Ellerton, 164

Hymns for Children, Neale, 155

Hymns from the Heart, Cash, 268

Hymns for Little Children, Alexander, 164

Hymns of Praise and Love, Monsell, 158

Hymns for the Sick, Neale, 155

Hymns through the Centuries, Lewis, 137

Hymns for the Young, Neale, 155

"I Am Praying for You, Lord," Sankey, 161

"I Am a Servant," Norman, 243

"I Am Thine, O Lord," Crosby, 163

"I Am Trusting Thee, Lord Jesus," Havergal, 160

I Believe, Jackson, 226, 238

"I Can Put My Trust in Jesus," Jackson, 226

"I Do Believe," 152

"I Gave My Life for Thee," Havergal, 160

"I Heard the Voice of Jesus Say," Bonar, 164

"I Just Feel like Something Good Is About to Happen," Gaither, 198

"I Know that My Redeemer Liveth," Pound, 196

"I Lay My Sins on Jesus," Bonar, 164

"I Love You," Norman, 243

I Saw the Light, Williams, 267, 280

"I See Thee Face to Face," Bonar, 164

I Stood on the Banks, Cleveland, 227

"I Will Bless the Lord," Hernandez, 201

"I Will Call Upon the Lord," O'Shields, 199

"I Will Serve Thee," Gaither, 198

"I Wish We'd All Been Ready," Norman, 243

"I Worship Thee, Most Gracious God," Faber, 159

"If Thou but Suffer God to Guide Me," Winkworth, 165

"If You See My Savior," Dorsey, 225

Ignatius of Antioch, 12

Imperial Mass, Haydn, 93, 94, 106

Imperials, the, 230, 238

In the Beginning, Copland, 180, 191

"In the Beginning, God," Ellington, 276

In Ecclesiis, Gabrieli, 63, 66

"In the Garden," Miles, 197

"In the Sweet By and By," Rogers, 265

Infancy of Christ, The, Berlioz, 109

instrumental music, 199–200
> chant and, 22–24
> instrumental worship, 7
> organs, 48, 77
> the Renaissance and, 48, 53

Ionian mode, 64

Isaac, Heinrich, 56

isorhythms, 43

Israel in Egypt, Handel, 80

It Is No Secret, Hamblen, 267, 280

"It Is Well with My Soul," Bliss, 159

"It Took a Miracle," Peterson, 197

"It Won't Be Long," Crouch, 228

Ives, Charles, 151, 179–80, 188, 191

Jackson, Mahalia, 226, 238

Janácek, Leos, 175

Jars of Clay, 255–56

Jars of Clay, Jars of Clay, 256

jazz, 275–78

Jeanne d'Arc au bûcher, Honegger, 176

Index

Jefferson, Thomas, 179

Jehovah quam multi sunt hostes, Purcell, 72

Jerome, 21

"Jerusalem the Golden," Neale, 155

"Jesus Calls Us," Alexander, 164

Jesus Freak, DC Talk, 255, 259

Jesus Is the Best Thing, Cleveland, 227

"Jesus Is Tenderly Calling," Crosby, 163

"Jesus Keep Me Near the Cross," Crosby, 163

"Jesus, Lover of My Soul," Ives, 180

"Jesus, Lover of My Soul," Wesley, C., 139

"Jesus Loves Even Me," Bliss, 159

"Jesus Loves Me This I Know," Bradbury, 157

Jesus movement, 241, 243

"Jesus, Name Above All Names," Hearn, 199

"Jesus, Priceless Treasure," Winkworth, 165

"Jesus Saves Today," Jones, 269

"Jesus Shall Reign," Watts, 134

"Jesus, We Just Want to Thank You," Gaither, 197

Jewish music, 4–7

Job (A Masque for Dancing), Vaughan Williams, 178

Johannes de Muris, 38

John Michael Talbot, Talbot, 273

John of Salisbury, 40

John XXII, Pope, 33

"Join All the Glorious Names," Watts, 136

Jones, George, 268–69

Jones, Nancy Sepulvada, 268

Josquin Desprez, 56–57, 66

Joy to the World, Smith, C., 269

"Joy to the World," Watts, 134, 136

"Joyful, Joyful, We Adore Thee," Van Dyke, 136

Jubal, 5

Judgement, The, Elgar, 123

"Just as I Am, without One Plea," Elliott, 154, 167

"Just as I Am, without One Plea," Ives, 180

"Just as I Am, without One Plea," Bradbury, 158

Juvenile Psalmist, The, Mason, 156

Kaiser, Kurt, 199

Kanawa, Kiri te, 79

Keaggy, Phil, 245

keys, major and minor, 64

"King is Coming, The," Gaither, 198

Kingdom, The, Elgar, 123

Kingsmen, the, 230

Knox, John, 132, 141

Kodály, Zoltán, 175, 191

Lafferty, Ken, 199, 215

Landini cadence, 46

Landini, Francesco, 46

Lassus, Orlandus, 62, 66

Latin music, 278

lauda, 61

Laudate pueri dominum, Byrd, 63

"Lay Some Soul upon My Heart," Sankey, 161

Le Roi David, Honegger, 175–76

Le tombeau resplendissant, Messiaen, 186

Lead Me On, Grant, 252

"Leaning on the Everlasting Arms," Hoffman, 196, 215

Lee, Ann, 143

Legendes, Liszt, 119

L'Enfant Prodigue, Debussy, 175

Léonin, 38–39

Les Dialogues des Carmelites, Poulenc, 183–84

"Let All that Is within Me," Harrell, 201

"Let's Just Praise the Lord," Gaither, 198

Levine, James, 91

Lewis Family, 265–66, 280

Lewis, J. Reilly, 137

Licciardello, Carman, 248–49

"Lift Up Your Heads, Ye Mighty Gates," Winkworth, 165

Light in the Wilderness, The, Brubeck, 277

"Light of the World, We Hail Thee," Monsell, 158

Lighten Up, McGuire, 245

"Like a River Glorious," Havergal, 160

Liszt, Franz, 109, 118–19, 125, 175

"Little Community Church," Monroe, B., 265

"Live the Mystery," Card and Talbot, 274

Long Tunes, 142

"Lord Be with Us Every Day, The," Ellerton, 164

Lord Help Me, Cleveland, 227

"Lord, Listen to Your Children Praying," Medema, 199

"Lord of the Living Harvest," Monsell, 158

Lord Nelson Mass, Haydn, 93, 94, 106

"Lord, Speak to Me," Havergal, 160

Lord's Supper, The, Talbot, 273, 280

Love Can Do, Grant, 248

Love Center Choir, 228

"Love Divine, All Loves Excelling," Wesley, C., 139

Love Feast of the Twelve Apostles, The, Wagner, 109

Love and Mercy, Troccoli, 250

"Love Song for a Savior," Jars of Clay, 256

Lowry, Mark, 198

Luther, Martin, 56, 57, 127, 129–30, 134, 145, 148

Lutheran churches, 201, 205–6

Lux Christi, Elgar, 122

McDonald, Gene, 198

McGinnis, Will, 255

McGuire, Barry, 245

Machaut, Guillaume de, 44–45

McIntosh Country Shouters, 150

McKeehan, Toby, 255

Madrigali spirtuali, 61

madrigals, 46

Magnificat, Bach, J.S., 31, 82, 83–84, 87

Magnificat, Monteverdi, 70

Magnum Opus Musicum, Lassus, 62

Magnus liber organum, 38

"Majesty," Hayford, 199, 215

Make His Praise Glorious, Patty, 249, 259

Man and His Music, A, Hamblen, 267

Mandrell, Barbara, 268, 280

Mansion Builder, 2nd Chapter of Acts, 245

Mary I, 132

Mason, Lowell, 135, 136, 155–56, 167

mass

    Catholic Church and the, 26–28

    the classical mass, 90–91

    Schubert's masses, 109–11

Mass in A-flat Major, Schubert, 111

Mass in B Minor, Bach, J.S., 58, 82, 83, 84, 87, 175

Mass in B-flat Major, Schubert, 110

Mass of the Bells, Peloquin, 203

Index

Mass, Bernstein, 180–81

Mass in C Major, Beethoven, 103–4, 106

Mass in C Major, Mozart, 97

Mass in C Major, Schubert, 110

Mass carminum, Obrecht, 55

Mass of Creation, Haugen, 203, 215

Mass in D Major, Dvořák, 120

Mass in E Minor, Bruckner, 119, 125

Mass in E-flat Major, Schubert, 111, 125

Mass in F Major, Bruckner, 119

Mass in F Major, Schubert, 110

Mass in G Major, Poulenc, 183

Mass in G Major, Schubert, 110

Mass in G Minor, Vaughan Williams, 178

Mass of Light, Haas, 203

Mass, Stravinsky, 183

Master and the Muscian, The, Keaggy, 245

measured song, 22

Medema, Ken, 199

medieval polyphony, 33–35

    first composers of polyphony, 38–39

    mensuration, 41–42

    music of Burgundy, 47

    need for new rhythmic notation, 36–37

    the "new art," 42–44

    new musical forms, 39–41

    organum, 35–36

    the Trinity, 37–38

melisma passages, 29

Mendelssohn, Felix, 86, 111–13, 125, 136

Menotti, Gian-Carlo, 184–85, 191

mensuration, 41–42

Messe de Notre Dame, La, Machaut, 45–46

Messiaen, Olivier, 185–87, 191

Messiah, Handel, 76, 80–81, 87, 95, 141

Methodist churches, 201, 211

    Moravians and Methodists, 138–40

Mighty Clouds of Joy, 230

"Mighty Fortress Is Our God, A," Luther, 145

Miles, C. Austin, 197

minimalism, 188–89

Miriam's Song of Victory, Schubert, 110

Missa Bossa Nova, Scholtes, 203

missa brevis, 90

Missa Brevis K. 192, Mozart, 97–98, 106

Missa Caput, Obrecht, 66

Missa de Americas, Hurd, 203, 215

Missa Pange Lingua, Desprez, 66

Missa Papae Marcelli, Palestrina, 57, 60

Missa Prolationum, Ockeghem, 66

Missa Renovata, Wuorinen, 190

Missa se la face ay pale, Dufay, 49

Missa sine nomine, 53

Missa Solemnis, Beethoven, 91, 102, 103, 104, 105, 175

Missa in tempore belli, Haydn, 93

modern classical composers, 171–72

    composers, 176–87

    a continuation of nationalism, 174–76

    sacred classical music at the end of the 20th century, 187–90

modes, framework of, 64

monastic life, 24–25, 28

monophonic music, 8, 22

Monroe, Bill, 265

Monroe, Charlie, 265

Monsell, John Samuel Bewley, 158

Monteverdi, Claudio, 69–70, 87

Montgomery, James, 154

Moody, Dwight Lyman, 160–61, 163

Moravians, 138–40, 143

More Power to Ya, Petra, 254, 259

Mors et Vita, Gounod, 118

"Moses," Norman, 243

motets, 40, 55, 56

Mother Ann Lee. See Lee, Ann

"Move on Up a Little Higher," Jackson, 226

Mozart, Wolfgang Amadeus, 89, 90, 96–100, 106

Much Afraid, Jars of Clay, 256

Music from Ancient Rome, Synaulia, 9

Musica enchiriadis, 35

musica ficta, 43

musica reservata, 61

"My Faith Looks Up to Thee," Mason, 156, 167

"My God," Audio Adrenaline, 255

"My God, My Father, while I Stray," Elliott, 155

"My Hope Is Built on Nothing Less, Bradbury, 158

"My Savior First of All," Crosby, 163

Myers, Robert Manson, 80

National Baptist Convention, 225

Nativité du Seigneur, Messiaen, 186

Neale, John Mason, 155

"Nearer the Cross," Crosby, 163

"Nearer My God to Thee," Mason, 156

Negro spirituals, 144–45, 149–51

neumes, 19

"Never Further than Thy Cross," Bradbury, 158

New Covenant, Fischer, 272

New Earth, The, Talbot, 273

New World Symphony, Dvorák, 120

New-England Psalm Singer, 144

Newsboys, 256

Newton, John, 140, 145

Nicolai, Philipp, 130

"Ninety and Nine, The," Sankey, 161, 167

No Compromise, Green, 248, 259

"No, Not Despairingly," Bonar, 164

"No One Understands like Jesus," Peterson, 197

Norfolk Rhapsodies, Vaughan Williams, 270

Norman, Jessye, 91

Norman, Larry, 239, 242–43, 259

Not Ashamed, Newsboys, 256

Not of this World, Petra, 254

notation, 13–14

    baroque composers and, 73

    chant and, 19–20

    florid organum and rhythmic notation, 36–37

    the Greeks and, 7–8, 13

    shape note hymns, 152–53

    sharps and flats, 43–44

Nothing but Praise, Holm, 244, 259

Notre Dame, 38–39

"Now God Be with Us," Winkworth, 165

"Now the Laborer's Task Is O'er," Ellerton, 164

"Now Thank We All Our God," Rinkart, 145

"Now Thank We All Our God," Winkworth, 165

O Clap Your Hands, Vaughan Williams, 178

"O, for a Closer Walk with God," Cowper, 141

Index

"O Come and Mourn with Me Awhile," Faber, 159

"O Come, O Come, Emmanuel," Neale, 155

"O, for a Thousand Tongues," Wesley, C., 139, 145

"O Holy Savior, Friend Unseen," Elliott, 155

"O How the Thought of God Attracts," Faber, 159

"O Lord Our Lord, How Majestic Is Your Name in All the Earth," Smith, M. W., 250

"O Love, Divine and Golden," Monsell, 158

"O Sacred Head Now Wounded," Clairvaux, 128

O Taste and See, Vaughan Williams, 178

O vos omnes, Sancta Civitas, Vaughan Williams, 178

Oatman, Johnson, 196

Obrecht, Jacob, 55, 66

Ockeghem, Johannes, 55, 66

Ode for Saint Cecilia's Day, Purcell, 72, 87

Odes of Solomon, 12

O'Donnell, James, 182

"Oh, Happy Day," Hawkins, 233

"Old Country Church, The," Pals, 271

Old Hundredth, Vaughan Williams, 178

Old Rugged Cross, Stoneman Family, 271

"Old Rugged Cross, The," Bennard, 197, 215

Olney Hymns, 140

On Music, Augustine, 20

"Once in Royal David's City," Alexander, 164

"One Way," Norman, 243

"Only a Look," Roberta Martin Singers, 230, 238

oratorios, 75–76
 Mendelssohn's, 111–13

Orfeo, Monteverdi, 70

Orff, Carl, 176

organum, 35–36

Origen, 12

origins of sacred music, 3–4, 13–14
 the earliest Christian music, 8–11
 Greek contributions, 7–8
 the Jews and Greeks, 4–5
 the music of Jewish worship, 5–7
 music in the persecuted church, 11–13

O'Shields, Michael, 199

Osiander, Lucas, 130–31

Owen, Wilfred, 185

Owens, Jimmy, 199

Oxford Book of Carols, Vaughan Williams, 177

Oxford Camerata, 45

"Packing Up," Ward, 227

Palestrina, Giovanni Pierluigi da, 57, 59–60

Pals, Georgia, 271

parachurch ministries, 213

Paris, Twila, 250–51

"Pass It On," Kaiser, 199

passions, 76–77

Pater Noster, Stravinsky, 183

Patty, Sandi, 249–50, 259

Paukenmesse, Haydn, 93, 106

Paul, 3, 9–11

Peace, Be Still, Cleveland, 227

"Peace, Be Still," Gaither, 198

Peaceable Kingdom, The, Thompson, 196

Peloquin, Alexander, 203

Penderecki, Krzysztof, 124, 189, 191

pendulum theory of music history, 17

Penitential Psalms, Lassus, 62, 66

Pentecostalism, 200, 201

perfectio, 38

Pérotin, 38–39

"Perseverance of the Saints," Supertones, 257

Peter, Paul, and Mary, 273

Peterson, John W., 197, 215

Petra, 254, 259

Petrucci, Ottaviano dei, 54

Petrushka, Stravinsky, 181

Phillips, Philip, 193, 222–23

Pietism, 133

Pilgrim's Progress, The, Vaughan Williams, 178

pitch, 64

plainchant/plainsong, 22, 54

Plato, 7

Pliny the Younger, 11–12

plygain singing, 141

Polyeucte, Gounod, 118

polyphonic music, 22

polyphony. See medieval polyphony

Poulenc, Francis, 183–84

Pound, Jessie, 196

praise bands, 200

praise choruses, 197–99

"Praise to the Lord, the Almighty," Winkworth, 165

"Prayer Is the Soul's Sincere Desire," Montgomery, 154

Prayers of Kierkegaard, Barber, 184

"Precious Lord, Take My Hand," Dorsey, 225, 238

Prelude no. 1 in C Major, Bach, 118

Presbyterian churches, 201, 207–8

Presley, Elvis, 232, 241

"Prince of Peace, Control My Will," Bradbury, 158

"Prince of Peace," Ward, 227

Princely Players, 150

printing press, music and the, 53–54

Proclus, bishop of Constantinople, 21

Protestant Church

    congregational music among Protestant denominations, 204–12

    hymns, 136

    Protestant composers, 58, 59, 71

Proulx, Richard, 203

Psalm 150, Bruckner, 119

Psalms of David, Schütz, 71

Psalms and Hymns, Watts, 144

Psalmus Hungaricus, Kodály, 175, 191

Purcell, Henry, 71–73, 87

Pure Attraction, Troccoli, 250

Puritans, 132, 142

Pythagoras, 7, 8

Quartet for the End of Time, The, Messiaen, 186

"Raindrops Keep Falling on My Head," Thomas, 245

Rainey, Ma, 225

"Raise the Strain," Neale, 155

Rambo, Buck, Dottie, and Reba, 233, 238

rap music, 255

Ravel, Maurice, 124, 175

Real to Reel, Stookey, 273

Rebecca, Franck, 121

Redemption, Franck, 121–22

Redemption, Gounod, 118

Reformation, the, 57–59, 127

Index

congregational music in the early Reformation, 130–31

Rejoice in the Lamb, Britten, 185

"Rejoice in the Lord," Purcell, 72

Renaissance, the, 47–48, 51–52
  composers, 55–57, 62–63
  the Counter-Reformation, 59–60
  heading toward the baroque, 63–66
  the printing press, 53–54
  the Reformation, 57–59
  rise in national styles, 60–61
  the secular in the sacred, 52–53

Requiem, Berlioz, 117–18

Requiem, Brahms, 31, 114–15

Requiem Canticles, Stravinsky, 183

Requiem, Dvořák, 117, 120, 125

Requiem, Fauré, 116, 125

requiem mass, 27

Requiem Mass in D Minor, Mozart, 97, 99–100, 106, 113

Requiem, Verdi, 115–16, 125

requiems, 113–18

"Rescue the Perishing," Crosby, 163

"Resolution," Supertones, 257

responsorial singing, 5–6

"Return, O Wanderer, Return," Bradbury, 158

Revival in the Land, Carman, 249

rhythms, 65

ricercar, 61

Richey, Paul, 269

Rinkart, Martin, 135, 145

Rise Again, Holm, 244

Rite of Spring, Stravinsky, 181

Roberta Martin Singers, 230, 238

"Rock of Ages," Hastings, 157

rococo period of music, 89

Rodeheaver, Homer Alvan, 193, 223

Rogers, Roy, 265

Roman, Lulu, 269

romantic period, 100–101, 107–8
  Brahms Requiem, 113–15
  crisis of faith, 108–9
  Mendelssohn's oratorios, 111–13
  Schubert's masses, 109–11

Root, George Frederick, 157–58

Russell, Johnny, 269

Ruth, Franck, 121

Rutter, John, 196, 215

Ryman Auditorium, 264

Ryman, Thomas Greene, 264

sacred harp singing, 153

sacred music
  the church fathers and, 20–22
  See also origins of sacred music

"Safe in the Arms of Jesus," Crosby, 163

Saint François d'Assise, Messiaen, 186

Saint John Passion, Handel, 78

St. Louis Jesuits, 203

Saint Ludmila, Dvořák, 121

Saint Luke Passion, Penderecki, 124, 189, 191

Saint Matthew Passion, Bach, J.S., 79, 83, 84–85, 86, 112

Saint Nicolas, Britten, 185

Saint Paul, Mendelssohn, 112

Samson, Handel, 80

Samuel, Claude, 186

Sankey, Ira David, 160, 161, 163, 167, 223

SATB (soprano, alto, tenor, bass), 53, 196

Saul, Handel, 80

"Savior, Again to Thy Dear Name We Raise," Ellerton, 164

"Savior, Again to Thy Dear Name We Raise," Vaughan Williams, 177

"Savior, Like a Shepherd Lead Us," Bradbury, 158

Scenes from the Saga of King Olaf, Elgar, 122

Schoenberg, Arnold, 43, 124

Scholtes, Peter, 203

Schubert, Franz, 109–11, 125

Schumann, Robert, 101

Schutte, Dan, 201

Schütz, Heinrich, 59, 70–71, 72–73, 87

Scottish congregations, 141–42

2nd Chapter of Acts, 245, 259

Second Vatican Council, 202

secular music

    growth of, 48

    relationship of gospel music to, 231–32

    the Renaissance and sacred vs. secular, 52–53

Seeds, McGuire, 245

"Seek Ye First," Lafferty, 199, 215

Sensational Nightingales, 230

Separatists, 132, 133

Sequences, Hymns and Other Ecclesiastical Verses, Neale, 155

sequencing, 29

"Sermon on the Mount," Brubeck, 277

Sermon, a Narrative and a Prayer, A, Stravinsky, 183

Seven Last Words of Jesus, Schütz, 71, 87

Seventh-Day Adventist churches, 208–9

Shakers, the, 143

"Shall We Gather at the River?" 152

Shall We Gather at the River? Lewis Family, 266

shape note hymns, 152–53

sharps and flats, 43–44

Shea, George Beverly, 193, 223–24

"Shelter in the Time of Storm, A," Sankey, 161

Sheltered in the Arms of God, Blackwood Brothers, 238

"Shepherd of Love," Peterson, 197

"Shine, Jesus, Shine," Hendricks, 201, 215

"Sign of the Judgment," McIntosh Country Shouters, 150

"666," Norman, 243

ska music, 256–57, 278

Skillet, 257, 259

Skillet, Skillet, 259

Slavonic Dances, Dvořák, 270

Sleepers, Awake! (Cantata no. 140), Bach, J. S., 83, 87

Slye, Leonard Franklin, 265

Smith, Alfred B., 197

Smith, Bessie, 225

Smith, Connie, 269

Smith, Kevin, 255

Smith, Michael W., 250

Smith, Reggie, 198

"So I Send You," Peterson, 197

So Much 2 Say, Take 6, 278, 280

Solti, Sir George, 79

Some Kind of Zombie, Audio Adrenaline, 255

"Something about Believin'," Ellington, 276

"Something about That Name," Gaither, 198

"Something Beautiful," Gaither, 198

Something New and Fresh, Stookey, 273

"Something within Me," Campbell, 224

Index

"Sometimes I Feel like a Motherless Child," 150, 167

Son Is Shining, The, The Rambos, 238

Sonets and Songs of Sadness and Piety, Byrd, 66

Song Pilgrimage Round the World, Phillips, 223

songbooks, the church's first, 12

Songs from the Heart, Patty, 249

Songs of Praise, Vaughan Williams, 177

Soul Stirrers, 230

Souls of the Righteous, The, Vaughan Williams, 178

Southern Harmony, The, Walker, 271

Sowerby, Leo, 196

Speer Family, 230

"Spend and Be Spent," Bonar, 164

spirituals, Negro, 144–45, 149–51

Spread Love, Take 6, 277

Stabat Mater, Dvořák, 120

Stabat Mater, Poulenc, 183

"Stand Up and Bless the Lord," Montgomery, 154

Standard, The, Carman, 249

"Star Spangled Banner, The," 249

Statesman, the, 230

Stavesacre, 257

Steppenwolf, 242

Still Life, Fischer, 272

Stonehill, Randy, 244

Stoneman, Ernest, 271

Stoneman Family, 271, 280

Stookey, Noel Paul, 273

Stravinsky, Igor, 124, 171, 181–83

Stuart, Mark, 255

Stubborn Love, Troccoli, 250

Summerly, Jeremy, 45

Sumner, Donnie, 198

Sunday, Billy, 161, 223

"Sunday Mornin' Country," 269

Sunday school hymns, 157

Supertones, 256–57, 259

Supertones Strike Back, 259

"Supreme God," Ellington, 276

"Surely Goodness and Mercy Shall Follow Me," Peterson, 197

Swan Silvertones, 230

"Sweet Hour of Prayer," Bradbury, 158

"Swing Low, Sweet Chariot," 150

"Swing Low, Sweet Chariot," Princely Players, 150

Symphony no. 3, Gorecki, 188–89

Symphony no. 5, Beethoven, 172

Symphony no. 7, Beethoven, 173

Symphony no. 9, Beethoven, 104

Symphony of Psalms, Stravinsky, 31, 124, 181, 182

Tait, Michael, 255

Take 6, 277, 280

Take Me Back, Crouch, 238

Take Me to Your Leader, Newsboys, 256

"Take My Life and Let It Be," Havergal, 160

"Take the World, but Give Me Jesus," Crosby, 163

Talbot, John Michael, 273–74, 280

Te Deum, Bruckner, 119

Te Deum laudamus, Augustine, 20

Te Deum, Vaughan Williams, 178

Tell 'Em Again, Holm, 244

"Tell Me the Story of Jesus," Crosby, 163

tenor, 36

texture and rhythm, 65

Tharpe, Rosetta, 226

"There Is a Fountain Filled with Blood," Cowper, 141

"There Is a Green Hill Far Away," Alexander, 164, 167

"There Is a Land of Pure Delight," Watts, 134, 145, 157–58

"There'll Be Peace in the Valley for Me," Dorsey, 225

"There's Something about That Name," Gaither, 198, 215

"There's a Wideness in God's Mercy," Faber, 159

XIIIth Psalm, Liszt, 118–19

"This Is the Day of Light," Ellerton, 164

This Means War! Petra, 254

Thomas, B. J., 245

Thompson, Randall, 196

"Though Your Sins Be As Scarlet," Crosby, 163

Thrasher Brothers, 230

Three Sacred Choruses, Stravinsky, 183

Threni, Stravinsky, 183

Thy Word, Grant, 248

Tinctoris, Johannes, 52

Tindley, Charles Albert, 224, 225, 238

"'Tis the Blessed Hour of Prayer," Crosby, 163

"'Tis a Gift to Be Simple," 143, 145

To the Bride, 2nd Chapter of Acts, 245, 259

To Hope, a Celebration, Brubeck, 277

tonic pitch, 64

"Tonight," Supertones, 257

Tower of Babel, The, Franck, 122

Tower of Babel, The, Stravinsky, 183

Trinity, the, 37–38

Troccoli, Kathy, 250

Trois Petites Liturgies de la Présence Divine, Messiaen, 186, 187, 191

tropes, 28

Trust in God, Cleveland, 238

"Trusting Jesus," Sankey, 161

"UFO," Norman, 243

"Under His Wings," Sankey, 161

Unguarded, Grant, 252

Unveiled Hope, Card, 275, 280

Upon This Rock, Norman, 243, 259

van Dyke, Henry, 136

Vaughan Williams, Ralph, 176–79, 191

Vaughn, James D., 227

Verdi, Giuseppe, 115–16, 125

Vespers, 25

Vespers, Monteverdi, 25, 70, 87

Vienna Boys' Choir, 92

Vienna Philharmonic, 91

Vitri, Philippe de, 42–43

Vivaldi, Antonio, 74–75, 87

Voice of the Holy Spirit, The, Brubeck, 277

Wade in the Water: African American Sacred Music Traditions, 150

Wagner, Richard, 43, 109

Wake-Up Call, Petra, 254

Walker, Billy, 269, 271

Walton, William, 184, 191

War Requiem, Britten, 185

Ward, Clara, 227, 230

Ward, Matthew, 245

Ward Singers, 230

Index

"Watchman, Tell Us of the Night," Heber, 154

Waters, Ethel, 224

Watts, Isaac, 128, 133–34, 135, 136, 140, 145, 156

Wayne, John, 266–67

"We Are So Blessed," Gaither, 198

"We Will Glorify the King of Kings," Paris, 251

"We'll Understand It Better By and By," Tindley, 224, 238

"Were You There When They Crucified My Lord?" 150

Wesley, Charles, 128, 136, 138–40, 145, 156

Wesley, John, 138–40

Wesley, Samuel, 138

"What a Friend We Have in Jesus," Ives, 180

"What Would You Give in Exchange for Your Soul?" Monroe, B., 265

"When I Survey the Wondrous Cross," Watts, 134

"When I Wake Up in Glory," Jackson, 226

"When the Roll Is Called up Yonder," Black, 196–97

"Where Are the Hebrew Children?" 152, 167

"Where Can I Go?" Roberta Martin Singers, 230

White, Benjamin Franklin, 153

Whitefield, George, 144

Whittle, W. D., 159

"Who Is on the Lord's Side?" Havergal, 160

Whole Booke of Psalms Faithfully Translated in English Metre, The, 142–43, 152

"Wicked Path of Sin," Monroe, B., 265

"Will Jesus Find Us Watching?" Crosby, 163

Williams, Hank, 267, 280

Winans, BeBe and CeCe, 234

Wings over Jordan, 230

Winkworth, Catherine, 165

"Wonderful Words of Life," Bliss, 159

Wuorinen, Charles, 189–90

You Gave Me Love, Thomas, 245

Young, Jeremy, 203

Zinzendorf, Count Nicolaus, 138

Zwingli, Huldrych, 131

DEMCO